REDISCOVERING CONFUCIANISM

Mencius, ca. 371–ca. 289 BC

REDISCOVERING
CONFUCIANISM

A MAJOR PHILOSOPHY OF LIFE IN EAST ASIA

TORBJÖRN LODÉN

**GLOBAL
ORIENTAL**

REDISCOVERING CONFUCIANISM
A MAJOR PHILOSOPHY OF LIFE IN EAST ASIA

Torbjörn Lodén

First published 2006 by

GLOBAL ORIENTAL LTD
PO Box 219
Folkestone
Kent CT20 3WP
UK

www.globaloriental.co.uk

© 2006 Torbjörn Lodén

British Library Cataloguing in Publication Data
A CIP catalogue entry for this book is available
from the British Library

ISBN 1-901903-53-2

Set in Bembo 11 on 12pt by Servis Filmsetting Ltd, Manchester
Printed and bound in England by Antony Rowe Ltd, Chippenham, Wilts

CONTENTS

v

CONTENTS

PREFACE

Writing this I am seated on a flight back to Sweden after spending nine months as a visiting scholar in Hong Kong. Around me are people from Hong Kong, Mainland China, Germany and England. Today cross-cultural contacts are not abstract facts, they are part of our everyday experience. The increasing exposure to 'foreign' cultures may give rise to misunderstanding and conflict, but also offers unprecedented opportunities to enrich our lives. What is more, some awareness of the enormous repositories of experience and wisdom that different cultural traditions represent may help us discover unity in diversity as an essential characteristic of the human condition.

This book is intended to offer the reader some insight into Confucianism as one of the world's great spiritual and intellectual traditions. Assuming no prior knowledge about Confucianism, it has been written for anyone with an interest in the subject. It is also my hope that it may be of interest as a textbook for university courses on Asian thought and religion.

In recent years, many excellent studies of different aspects of Confucianism have appeared in English. There are also a few general introductions to the subject in English. Yet, I am optimistic that there may be a room for one more broadly-based introduction, written by someone who sees himself as standing outside the tradition trying to present a concise factual account which opens up a perspective on the multi-dimensional character of Confucian theory and praxis.

This book, therefore, is no more than an attempt to highlight some of the major landmarks in the vast Confucian landscape. In order to facilitate further study I have appended a bibliography of

'Further reading' at the end of each chapter. I have only included titles in English, since I assume that most readers will be English speakers. However, since some readers may be students of Chinese, I have added Chinese characters for Confucian writings in Chinese as well as for all Confucian thinkers and scholars mentioned in the text.

Torbjörn Lodén

ACKNOWLEDGEMENTS

W ork on this book – at first somewhat differently conceived – began in Stockholm several years ago. But it was only during the past year in Hong Kong, when I was a visiting fellow at the Centre for Cross-Cultural Studies at City University of Hong Kong, that it gained its final form. I am greatly indebted to the director of the Centre for Cross-Cultural Studies, Professor Zhang Longxi, for inviting me to spend an extended period of time at City University. This offered me an exceedingly stimulating environment in which to read and write about Chinese culture. At City University of Hong Kong I am also most grateful to Professor Cheng Pei-kai and his staff at the Chinese Civilization Centre of City University for inviting me to attend many extremely stimulating lectures and seminars and for helping me in some very concrete ways. In particular, I am indebted to Ms Winnie Lee and Ms Janet Cheung for helping me locate and scan the illustrations in this book.

Professor Chang Hao at the Hong Kong University of Science and Technology and Professor Göran Malmqvist, my teacher and good friend in Stockholm, have been kind enough to read my manuscript and offer many invaluable suggestions, which have helped me avoid several errors and improve the quality of the book. My student, Dr Ane Schei in Stockholm, has pointed out numerous inconsistencies and typos in the text that I have corrected. For all remaining mistakes and weaknesses I bear, of course, the sole responsibility.

LIST OF PLATES

INTRODUCTION

Confucianism, a major intellectual and spiritual tradition in the world, emerged during the first millennium BC and became one of the pillars of Chinese civilization. Its influence has extended far beyond the borders of China, into Korea, Japan, Vietnam and large parts of Southeast Asia. It has been not only a philosophy of life for hundreds of millions of people but also a guiding ideology for states, for example the Chinese empire and the governments of contemporary Singapore and South Korea.

The main purpose of this book is to give a brief outline of Confucianism as a system of ideas and beliefs that have evolved during the past three millennia. But at least to someone who does not consider himself a Confucian believer it does not seem possible to define Confucianism in terms of one set of ideas and beliefs. Rather, Confucianism appears as a continuing discussion of certain basic themes that were defined at an early stage: How is harmony achieved in the world? How do human beings fully develop their potential? In the course of history some themes have also been added. For example, should we seek for the important existential truths mainly within ourselves, through introspection, or through the study of the external world? And closely related to this: what should come first, moral cultivation or intellectual inquiry?

The Confucian discussion has proceeded upon certain assumptions or postulates concerning the human condition. The most important of these has been the belief that it is in the power of humans to improve themselves and the world – without recourse to a deity whose existence and behaviour transcend human understanding. In this sense we may speak about a Confucian humanism.

1

We may also think of the Confucian discussion as making use of its own language or discourse. In the Confucian discourse we meet such terms as 'goodness' or 'humanity' (*ren* 仁), 'righteousness' (*yi* 義), 'reciprocity' or 'altruism' (*shu* 恕) etc., which are central and have acquired special meanings in the Confucian discussion.

One reason for regarding Confucianism as a continuous discussion of certain themes, proceeding on the basis of certain postulates concerning the human condition and thereby creating a discourse of it own, is to draw attention to the many different and even contradictory strands and tendencies that it encompasses. Just as in the case of, for example, Christianity, this multifariousness adds to the richness and vitality of the tradition, although to some adherents with somewhat fundamentalist inclinations it may – just as in the Christian case – seem important to define *true* Confucianism as one consistent set of doctrines.

Approaching Confucianism as an ongoing discussion, we may draw intellectual and spiritual nourishment from it and we may marvel at its richness and complexity. Something that adds complexity to the Confucian tradition is the tension within it between what we may refer to, for want of better terms, as 'meaning' and 'function'. On the one hand we may focus on the meaning and validity of Confucian ideas and beliefs, and we may assume that this has been the main focus of serious philosophers and thinkers interested in Confucianism. On the other hand, we may study the function of Confucianism as a moral-spiritual praxis, giving existential meaning to the lives of millions of people, and an ideology serving certain ideological and political purposes.

For many centuries in China and elsewhere Confucianism was a state philosophy or ideology, in whose name all policies had to be legitimized. But so dominant was its position that critics of the prevailing order also used it to legitimize their social criticism in Confucian terms.

The relationship between Confucianism as meaning and function respectively is intricate but also offers a fruitful perspective from which to approach it.

Is Confucianism a Religion or a Philosophy?

In its function as a moral-spiritual praxis Confucianism shares many characteristics with the great world religions. Indeed, Confucianism has also often been classified as a religion.[1] But is it really a religion? That depends very much on how we wish to define the term 'religion'.

So what does 'religion' mean? Does it have a specific meaning in the Chinese context? In pre-modern China there was no term that corresponded closely with the European notion of 'religion'. This does not mean that there were no religions in China or East Asia, but it does mean that the distinction between religions and other worldviews and philosophies of life was not in focus.

In European tradition, and even more so in the modern world, the notion of 'religion' has been understood in different ways and this is a major reason why some scholars think of Confucianism as a religion while others say that it is not.[2] In broad outline it seems that definitions of religion tend to focus on three aspects. First, it is often related to 'the belief in and worship of a superhuman controlling power, especially a personal God or gods'[3]. Second, some definitions focus on a certain way of relating to some doctrines or to the world: faith, devotion, belief are words that are often used to describe this religious attitude. Third, religions are often taken to offer a total, or holistic, perspective of the human condition.

If we try to relate these aspects to Confucianism, it is important to bear in mind that Confucians do not believe in any personal God. It is true that the notion of 'Heaven' (*tian* 天) plays an important role

---

[1] Confucianism is treated in authoritative dictionaries of religion, such as *The Encyclopedia of Religion*, ed., Mircea Eliade, London: Collier Macmillan, 1993 and The *Oxford Dictionary of World Religions,* ed. John Bowker, Oxford & New York: Oxford University Press, 1997. See also e.g. Arvind Sharman, *Our Religions*, San Francisco: Harper, 1993, which includes a long chapter about Confucianism by Professor Tu Wei-ming; Hans Küng and Julia Ching, *Christianity and Chinese Religion*, New York: Doubleday, 1989. Both the influential theologian Hans Küng and the sinologist Julia Ching regard Confucianism as a religion.
[2] For an introduction to the question of the meaning of 'religion', see 'The Study and Classification of Religion', in *The New Encyclopedia Britannica. Macropedia*, Vol. 26, 1991, pp. 509–529.
[3] *Oxford Dictionary Thesaurus*, Oxford and New York: Oxford University Press, 2001, p. 1089.

in Confucian thought and that this notion in pre-Confucian times was often described as a deity. In mainstream Confucianism, however, the meaning of 'Heaven' comes very close to the notion of 'nature', or 'the natural world', and although ethical principles according to Confucianism are somehow anchored in 'Heaven', consciousness seems not to have been one of heaven's attributes. Also Confucian thinkers do not seem to have been very interested in questions as to what is beyond our mundane existence, for example whether humans can somehow continue to exist after death. When Confucius himself was once asked about life after death he answered: 'Till you know about the living, how are you to know about the dead?'[4]

Yet, it is more difficult to deny categorically that Confucians believe in some 'superhuman controlling power'. Confucians have generally held that the fundamental ethical principles are somehow inherent in the universe and that acting against them will have harmful consequences. The notion of the 'Mandate of Heaven' (*tian ming* 天命) is one concrete expression of this belief. However, the emphasis is not on the 'controlling power' of superhuman forces but rather on the ability and obligation of humans to conform to the ethical principles that are anchored in the natural world beyond man.

If we move on to the second aspect of religion that we have here drawn attention to, it seems quite clear that we may describe the way Confucians relate to the Confucian doctrines in terms of 'faith', 'devotion', 'reverence' etc.

Finally, there is no doubt that Confucianism offers a total, or holistic, perspective on the human condition. It defines universally valid objective values which are anchored in the very order or structure of the universe.

Thus, in some important ways Confucianism differs from traditions that we generally describe as religions. In some other ways, however, Confucianism does indeed possess characteristics that we associate with religions. To be Confucian is to subscribe to a worldview and a philosophy of life with universalistic claims which offers

---

[4] *The Analects*, 11:11. Arthur Waley, *The Analects of Confucius*, London: George Allen & Unwin, 1938, p. 155.

guidelines for all aspects of human life, and the precepts of this creed are eternal, somehow anchored in the universe and beyond the control of man; it is even tempting to say that they are divine.

In modern times, and in the wake of the encounter with European culture, people in China and other parts of East Asia have discussed whether Confucianism should be considered a religion, and even today Chinese scholars have different opinions about this.[5]

Thus, it seems that the question, whether Confucianism should be classified as a religion or not, depends in the final analysis on our definition of 'religion'. But in responding to the question, it is important to acknowledge certain differences within the Confucian tradition that are significant.

The word 'Confucianism' is a European coinage naming this intellectual and spiritual tradition after its most famous representative, Confucius, the Latinized form of Kong Zi 孔子 or Kong Fu Zi 孔夫子 – 'Master Kong' – who is supposed to have lived from 551 to 479 BC. His real name was Kong Qiu 孔丘. In Chinese this school, which more than two thousand years ago was classified as one of the Hundred Schools of Thought that contended during the latter half of the first millennium BC, is referred to as *Rujia* 儒家, i.e. the 'School of Scholars'. After the encounter with the West the distinction between the School of Scholars (*Rujia*) and the 'Teaching of the Scholars' (*Rujiao* 儒教) began to be used to distinguish between Confucianism as philosophy and religion respectively.

Within the Confucian tradition there is indeed a basis for making such a distinction. In addition to the intellectual discussion of the meaning of Confucian ideas, there developed early in China also certain rituals having to do with Confucianism. For example, innumerable temples in Confucius' honour were built in China and other countries, where sacrifices and other rituals took place that must be called Confucian.

In this context the distinction between élite culture and popular culture is significant. As part of élite culture the distinguishing features of Confucianism have been significant and generally

---

[5] See, e.g., Ren Jiyu, 'Chu Hsi and Religion', in Wing-tsit Chan ed. *Chu Hsi and Neo-Confucianism*. Honolulu: University of Hawaii Press, 1986, pp. 355–76.

upheld, but as part of popular religion Confucian rituals and ceremonies have often been mixed with Buddhist and Daoist practices. Certainly, it has not been unknown over time for Confucius, Lao Zi and the Buddhist Goddess of Mercy Guanyin to have been worshipped at one and the same time and in one and the same place.

Those who deny that Confucianism is a religion usually prefer to describe it as a 'philosophy'. Since the word philosophy is generally used in a very broad sense to refer to 'the study of the fundamental nature of knowledge, reality and existence', this characterization would appear quite natural. Yet there are also scholars who on the basis of more narrow definitions of 'philosophy' as referring specifically to the modes of philosophical thought that developed in Europe and produced some rather specific modes of discourse that we may refer to in such terms as logic, ontology, epistemology and ethics, do not like to characterize Confucianism as a philosophy.

The question whether Confucianism is to be considered a philosophy is largely a matter of the definition of the word 'philosophy'. However, we should be aware that the choice of definition may not be an entirely innocent matter but may indeed have some consequences that we should consider before deciding upon a definition. If we choose a broad enough definition of philosophy to include everything from European philosophy, Buddhist thought to Confucianism, then it is likely to promote interest in comparisons and direct our attention, not only to features that divide different traditions, but also to shared features or efforts, in different cultural contexts, to produce coherent visions of the world and of the human predicament itself. On this basis I prefer a broad definition of philosophy. I also cannot see any decisive reason not to define religion in broad enough terms to include Confucianism among the world religions – as long as this does not mean that we start projecting religious features on to Confucianism which are not really present.

Here the focus will be on the evolution and meaning of the Confucian ideas and beliefs and their ideological functions rather than on Confucianism's existential, moral-spiritual praxis. This does not mean that the latter should be seen as less important than the former. Rather, it springs from a desire to give a presentation, which is at the same time serious and easily accessible, of the core intellectual elements of the Confucian tradition and some ideological functions that these have performed.

The Confucian Canon

Confucianism, or the School of Scholars, became talked about as one of the Hundred Schools of Thought that contended during the latter half of the first millennium BC. However, the figure one hundred must be taken *cum grano salis*. In *The Records of the Grand Historian* (*Shiji* 史記) – the first great work of history in China from the first century BC – six major schools are discussed: the Confucians, the Mohists, the Daoists, the Legalists, the School of Names and the Yin-Yang School. In the *History of the Han Dynasty* (*Hanshu* 漢書) from the first century AD, which contains the first extant Chinese bibliography, four more schools were added: the Diplomatists, the Eclectics, the Agrarians and the Story-Tellers, but then the author adds that only nine of these are worth considering, implying that the Story-Tellers are not important.[6]

In the development of Confucianism a number of texts considered as sacred and referred to as 'classics' (*jing* 經) have played a central role. Confucians have explained the meaning of their ideas and beliefs with reference to these classics, and controversies over the true meaning of Confucian ideas and beliefs have therefore generally taken the form of debates over the true interpretation of some passages in the classics.

As an ideological orthodoxy, the government of the Chinese empire put a lot of effort into defining and upholding the true interpretation of these texts. To understand and subscribe to the orthodox interpretation was for many centuries a prerequisite for someone who wanted to serve the empire in any official capacity. To challenge that interpretation which at a certain time was defined as correct was a serious crime.

---

[6] Each work listed under each of these schools is also referred to as a 'school'. If we count these we will arrive at the imposing figure of 190 schools.

The significance of the notion of classics in Chinese intellectual history can hardly be exaggerated. The status of a text as a classic meant that every word in it was correct; the point was not to evaluate what was written in the text but to understand it correctly and learn from it. The notion of 'Six Arts' (*liuyi* 六藝, often translated as 'Six Classics') – *The Poetry* (*Shi* 詩), *The Documents* (*Shu* 書), *The Rites* (*Li* 禮), *The Changes* (*Yi* 易), *The Spring and Autumn Annals* (*Chunqiu* 春秋) and *The Music* (*Yue* 樂) – has traditionally been taken to date back at least to the time of Confucius. This is questionable, but at least it existed before the first emperor of the Qin Dynasty (221–206) who unified China in 221 BC. He and his associates were vehemently opposed to Confucianism, so in 213 he ordered that all heretical texts should be handed in to the state and be burnt.

The Confucian writings were indeed considered heretical – the emperor went so far as to order that a number of Confucian scholars be buried alive. The burning of the books that ensued had far-reaching consequences for China's cultural history. As a result of the burning the question of the authenticity of different versions of ancient texts became even more difficult than it would otherwise have been.

In the Former Han Dynasty (206–25 BC), Confucianism became the ideological orthodoxy of the empire, and then the notion of Six Classics was still familiar. But one of them – *The Classic of Music* – could no longer be found, and as for the other five it was uncertain how close the extant versions were to the original ones.

Emperor Wu (reigned 141–88 BC) adopted the policy of 'banning the hundred schools while recognizing only the Confucians' and established the Five Classics as the official canon. In 124 BC a Grand Academy (*Taixue* 太學) was set up and learned masters of the classics were appointed 'academicians' with the task of defining and explaining the orthodox doctrines. The title of the academicians in Chinese was *boshi* 博士 – 'scholars of wide learning' – which is the word later used for 'doctor'.

Let us take a brief look at the Five Classics, which were to remain important parts of the Confucian Canon until modern times:

First, there was *The Classic of Poetry*, in Chinese *Shijing* 詩經, also known in English as the *Book of Odes* or the *Book of Songs*, a collection of 305 poems which may be dated between ca. 1000 and ca. 600 BC. According to tradition Confucius selected these 305 poems out of three thousand to be used for educational purposes, but this is highly questionable. The poems are arranged in four groups: (i) 'State Airs' (*Guofeng* 國風) contains 160 folk songs dealing with the daily lives of people in 15 states in the north; (ii) 'Small Elegance'(*Xiaoya* 小雅) contains 74 odes dealing with subjects of 'high culture'; some of them have been interpreted as criticism of the authorities; (iii) 'Great Elegance' (*Daya* 大雅) contains 31 poems that deal with the Zhou state and the overthrow of the Shang; (iv) 'Hymns of Praise' (Song 頌) contains sections dealing with religious rites, feasts or musical performances in the states of Zhou, Lu and Shang. Among the translations that exist I would recommend those by Arthur Waley and Bernhard Karlgren.[7] In terms of combining literary elegance with accuracy Arthur Waley's translation remains unsurpassed. Karlgren offers a more scholarly translation, which should be studied in conjunction with his glosses, which help the reader penetrate deeper into the text.

Second, there was *The Classic of Documents*, sometimes known in English as *The Book of Documents* or *The Book of History*, in Chinese *Shujing* 書經 or *Shangshu* 尚書, the earliest work of history in Chinese tradition. It deals with historical and political events of the Three Dynasties, i.e. the Xia, the Shang and the Zhou. This work exists mainly in two different versions, one referred to as the New Text version and the other as the Old Text version. Some parts of it probably date back to the very beginning of the Zhou Dynasty about one thousand years BC, while parts of the Old Text version are today generally considered to be forgeries from the fourth century AD.

James Legge's copiously annotated translation, which includes both versions, gives us a good idea of how the *Book of History* was oftentimes meant to be understood according to the ideological orthodoxy. Bernhard Karlgren set himself the task of translating as accurately as possible those parts that he considered most likely to

---

[7] For bibliographical data on these translations, see below under 'Further Reading'.

be authentic, and so his translation includes 28 chapters whereas the Old Text version contains altogether 58 chapters. As in the case of the odes, he has published illuminating glosses on difficult parts of the text in a separate volume.[8]

Third, there was *The Book of Rites* (*Liji* 禮記), a work probably quite different from the *Rites* classic referred to as one of the Six Classics in pre-Qin times. Its contents are quite diverse. One chapter on music – 'Treatise on Music' (*Yueji* 樂記) has been very important in the Confucian discussions on metaphysics. Other chapters contain information about ancient rites and practices. Two chapters – the 'Great Learning' (*Daxue* 大學) and 'The Doctrine of the Mean' (*Zhongyong* 中庸) were in the Song Dynasty selected to be part of the core of the Confucian canon, *The Four Books* (*Sishu* 四書).

Fourth, there was *The Classic of Changes*, often referred to as *The Book of Changes*, in Chinese *Yijing* 易經. This work consists of two main parts, a handbook for divination, which we may refer to as the *Zhouyi* 周易, and the 'Commentaries' or 'Ten Wings' (*Shiyi* 十翼). One of these in particular, 'The Appended Words'' (*Xici* 系辭) outlines a metaphysics which has played a very important role in Confucianism, not least for the Neo-Confucianism that developed during the Tang and Song Dynasties. In the Confucian interpretation of *The Classic of Changes*, these parts have been taken to constitute a whole; the book of divination has been interpreted in the light of the Ten Wings. Historically, these texts were separate. The origins of the material in the book of divination probably go back at least to as early as the ninth century BC, whereas 'The Ten Wings' probably date back to the first three centuries BC.

The manual for divination is arranged under 64 so-called hexagrams. One hexagram consists of six lines, and one line may be broken (this line is called *yin* 陰) or unbroken (this line is called *yang* 陽). If all possible combinations of hexagrams consisting of *yin* and *yang* lines are calculated the result will be 64, and so there are altogether 64 hexagrams. The *yin* and *yang* lines, the hexagrams (which may have been an expanded version of trigrams,

---

[8] Bibliographical data concerning these works by Bernhard Karlgren and Waley, see below under 'Further Reading'.

'threeliners') go back to ancient divination practices from the Shang Dynasty, when yarrow sticks were used as tools to receive oracle messages. *The Classic of Changes* is important not only in the Confucian but also in the Daoist tradition.

There exist numerous translations of *The Classic of Changes* into English and other foreign languages. Among recent translations I would like to draw attention to two in particular. Professor Richard Lynn has translated this classic together with the famous and influential commentary by Wang Bi 王弼 (226–249).[9] In 1973 a copy of *The Classic of Changes* dating back to the second century BC was found during the excavation of a tomb in Mawangdui in Hunan province. This discovery is of great significance for our understanding of the history of this text, and it has been rendered into English by Edward Shaughnessy.[10]

Fifth and finally there was *The Spring and Autumn Annals*, in Chinese *Chunqiu* 春秋, a terse chronicle of events in the state of Lu in present-day Shandong province during the Spring and Autumn period from 722 to 481 BC.

These Five Classics were to remain a central part of the Confucian Canon for more than two thousand years, albeit in somewhat different versions.

In the Later Han Dynasty the Five Classics became the Seven Classics, *The Analects of Confucius* – in Chinese *Lunyu* 論語 – and *The Book of Filial Piety* – in Chinese *Xiaojing* 孝經 – were added to the list. *The Analects of Confucius* contains recorded conversations with Confucius and his disciples and constitutes the most reliable source we have about Confucius and his ideas. *The Book of Filial Piety* is a text that exemplifies and extols the virtue of this central Confucian value.

In the Tang Dynasty Nine Classics were inscribed on stone tablets, and they were the Five Classics of the Former Han Dynasty plus three commentaries on *The Spring and Autumn Annals* – namely the commentaries known as *Gongyangzhuan* 公羊傳, *Guliangzhuan* 穀梁傳. and *Zuozhuan* 左傳 – and the *Rites of Etiquette and Ceremonial*,

---

[9] See below under 'Further Reading'.
[10] See below under 'Further Reading'.

in Chinese *Yili* 儀禮, which in the Han canon had been a chapter in the *Book of Rites*.

In chapter three we shall see how the three commentaries on the *Spring and Autumn Annals*, were to play a key role in a major controversy in Chinese intellectual history dealing with the contents and authenticity of the Old Text School and New Text School.

Later, the Nine Classics became the Twelve Classics when *The Analects of Confucius* and *The Book of Filial Piety* were again added to the list and when the *Erya* 爾雅 (the oldest Chinese dictionary) also became classified as a 'classic'.

In the Song Dynasty the *Mencius – Meng Zi* 孟子, which records conversations that this important Confucian philosopher had with his disciples and with various rulers as well as other people, became the thirteenth classic.

In the Song Dynasty the great Neo-Confucian philosopher and synthesizer of Confucian thought Zhu Xi 朱熹 (1130–1200) singled out four texts as the core of the Confucian canon and they have since been known as the *Four Books: The Great Learning, The Doctrine of the Mean, The Analects of Confucius* and *Mencius*. Out of these texts which are ordered according to their length, from the shortest to the longest, the first two are actually chapters from the *Book of Rites*.

The Great Learning should give the student a good foundation for learning. The core of the book may be described as how to cultivate one's own moral virtue and at the same time exert moral influence on others. Traditionally it has been believed to be the work of a disciple of Confucius, Zeng Zi 曾子. *The Doctrine of the Mean* is one of the most profound texts of the Confucian canon exploring how one should cultivate oneself and strive for sagehood. The Way – *dao* 道 – plays a very important role in this text, where it is defined in terms of 'centrality' (*zhong* 中) and 'harmony' (*he* 和).[11]

In the late-fourteenth century Zhu Xi's Neo-Confucianism became the ideological orthodoxy upheld by the state and from then on until the end of the empire Zhu Xi's edition of the

---

[11] Translations of *Daxue* and *Zhongyong* are found in Wing-tsit Chan, *A Source Book in Chinese Philosophy,* Princeton: Princeton University Press, 1963, pp. 84–114.

Four Books – *Collected Annotations on the Four Books* (*Sishu jizhu* 四書集注) – remained the core of the Confucian canon.

Further reading

On the meaning and function of ideas

Hirsch, E.D. *The Aims of Interpretation*. Chicago: University of Chicago Press, 1976.

Popper, Karl. 'Three Worlds.' In Sterling M. McMurrin ed. *The Tanner Lectures on Human Values*. Salt Lake City and Cambridge: University of Utah Press and Cambridge University Press, 1980. pp. 141–167.

Idem. *Unended Quest*, London: Routledge, 1974, pp. 180–187.

Is Confucianism a religion?

Bowker, John. *Oxford Dictionary of World Religions*. Oxford & New York: Oxford University Press, 1997.

Eliade, Mircea ed. *The Encyclopedia of Religion*. London: Collier Macmillan, 1993.

Ren Jiyu. 'Chu Hsi and Religion.' In Wing-tsit Chan ed. *Chu Hsi and Neo-Confucianism*. Honolulu: University of Hawaii Press, 1986, pp. 355–76.

Sharman, Arvind. *Our Religions*. San Francisco: Harper, 1993.

'The Study and Classification of Religion.' In *The New Encyclopedia Britannica*. *Macropedia*, Vol. 26, 1991. pp. 509–529.

Küng, Hans and Julia Ching. *Christianity and Chinese Religion*. New York: Doubleday, 1989.

General studies of Confucianism

Creel, H.G. *Chinese Thought from Confucius to Mao Tse-tung*. Chicago: University of Chicago Press, 1953.

Elman, Benjamin A. et al eds. *Rethinking Confucianism: Past and Present in China, Japan, Korea, and Vietnam*. Eds. Benjamin A. Elman, John B. Duncan and Herman Ooms. Los Angeles: UCLA Asian Pacific Monograph Series, 2002.

Fung, Yu-lan. *A Short History of Chinese Philosophy: A Systematic Account of Chinese Thought From its Origins to the Present Day*. New York: Simon & Schuster, 1976. (1st ed 1948)

Idem. *A History of Chinese Philosophy*. I-II. Princeton: Princeton University Press, 1952–1953.

Nivison, David S. *The Ways of Confucianism: Investigations in Chinese Philosophy*. Edited with an introduction by Bryan W. Van Norden. Chicago: Open Court, 1996.

Nivison, David S., ed. *Confucianism in Action*. Edited by David S. Nivison and Arthur F. Wright, with contributions by Wm. Theodore De Bary et al. Stanford: Stanford Univertsity Press, 1959.

Oldstone-Moore, Jennifer. *Confucianism: Origins, Beliefs, Practices, Holy Texts, Sacred Places*. Oxford and New York: Oxford University Press, 2002.

Yao, Xinzhong. *An Introduction to Confucianism*. New York: Cambridge University Press, 2000.

The Confucian Classics
A. General

Loewe, Michael ed. *Early Chinese Texts: A Bibliographical Guide*. Berkeley: Society for the Study of Early China: Institute of East Asian Studies, 1993.

Wilkinson, Endymion Porter. *Chinese History: A Manual*. Cambridge, Mass.: Harvard University Asia Center for the Harvard-Yenching Institute, 2000. pp. 475–479.

B. Individual Classics

1. *The Classic of Poetry* (*Shijing* 詩經)

For an introduction, see Michael Loewe's entry in *Early Chinese Texts: A Bibliographical Guide*, pp. 415–423. See also Stephen Owen's 'Preface' and Joseph R. Allen's 'Postface' to *The Book of Songs. The Ancient Chinese Classic of Poetry*, translated from the Chinese by Arthur Waley; edited with additional translations by Joseph R. Allen, New York: Grove Press, 1996.

Translations

Karlgren, Bernhard. *The Book of Odes: Chinese Text, Transcription and Translation*. Stockholm: Museum of Far Eastern Antiquities, 1950.

Waley, Arthur. *The Book of Songs. The Ancient Chinese Classic of Poetry*. Translated from the Chinese by Arthur Waley; edited with additional translations by Joseph R. Allen, New York: Grove Press, 1996.

Studies

Karlgren, Bernhard. *Glosses on the Book of Odes*. Stockholm: Museum of Far Eastern Antiquities, 1970.

2. *The Classic of Documents* (*Shujing* 書經)

For an introduction, see Edward Shaughnessy's entry in *Early Chinese Texts: A Bibliographical Guide*, pp. 376–389.

Translations

Karlgren, Bernhard. *The Book of Documents*. Stockholm: Museum of Far Eastern Antiquities, 1950.

Legge, James. *The Book of History*. In *The Chinese Classics*, Vol. III, Parts I and II. Taipei: SMC publications, 1991. 1st ed. 1865.

Studies

Karlgren, Bernhard. *Glosses on the Book of Documents*. Stockholm: Museum of Far Eastern Antiquities, 1970.

3. *The Book of Rites* (*Liji* 禮記)

For an introduction, see Jeffrey K. Riegel's entry in *Early Chinese Texts: A Bibliographical Guide*, pp. 293–297.

Translations

Legge. James. *Li chi: Book of Rites: An Encyclopedia of Ancient Ceremonial Usages, Religious Creeds, and Social institutions*. Edited with an introduction and study guide by Ch'u Chai and Winberg Chai. New Hyde Park, N.Y.: University Books, 1967. First edition of Legge's translation published by Oxford University press in 1885 as volumes XXVII and XXVIII of *The Sacred Books of the East*.

Two Chapters in The Book of Rites – *The Great Learning* (*Daxue* 大學) and *The Doctrine of the Mean* (*Zhongyong* 中庸) – became in the Song dynasty two of the Four books. Translations of *The Great Learning* and *The Doctrine of the Mean* are found in Wing-tsit Chan, *A Source Book in Chinese Philosophy*, Princeton: Princeton University Press, 1963, pp. 84–94 and 95–114. English translations of these two works are also found in James Legge, *The Chinese Classics*. Vol. 1. Taipei: SMC Pub., 1991. Reprint of Oxford University Press edition from 1893.

4. *The Classic of Changes* (*Yijing* 易經)
For an introduction, see Edward Shaughnessy's entry in *Early Chinese Texts: A Bibliographical Guide*, pp. 216–228. For a bibliography of translations and studies, see Edward Hacker et al., *I Ching: An Annotated Bibliography. By Edward Hacker, Steve Moore, and Lorraine Patsco*. New York: Routledge, 2002.

Translations
Lynn, Richard John. *The Classic of Changes. A New Translation of the I Ching as Interpreted by Wang Bi*. New York: Columbia University Press, 1994.
Shaughnessy, Edward L. *I Ching: The Classic of Changes*. Translated with an introduction and commentary by Shaughnessy. New York: The Ballantine Publishing Co., 1996.

Studies
Peterson. Willard J. 'Making Connections: "Commentary on the Attached Verbalizations" of the *Book of Changes*. In *Harvard Journal of Asiatic Studies*, 42:1, pp. 67–116.

5. *The Spring and Autumn Annals* (*Chunqiu* 春秋)
For an introduction, see Anne Cheng's entry in *Early Chinese Texts: A Bibliographical Guide*, pp. 67–76.

Translation
Legge, James. *The Chinese Classics*. Vol. 5. Taipei: SMC Pub., 1991. First edition Hong Kong: London Missionary Society, 1872. A number of errata listed by James Legge have been corrected in the text. With concordance tables to later translations in English, French, and German.

6. *The Analects of Confucius* (*Lunyu* 論語)
For bibliographical references concerning translations and studies of the *Mencius*, see below chapter 2.

7. *The Book of Filial Piety* (*Xiaojing* 孝經)
For an introduction, see William G. Boltz' entry in *Early Chinese Texts: A Bibliographical Guide*, pp. 141–153.

Translation

Legge, James. *The Sacred Books of China: The Texts of Confucianism.* Vol. 1. New York: Gordon Press, 1976. First edition Oxford: Claendon Press, 1879.

8. *Gongyangzhuan* 公羊傳,

For an introduction, see Anne Cheng's entry in *Early Chinese Texts: A Bibliographical Guide*, pp. 67–76.

Partial translation

Malmqvist, Göran. 'Studies on the Gongyang and Guuliang Commentaries, I–III. In *Bulletin of the Museum of Far Eastern Antiquities*, No. 43, 1971, pp. 67–222; No. 47, 1975, pp. 19–69; and No. 49, 1977, pp. 33–215.

9. *Guliangzhuan* 穀梁傳

For an introduction, see Anne Cheng's entry in *Early Chinese Texts: A Bibliographical Guide*, pp. 67–76.

Partial translation

Malmqvist, Göran. 'Studies on the Gongyang and Guuliang Commentaries, I–III. In *Bulletin of the Museum of Far Eastern Antiquities*, No. 43, 1971, pp. 67–222; No. 47, 1975, pp. 19–69; and No. 49, 1977, pp. 33–215.

10. *Zuozhuan* 左傳

For an introduction, see Anne Cheng's entry in *Early Chinese Texts: A Bibliographical Guide*, pp. 67–76.

Translation

Legge, James. *The Chinese Classics.* Vol. 5. Taipei: SMC Pub., 1991. First Hong Kong: London Missionary Society, 1872. A number of errata listed by James Legge have been corrected in the text. With concordance tables to later translations in English, French, and German.

11. *Rites of Etiquette and Ceremonial* (*Yili* 儀禮)

For an introduction, see William G. Boltz entry in *Early Chinese Texts: A Bibliographical Guide*, pp. 234–243.

Translation

Steele, John. *The I li, or Book of Etiquette and Ceremonial.* London: Probsthain and Co., 1917. 2 vols.

12. *Erya* 爾雅

See W. South Coblin's entry to *Early Chinese Texts: A Bibliographical Guide*, pp. 94–99.

Erya is a dictionary and so it is not surprising that there are no translations of this work.

13. *Mencius* (*Meng Zi* 孟子)

For bibliographical references concerning translations and studies of the *Mencius*, see below chapter 3.

1

CONFUCIANISM BEFORE CONFUCIUS

C onfucius talked about himself as a transmitter rather than a creator, and much of the core of Confucian thought goes back to the time before Confucius, more specifically to the first centuries after the Zhou people had conquered the Shang in the eleventh century BC.

If history begins with the emergence of written sources, then Chinese history begins with the Shang Dynasty which lasted from the seventeenth to the eleventh century BC. The written sources from the Shang that have been preserved are the so-called oracle bone inscriptions which tell us something about the religious practices of the time and some of the questions that were considered most important. The 'oracle bones' – actually shoulder blades of oxen or turtle shells – were used by diviners to seek answers to questions related to a wide variety of topics. In the words of the leading Western specialist on the oracle bones, David N. Keightley: '[f]ew significant aspects of Shang life were undivined'.[1] Questions could concern topics such as sacrifices, military campaigns, hunting expeditions, excursions, the ten-day week, the night or the day, the weather, agriculture, sickness, childbirth, distress or trouble, dreams, settlement, buildings orders, tribute payments, divine assistance or approval and requests addressed to ancestral or nature powers.[2]

---

[1] David N. Keightley, *Sources of Shang History: The Oracle-Bone Inscriptions of Bronze Age China,* Berkeley and Los Angeles: California University Press, 1985, p. 33.
[2] Ibid., pp. 33–35.

The diviner applied heat to a hollow that had been carved in the oracle bone, which then cracked, and the crack was seen as a response to the question. The diviner was able to interpret the response and so inscribed his question as well as the answer. In the divinations we find many references to the 'High God' (Di 帝), also called 'Lord on High (Shangdi 上帝), the preeminent deity of the Shang people, who was later in the Zhou dynasty to be replaced by 'Heaven' (tian 天).

Scholars who have studied the oracle bones have been struck by the pervasiveness of ancestor worship. The focus on ancestors and the family, viewing the family as a microcosm of the world and discussing ethical and political questions in perspective of the hierarchical family relations are themes that figure prominently in the Confucian tradition and which we will get back to in this book. However, the oracle bone inscriptions as such do not play any role in Confucianism, since they seem to have been unknown to Confucius and his contemporaries and, strangely enough, were rediscovered only on the eve of the twentieth century.

Today we know through the results of archaeological excavations that ancestor worship in China is much more ancient than the oracle bones known today. We may therefore say that Confucianism has incorporated ancient elements from pre-historic times.

The historical lessons that Confucius wanted to transmit were largely based on what we would consider legends and myths. According to one of these legends, which are exceedingly rich and of which there are several versions, the universe had been created by Pan Gu 盤古, who separated Heaven and Earth.

Later, there appeared three sovereigns: Fu Xi 伏犧, Shen Nong 神農 and Huang Di 黃帝. Fu Xi invented the script and many forms of arts and crafts, for example the system of divination later recorded in *The Classic of Changes*; Shen Nong was the father of agriculture; and Huang Di, or the Yellow Emperor, was the ancestor of later kings and aristocrats. Sometimes he – and another mythological figure Yan Di 炎帝 – have been taken as the ancestors of all Han-Chinese people, the Han being the major ethnic group in China.

The Three Sovereigns were followed by the Five Emperors and three of these were Yao 堯, Shun 舜 and Yu 禹. As sages or sage-kings, Yao and Shun have remained preeminent paragons of virtue in the Confucian tradition. As a ruler Yao abdicated and ceded his throne to Shun rather than to his son, and Shun, too, abdicated in favour of the capable Yu, who tamed the rivers and solved the problem of floods. The theme of abdication in favour of a virtuous and capable successor, instead of ceding the throne to one's son, has remained important in Confucian thought as an example of virtuous behaviour of rulers.

The view of abdication may be seen as an expression of a cluster of core Confucian values. One of these has to do with moral virtue, which is considered the most important quality in a human being. Ideally, the world should be ruled by the example of a virtuous ruler who does not need to resort to the use of force and rewards and punishments. This is indeed the very definition of a 'sage-king' (*sheng wang* 聖王), a central concept in Confucian political thought. Another value has to do with the supremacy of merit over descent. The important thing is how you use your talents and what kind of a person you become, not what family you come from. To some extent we may describe the Chinese state as a meritocracy – a country where merit ruled – since, although the imperial succession within one and the same dynasty was based on descent, the recruitment of government officials was based on examinations where the candidates were anonymous to those who corrected their exam papers. This meritocracy was very much legitimized in Confucian terms.[3]

The values of virtue and merit were part of the foundation of what has been referred to as culturalism, i.e. the notion that anyone, no matter what their ethnic or family background, can become a good Confucian and even a sage. The sage-king Shun himself was held up as an example of this, since he was a descendant of the 'Northern barbarians'. This notion was to serve the Chinese empire well, since it could be used to legitimize its universalistic

---

[3] The concept 'meritocracy' became known through Michael Young's study of the effects of education as part of modernization in the West. See his classical work *The Rise of the Meritocracy, 1870–2033: An Essay on Education and Equality*, London: Thames and Hudson, 1958. But the concept may no doubt also be applied to pre-modern China.

pretensions: everybody in the world was a potential Confucian and Chinese; to be Confucian and Chinese was in the final analysis the same thing as to be civilized.

The mythological ruler Yu was succeeded by his son Qi 啟, and with him began, according to the traditional historiography, the Xia dynasty which lasted for some four hundred years into the seventeenth century BC, when it was succeeded by the Shang. The last ruler of the Xia was allegedly the tyrant Jie 桀, who was overthrown by King Tang 湯, the founder of the Shang.

With the rise of critical historiography in China in the early twentieth century there emerged the slogan to 'doubt antiquity', and the historians who represented this new trend became known as 'the school of antiquity doubters' (*yigupai* 疑古派).[4] These historians rejected the legends about the origin of the universe and of China as fictitious. They even denied the historical existence of the Xia dynasty. Their contribution to Chinese scholarship can hardly be overestimated; they did in China what Ranke and like-minded historians did in Europe. Yet dismissing the legends as fictitious should not mean that they are insignificant. On the contrary, shaping historical consciousness in China during more than two thousand years they have been extremely important. To the credit of the 'antiquity doubters' we should also say that their work paved the way for the study of the ancient legends and myths as legends.

To deny the existence of the Xia dynasty was correct on the basis of the evidence that was available in the early twentieth century. With the tremendous advances in the field of archaeology during the past century, however, much new evidence has been unearthed which suggests that there may after all have existed a Xia dynasty.

According to the traditional historical account, the Xia was overthrown because its last ruler was a tyrant, and the same pattern re-emerged with the transition from the Shang to the Zhou

---

[4] The most famous representative of this group of historians was Gu Jiegang 顧頡剛 (1893–1980), who edited the *Gushibian* 古史辨 (Discussions on ancient history). Concerning Gu Jiegang see Laurence Schneider, *Ku Chieh-kang and China's New History: Nationalism and the Quest for Alternative Traditions*, Berkeley : University of California Press, 1971.

Dynasty. The last ruler of the Shang – Zhou Xin 紂辛 – was described by the Zhou rulers as a tyrant disliked by the people who lost the Mandate of Heaven to the state of Zhou.

The first part of the Zhou Dynasty, lasting from ca. 1040 BC until 771 BC when the capital was situated in the valley of the river Wei in near present-day Xian in Shaanxi province, is often referred to as the Western Zhou. As a result of barbarian invasions from the West, the Zhou had to move their capital in 771 to Zhengzhou near present-day Luoyang in Henan province. The period which began in 771 and lasted until the final collapse of the Zhou in 256 BC – just a few decades before the Qin created the first unified Chinese empire – is called Eastern Zhou.

During the Eastern Zhou we meet with the two periods, the Spring-and-Autumn Period (722–481 BC), and the Warring States Period (403–221 BC). The Spring-and-Autumn Period covers the period of the annals of the state of Lu in present-day Shandong province which bear the same name, *Chunqiu* 春秋, and which are traditionally attributed to Confucius.

The prevailing political order of the Western Zhou has often been described as feudal, since the Zhou King, who was in possession of the Mandate of Heaven, enfeoffed vassals with states to rule. There emerged a nobility allegedly divided into five ranks: 'duke' (*gong* 公), 'marquis' (*hou* 侯), 'earl' (*bo* 伯), 'viscount' (*zi* 子), and 'baron' (*nan* 男). The order of the early Zhou was a model to emulate for the Confucians, but this original order gradually degenerated. The vassal states asserted their independence vis-a-vis the Zhou and there was strife among them. Their leaders acted not as sages but became 'hegemons' (*ba* 霸), i.e. they relied for their rule on force rather than on their own good example.

The description of the Zhou as a continuing process of degeneration of an original ideal state of harmony into strife, disintegration and hardship for the people is not uncontroversial; there is no doubt that this was also a period of development and in some sense progress. Production techniques as well as administrative structures became more advanced. Yet what is important in this context is the Confucian *perception* of degeneration. It was this perception, and the notion of a truly Golden Age when all under Heaven was ruled by sage-kings such as Yao and Shun, that provided a fundamental point of departure for the Confucians: the task facing them as spiritual leaders was to point out the way to renewed order and harmony.

The Classic of Documents

The transition from the Shang to the Zhou was described in *The Classic of Documents,* where we meet for the first time the notion of the 'Mandate of Heaven' (*tian ming* 天命), which has been at the very core of Confucianism, particularly in its role as state ideology. According to this idea, the king was the 'Son of Heaven' (*tian zi* 天子) who had received the 'Mandate of Heaven' to rule 'all under Heaven' (*tian xia* 天下), i.e. the whole world. Just as Heaven was the supreme ruler in the divine world, so the 'King' (*wang* 王) ruled under Heaven, but only by virtue of the Mandate of Heaven.

When the King of Zhou received the mandate, Heaven made this clear by arranging a solar eclipse, and later it became a central concern for Confucians to know for sure when one ruler and his dynasty had lost the mandate and another one had gained it. At the time of transition from one dynasty to another, unusual natural phenomena could always be observed. Moreover, in the Confucian tradition the loss of popular support has often been taken as a sign – or cause – of the loss of the Mandate of Heaven.

When in modern times the Western notion of 'revolution' was to be translated into Japanese and Chinese, it was rendered as *geming* 革命, which literally means 'change mandate'. This we may see as testimony to the centrality in Chinese thought of the notion of a heavenly mandate.

The Classic of Documents contains some rather terse historical and political treatises, which have been immensely important for the formation of Confucian thought. Reading through it we may discern a number of themes which would later form part of the core of Confucian thought. It deals largely with history, but the purpose is to draw lessons from history. Therefore, we can also say that it is a book of statecraft. In this it anticipates a major trend in later

Confucian thought: to use history as 'a mirror' of one's own time and of the future. In the chapter 'Shao gao' 召誥, we may read:

> We should not fail to mirror ourselves in the lords of Xia; we likewise should not fail to mirror ourselves in the lords of Yin [i.e. the later part of the Shang]. We do not presume to know and say: the lords of Xia undertook Heaven's mandate so as to have it for so-and-so many years; we do not presume to say: it could not be prolonged. It was that they did not reverently attend to their virtue, and so they prematurely renounced their mandate. We do not presume to know and say: the Lords of Yin received Heaven's mandate so as to have it for so-and-so many years; we do not know and say: it could not be prolonged. It was that they did not reverently attend to their virtue, and so they prematurely threw away their mandate.
>
> Now the king has succeeded to and received their mandate. We should then also remember the mandates of these two states [i.e. Xia and Yin], and in succeeding to them equal their merits. Now the king starts to undertake the mandate.[5]

In this section it is the famous Duke of Zhou, one of the major political figures of the early Zhou Dynasty held up as a paragon of virtue by Confucius, who is speaking. The fate of the states of Xia and Yin – Yin we now generally refer to as late Shang – shows that the Mandate of Heaven can be gained but also be lost. Later, throughout the Confucian tradition, this has been a major theme: to study the fate of the Xia and the Shang dynasties and learn what they did right and what they did wrong in order to be able to retain the Mandate of Heaven.

As we can see from the passage just quoted, the way for a ruler to retain the mandate was to attend to his 'virtue' (*de* 德), a concept which in early times combined the meanings 'virtue' and 'force' or 'power'; in the course of the Confucian tradition the meaning 'force' or 'power' was weakened and it hardly exists in the modern Chinese language more than as an echo of this early usage. If a ruler was not virtuous, he would lose the mandate, and according to later Chinese historiography it was considered almost inevitable that an imperial dynasty would sooner or later lose it.

---

[5] Karlgren, *The Book of Documents,* pp. 49–50, modif.

How then could one know if a ruler was virtuous or not? The cynic might answer that these were only beautiful words to embellish the ugly reality of power politics: as long as a ruler stayed in power, he was virtuous; when he was overthrown the reason was said to be, to use the words of the Duke of Zhou that we just quoted, that he had not reverently attended to his virtue.

This cynical interpretation does indeed capture one aspect of the ideological use of the notion of the Mandate of Heaven, but it does not exhaust its meaning. This is an example of how we should be attentive to the discrepancy and tension between original meaning and function of Confucian notions.

If we read more about the mandate in the *Classic of Documents*, and then study how it was later explicated and commented upon in the Confucian tradition, we shall find that it is pointed out again and again that a ruler must be good to his people, protect them, create conditions for a good life in order to retain his mandate. Similarly, if rulers become selfish and only think of their own pleasure, then they will lose the mandate. Let us look at another passage, in the chapter 'Wu yi' 無逸:

> At the start, when he [Zu Jia 祖甲, ruler of Shang] came to the high position, then he knew the sufferings of the small people. He could give protection and kindness to the common people, and he dared not insult widowers and widows. Thus Zu Jia's enjoyment of the realm lasted for 33 years. [. . .] The kings who arose after this, during their whole life enjoyed ease; during their life they enjoyed ease and did not know the hardships of husbandry, they did not hear about the toilings of the small people. They were bent on being steeped in pleasure. After this there was none who had any chance of reaching a high age; some had ten years [on the throne], some seven or eight years, some five or six years, some four or three years.[6]

After this follows a long characterization of King Wen of Zhou – Wen Wang 文王 – one of the great paragons of Confucian virtue in the history of Chinese statecraft:

---

[6] Ibid., p. 58, modif.

24

King Wen was humble and submissive, he applied himself to peaceful achievements and to agricultural achievements.

He was finely mild and beautifully respectful, he cherished and protected the small people, he was kind and good to widowers and widows. From morning to the sun's being in the middle of its course and being in the west he had no time to eat at leisure. And thus he united and harmonized the myriad people.

King Wen dared not amuse himself in excursions and hunts. Together with the many states he managed the government. King Wen received the mandate in the middle of life, and his enjoyment of the realm lasted for fifty years.

The Duke of Zhou said: Oh, the succeeding king, who will continue the line from now, should not be excessive in wine and not licentious in excursions and hunting. Together with the myriad people he should manage the government.

Do not moreover say: today I will indulge in pleasure. That is not what the people comply with, it is not what Heaven approves of. The people of the age will greatly take as pattern the faults you have. Do not imitate the errors and disorders of the king of Yin, Zhou, and his disposition of one madly given to wine.

The Duke of Zhou said: Oh, I have heard that the ancient men informed and told each other, protected and cherished each other, taught and instructed each other. Among the people there were hardly any who imposed on each other or did cheating tricks. [. . .]

The Duke of Zhou said: Oh, from the Yin king Zhong Zong to Gao Zong and to Zu Jia and to our King Wen of Zhou, these four men pursued the course of wisdom. If somebody told them: the small people bear resentment against you and revile you, then all the more they paid careful attention to their virtue. As to their faults they said: that is my fault. When it truly was like this, they not only dared not bear anger [i.e. even welcomed criticism].[7]

We meet already in these early texts of *The Classic of Documents* strong belief in the power of the moral example. Maybe we can regard the fact, which we have already drawn attention to, that the word *de* 德 in ancient times combined the meaning 'virtue' and 'power' or 'force' as a reflection of the profound conviction of the power of virtue. In the *Classic of Documents* this theme recurs again

---

[7] Ibid., pp. 58–59, modif.

and again. Consider for example the following passage from the 'Yao dian' 堯典 chapter about the legendary sage-king Yao:

> He was able to make bright his lofty virtue, and so made affectionate the nine branches of the family. When the nine branches of the family had become harmonious, he distinguished and honoured the hundred clans (the gentry). When the hundred clans had become illustrious, he harmonized the myriad states. The numerous were amply nourished and prosperous and then became concordant.[8]

In the classical Confucianism of Confucius and Mencius, rule by moral example was said to characterize the sage-king, whereas the use of punishments was necessary for less perfect rulers and especially the so-called 'hegemons' (*ba* 霸) of the Zhou dynasty. However, in the *Classic of Documents* this distinction does not come forth very clearly. There is indeed, as we have seen, great emphasis on the power of the moral example, but again and again there are also references to punishments that were necessary:

> The King said: Oh, Feng, be careful and enlightened in regard to your punishments. If somebody has made a small offense, if it is not an offense by mishap but a persistence and he himself has committed what is unlawful according to his set purpose, even if his offense is small, then you cannot but kill him.[9]

The book even contains a whole chapter, containing twenty-two paragraphs, about punishment.[10] Interestingly, the concept of punishment is quite often ascribed to Heaven, which then appears rather like a God who may intervene in mundane affairs. In one context a king says: 'Now I execute Heaven's punishment.'[11] And again and again rulers of Zhou are quoted as telling their collaborators that 'Heaven is not to be relied upon', i.e. the mandate is uncertain. If a ruler does something wrong, Heaven will intervene and in effect punish him:

> The King spoke thus: [. . .] The merciless Heaven sends down injury on our house, without the slightest delay. [. . .] I am not perfected and

---

[8] Ibid., p. 1, modif.
[9] See the chapter 'Kang gao' 康誥, 8; ibid., p. 40, modif.
[10] The chapter 'Lü's punishments' (lü xing) 呂刑, ibid., pp. 74–78.
[11] Quoted from the chapter 'Gan shi' 甘誓, 3; ibid., p. 18 modif.

wise, leading the people to tranquility; how much less then should I be able to comprehend and know the commands of Heaven? Oh, I am a little child; I am as if I were to cross a deep water, I go and seek where I can cross. [. . .] When Heaven now sends down its inflictions [i.e. the difficulties in the Zhou house], he knows that our state has a flaw and that our people are not tranquil, and he says: 'we shall come back', and he even despises our Zhou state. [. . .] Heaven is not to be relied upon [i.e. the mandate is uncertain]. Do not dare now to change what has been determined. Moreover, when Heaven now sends down guilt on the state of Zhou [i.e. the sedition], and great troublemakers and disorderly neighbours attack us within the house, do you still not understand that the Heaven's mandate is not easy to keep?[12]

In the *Classic of Documents* we also find the notion made explicit that the Son of Heaven has the mandate to rule the whole world: 'The Son of Heaven is the father and mother of the people, and thereby is king over the whole world.'[13] We should also notice that the Son of Heaven is described as the mother and father of the people. This was also to remain as a core tenet of Confucian thought, i.e. the relationship between a sovereign and his subjects was compared to the relationship between father and son. In classical Confucianism the family is seen as a microcosm of 'all under Heaven'.

The main 'message' of *The Classic of Documents* is perhaps that rulers should follow the will of Heaven and be protective and kind to their people. If they are able to do this, they will retain the mandate and the people will follow them; if not, the people will be discontent and the mandate will be taken away from them. The focus is rather on the duties of the rulers than the duties of the 'common people'.

The Classic of Poetry

The *Classic of Poetry* is rich in its content and contains different kinds of poems, ranging from court hymns to love poetry. The

---

[12] See the chapter 'Da gao' 大誥, 1- 13; ibid., pp. 36–39, modif.
[13] Quoted from the chapter 'Hong fan' 洪範, 16; ibid., p. 32.

first poem in the collection reads in Arthur Waley's beautiful translation:

> 'Fair, fair', cry the ospreys
> On the island in the river
> Lovely is this noble lady,
> Fit bride for our lord.
>
> In patches grows the water mallow;
> To left and right one must seek it.
> Shy was this noble lady;
> Day and night he sought her.
>
> Sought her and could not get her;
> Day and night he grieved.
> Long thoughts, oh, long unhappy thoughts,
> Now on his back, now tossing on to his side.
>
> In patches grows the water mallow;
> To left and right one must gather it.
> Shy is this noble lady;
> With great zither and little we hearten her.
>
> In patches grows the water mallow;
> To left and right one must choose it.
> So shy is this noble lady;
> With gongs and drums we will gladden her.[14]

The spontaneous understanding of this poem is that it expresses a man's agonizing longing to be together with a woman he loves, a longing that inspires compassion in the reader. It is hard to see that the poem itself suggests that there is anything good or beautiful about the lovers being separated. But this is exactly what the orthodox Confucian interpretation has done to it: it has become a poem extolling the virtue of 'men and women being separate'. So this poem and its interpretation is another example of the tension between the meaning and function of the texts that make up the Confucian canon.

Many of the poems express the longing for love and beauty, sensuous pleasure, themes that were later often conspicuously absent

---

[14] Trans. Waley, *The Book of Songs*, pp. 5–6.

from the Confucian discussions. In the poem 'Of Fair Girls', the narrator rejoices in some rush-wool which he finds beautiful but which upon reflection is not beautiful in itself but only because it was given to him by the loveliest of 'fair girls':

> Of fair girls the loveliest
> Was to meet me at the corner of the Wall.
> But she hides and will not show herself;
> I scratch my head, pace up and down.
>
> Of fair girls the prettiest
> Gave me a red flute
> The flush of that red flute
> Is pleasure at the girl's beauty.
>
> She has been in the pastures and brought for me rush-wool,
> Very beautiful and rare.
> It is not you that are beautiful;
> But you were given by a lovely girl.[15]

In several poems we meet women who express their desire, sometimes with striking self-confidence as in the poem 'Gird Your Loins':

> If you tenderly love me,
> Gird your loins and wade across the Zhen;
> But if you do not love me –
> There are plenty of other men,
> Of madcaps maddest, oh!
>
> If you tenderly love me,
> Gird your loins and wade across the Wei;
> But if you do not love me –
> There are plenty of other knights,
> Of madcaps maddest, oh![16]

Not surprisingly, later Confucian commentators have found it difficult to explain such poems in terms of the rather negative Confucian view of independent women.

---

[15] No. 42; ibid., p. 36.
[16] No. 87; ibid, p. 72,

Of course many poems are much more Confucian in a conventional sense. Consider, for example, the following eulogy of the Duke of Zhou, one of the great paragons of virtue in Confucian tradition:

> Broken were our axes
> And chipped our hatchets.
> But since the Duke of Zhou came to the east
> Throughout the kingdom all is well.
> He has shown compassion to us people,
> He has greatly helped us.
>
> Broken were our axes
> And chipped our hoes.
> But since the Duke of Zhou came to the east
> The whole land has been changed.
> He has shown compassion to us people,
> He has greatly blessed us.
>
> Broken were our axes
> And chipped our chisels.
> But since the Duke of Zhou came to the east
> All the kingdoms are knit together.
> He has shown compassion to us people,
> He has been a great boon to us.[17]

Several poems contain references to Heaven and the way Heaven intervenes in the lives of people. Sometimes these references may appear rather fatalistic. Consider for example the poem entitled 'Northern Gate':

> I go out at the northern gate;
> Deep is my grief.
> I am utterly poverty-stricken and destitute;
> Yet no one heeds my misfortunes.
> Well, all is over now.
> No doubt it was Heaven's doing.
> So what's the good of talking about it?

---

[17] No. 157; ibid, p. 126.

The king's business came my way;
Government business of every sort was put upon me.
When I came in from outside
The people of the house all turned on me and scolded me.
Well, it's over now.
No doubt it was Heaven's doing.
So what's the good of talking about it?

The king's business was all piled upon me;
Government business of every sort was laid upon me.
When I came in from outside
The people of the house all turned upon me and abused me.
Well, it's over now.
No doubt it was Heaven's doing.
So what's the good of talking about it?[18]

One interesting poem expresses a longing for a better world:

Big rat, big rat,
Do not gobble our millet!
Three years we have slaved for you,
Yet you take no notice of us.
At last we are going to leave you
And go to that happy land;
Happy land, happy land,
Where we shall have our place.

Big rat, big rat,
Do not gobble our corn!
Three years we have slaved for you,
Yet you give us no credit.
At last we are going to leave you
And go to that happy kingdom;
Happy kingdom, happy kingdom,
Where we shall have our due.

Big rat, big rat,
Do not gobble our rice-shoots!
Three years we have slaved for you,

---

[18] Poem no 40; trans. ibid., p. 35.

Yet you did nothing to reward us.
At last we are going to leave you
And go to those happy borders;
Happy borders, happy borders,
Where no sad songs are song.[19]

This poem has been referred to as perhaps the earliest poetic expression in Chinese literature of 'the desire for a happy land or an ideal society'.[20] Traditionally, it has been taken as criticism of a ruler's 'greed' and 'heavy taxes' but also as expressing a desire 'to abandon the king for another land of happiness and virtue'.[21]

One section of this collection of poetry – the 'Great Elegance' (*Daya* 大雅) – contains some thirty poems most of which deal with 'big' subjects of history and legend. One of these entitled 'Birth to the People' tells us about Jiang Yuan who prayed that she would not remain childless and so trod on 'the big toe of God's footprint' and gave birth to Hou Ji, the inventor of agriculture and of the sacrifices.[22] Other poems in this section eulogize the early leaders of the Zhou. One typical example is the poem 'Renowned Was King Wen', the first stanza of which reads:

Renowned was King Wen,
Yes, high was his renown.
He united, he gave peace;
Manifold were his victories.
Oh, glorious was King Wen![23]

As we have seen, many of the poems in *The Classic of Poetry* express the thoughts, feelings and desires of individual people. Some of these were not easy to reconcile with the Confucian orthodoxy of later times. Therefore, with regard to many poems there evolved this discrepancy or tension between the original meaning and the orthodox interpretation.

---

[19] Poem no. 113; trans. Waley, pp. 88–89.
[20] See Zhang Longxi, 'The Utopian Vision, East and West', in *Utopian Studies*, Vol. 13, no. 1, 2002, p. 12.
[21] Zhang Longxi, ibid., p. 13
[22] For an English translation of this long poem – no. 245 – see Waley, pp. 244–247.
[23] No. 244; ibid., p. 241.

However, we should also bear in mind that in the Confucian tradition, since the earliest times, poetry has been conceived as opening up a window to the inner world of human beings: 'Poetry gives words to what the mind is intent upon' (*shi yan zhi* 詩言志). For the Confucian this was important. In the words of Stephen Owen, a leading specialist on Chinese poetry in the Western world:

> This seemingly innocuous statement had immense consequences; readers found in the *Songs* [i.e. *The Classic of Poetry*] not an 'art' of words, produced by a special class of human beings called 'poets', but rather a window into another person's heart, a person like themselves. Behind every song one might find some powerful concern – desire, anger, reverence, pain – set in its living context. Other Confucian classics treated outward things: deeds, moral precepts, the way the world worked. But *The Book of Songs* was the classic of the human heart and the human mind.[24]

This view of poetry as 'a window into another person's heart' combined with the conviction of Mencius and other Confucians that humans are basically good made the reading of poetry important for the Confucians as a way of 'educating the human heart back to its natural goodness'.[25] For this reason the reading of poetry in general and the poems of *The Classic of Poetry* in particular has remained a central concern for Confucians throughout the centuries.

Further reading

Historical background
Chang, Chih-kwang. *The Archaeology of Ancient China*. New Haven: Yale University Press, 1986.
Creel, H.G. *The Origins of Statecraft in China*. Chicago: University of Chicago Press, 1970.
Hsu, Cho-yun. *Ancient China in Transition: An Analysis of Social Mobility 722–222 BC*. Stanford: Stanford University Press, 1965.
Hsu, Cho-yun and Katheryn M. Linduff. *Western Chou Civilization*. New Haven: Yale University Press, 1988.

---

[24] Quoted from Owen's foreword to Waley, p. xv.
[25] Ibid., p. xiv.

Keightley, David N. *The Ancestral Landscape: Time, Space, and Community in Late Shang China*. Berkeley: University of California Press, 2000.

Idem., ed. *The Origins of Chinese Civilization*. London: University of California Press, 1983.

Idem. *Sources of Shang History: The Oracle-Bone Inscriptions of Bronze Age China*. Berkeley and Los Angeles: California University Press, 1985.

Li, Xueqin. *Eastern Zhou and Qin Civilizations*. New Haven and London: Yale University Press, 1985.

Loewe, Michael and Edward L. Shaughnessy eds., *The Cambridge History of Ancient China: From the Origins of Civilization to 221 B.C.,* Cambridge: Cambridge University Press 1999.

Schneider, Laurence. *Ku Chieh-kang and China's New History: Nationalism and the Quest for Alternative Traditions*. Berkeley : University of California Press, 1971.

Zhang Longxi. 'The Utopian Vision, East and West.' In *Utopian Studies*, Vol. 13, no. 1, 2002.

The Classic of Documents
For bibliographical data see above under 'Further Reading' in 'Introduction'.

The Classic of Poetry
For bibliographical data see above under 'Further Reading' in 'Introduction', p. 14.

2

CONFUCIUS: TRANSMITTER AND FOUNDING FATHER

Confucius was born in the small state of Lu in present-day Shandong province in Eastern China. He was a descendant of aristocrats and his great-grandparents had come to Lu from the state of Song, which was the descendant state of the Shang dynasty. However, his own parents and family were poor.

Confucius was a teacher and has been remembered as the great teacher in Chinese tradition. Today, adherents to his ideas are lobbying to persuade the United Nations to adopt the birthday of Confucius as international teacher's day.

He had a number of disciples and our most important source of knowledge of his ideas is, as we have seen, the book *Lunyu*, *The Analects*, which is a compilation of conversations Confucius had with his disciples and others.[1]

Specialists on his life and work still adhere to the traditional belief that Confucius lived from 551 to 479 BC, but because of the great distance in time we cannot be absolutely sure that these dates are accurate.

Confucius' mission as a teacher was to point out the way to restored harmony and order in the world. He was convinced that this could and should be done by emulating the principles enunciated by the mythical sage-kings Yao and Shun and the order

---

[1] There are very many translations of *The Analects*. My own favourite translation is still Arthur Waley's from 1938: *The Analects of Confucius*, London: George Allen & Unwin, 1938. If not otherwise indicated I have in this book adopted Waley's translation but changed the transcription of Chinese names and words according to the *Hanyu pinyin* system.

initiated by the legendary Duke of Zhou, characterized by an elaborate system of rites and ceremonies that had prevailed in the early
Zhou. He said:

> Zhou could survey the two preceding dynasties. How great a wealth
> of culture! And we follow upon Zhou.[2]

He found that in his own time this order had degenerated so that strife
and disorder, rather than harmony and order, prevailed under Heaven.
He admired in particular the legendary Duke of Zhou who, as he
thought, by developing the elaborate and glorious system of rites
and ceremonies had played a decisive role for the emergence of the
order of the early Zhou. He saw it as his task not so much to create
anything new as to transmit these experiences. In his own words:

> I have transmitted what was taught to me without making up anything
> of my own. I have been faithful to and loved the Ancients.[3]

After holding office in the state of Lu for a short period of time, he
wandered during thirteen years and visited a number of states to talk
to their leaders. In 484 BC he returned to his home state of Lu
where he spent his last years teaching.

Confucius' words in *The Analects* may appear unsystematic and frag-
mentary, even contradictory, and over the years the book has been
subject to innumerable interpretations. While there is no need to
argue that everything in the book is consistent, yet most people who
take the time to read it carefully and consider it get the feeling that it
does express a coherent vision of reality and the human predicament.

The best way to familiarize oneself with the ideas of Confucius is
to read *The Analects*, and here we shall on the basis of this book draw
attention to some of the main tenets of his thought.

Confucius the humanist

Confucius was primarily preoccupied with human problems: What
does it mean to be a human? How should we behave? According to

---

[2] *The Analects*, 3:14.
[3] Ibid. 7:1.

what principles should we act? How should society be organized? In modern terms we could say that he was a psychologist, a moral philosopher and a social philosopher and critic. From what we can read in *The Analects* it appears that he was not especially interested in other fields that are today considered important philosophical concerns, such as metaphysics, ontology, epistemology and logic.

The most fundamental value for Confucius was *ren* 仁, which has been rendered into English in many different ways, e.g. 'benevolence', 'goodness', 'human-heartedness', 'humanity', 'love', 'true manhood' etc. There can be no perfect translation of the term but it is essential to understand that it signifies goodness vis-a-vis other people; the Chinese character for *ren* consists of a 'human being' – *ren* 人 – and the figure 'two' – *er* 二. This brings out the interpersonal dimension of this virtue. In this book, 'good' or 'goodness' is generally used for *ren,* but in some instances it is also rendered as 'humane' and 'humanity'.

For Confucius, to be good is to be truly human. But to be truly human is very unusual, and he pointed out rather pessimistically:

> I for my part have never yet seen one who really cared for Goodness, nor one who really abhorred wickedness.[4]

As understood by Confucius, goodness seems to encompass several other 'minor' virtues. For example, he says:

> Zizhang asked Master Kong about Goodness [*ren*]. Master Kong said, He who could put the Five into practice everywhere under Heaven would be Good. Zizhang begged to hear what these were. The Master said, Courtesy, breadth, good faith, diligence and clemency. 'He who is courteous is not scorned, he who is broad wins the multitude, he who is of good faith is trusted by the people, he who is diligent succeeds in all he undertakes, he who is clement can get service from the people.'[5]

Confucius himself said that there was one thread binding his thought together, but he never clearly spelt out what this thread was. One of his disciples, Zeng Zi 曾子, said that by this expression

---

his master actually referred to 'loyalty' (*zhong* 忠) and 'consideration' (*shu* 恕). The passage in *The Analects* reads:

> The Master said, Shen! My Way has one (thread) that runs right through it. Master Zeng said, Yes. When the Master had gone out, the disciples asked, saying What did he mean? Master Zeng said, Our Master's Way is simply this: Loyalty, consideration.[6]

Zeng Zi's answer to the question what the one thread really refers to is confusing because loyalty and consideration are two things, not one. However, goodness being Confucius's paramount virtue, it has been suggested that actually goodness is the one thread and that loyalty and consideration are basic aspects of goodness.

'Loyalty', which is a translation of a Chinese word which has in recent years often been translated into 'conscientiousness' by specialists on Confucian thought, means to be loyal or true to others but also to oneself and to the true humanity in oneself.[7] In order to be true to oneself one must 'control' or 'master oneself'. Thus, to cultivate loyalty is to control oneself. Confucius explicitly said that goodness is to 'control oneself and return to the rites'.[8] 'Consideration', which is an English rendering of another difficult Chinese word *shu* 恕 now often translated as 'altruism', means to extend one's true self in one's behaviour towards other people or, in other words, to behave to others as a true human being should behave.[9]

More concretely, to be considerate means to apply the measure of the self, or the principle of reciprocity:

> Zigong asked saying, Is there any single saying that one can act upon all day and every day? The Master said, Perhaps the saying about

---

[6] Ibid., 4:15.
[7] Especially scholars in North America specializing on Neo-Confucianism often adopt the translation 'conscientiousness'. One example is the late professor Wing-tsit Chan, the most important translator in modern times of Chinese philosophical works into English. See his article 'On Translating Certain Chinese Philosophical Terms', in *A Source Book in Chinese Philosophy*, Princeton: Princeton University Press, 1969, pp. 783–791.
[8] 'keji fuli' 克己復禮, *The Analects*, 12:1; author's translation. Commentators in the Han dynasty, and their followers in the Qing Dynasty, interpreted the Chinese verb *ke* in this statement to mean something like 'control', while the Neo-Confucian Zhu Xi rather took it to mean something like 'conquer', 'master' or 'overcome'. The latter was more concerned with getting rid of the desires that he viewed as basically an evil part of the self.
[9] Those scholars who translate *zhong* into 'conscientiousness' tend to translate *shu* into 'altruism'. See, e.g., Wing-tsit Chan, p. 785–6.

consideration: 'Never do to others what you would not like them to do to you.'[10]

In view of the fact that presentations of Confucian thought often focus on its hierarchical tendency, and rightly so, it seems important to draw attention to the importance for Confucius of this principle of reciprocity, which is more akin to equality than to hierarchy.

However, Confucius does not argue that humans are all born equal:

> Highest are those who are born wise. Next are those who become wise by learning. After them come those who have to toil painfully in order to acquire learning. Finally, to the lowest of the common people belong those who toil painfully without ever managing to learn.[11]
> [. . .]
> The Master said, By nature, near together; by practice far apart.
> [. . .] It is only the wisest and the very stupidest who cannot change.[12]

Yet the distinction between the 'gentleman' or 'the superior man' (*junzi* 君子) and 'the small man' (*xiaoren* 小人), which is central in the thought of Confucius, seems mainly not to have been conceived of as innate: it was regarded as largely resulting from the degree of cultivation that a person undergoes.

A gentleman is not 'a vessel', i.e. he is not used as a means by others, whereas the small man is; the gentleman takes delight in what is morally good, whereas the small man seeks profit. This has later remained a core tenet of Confucian thought: in one's behaviour one should not be motivated by the search for profit or fame or status but by seeking what is good and right.

While the small man seeks profit and material goods, the gentleman is so preoccupied with spiritual things that he does not seem to worry much about his own material well-being. Confucius says:

> A gentleman, in his plans, thinks of the Way; he does not think of how he is going to make a living. Even farming sometimes entails times of

---

[10] *The Analects*, 15:24. (Waley has it as 15:23.)
[11] *The Analects*, 16:9.
[12] Ibid. 17:2–3.

shortage; and even learning may incidentally lead to high pay. But a gentleman's anxieties concern the progress of the Way; he has no anxiety concerning poverty.[13]

He was pessimistic in thinking that very few people can really succeed in putting spiritual values ahead of personal desires. For example, he once remarked that he had never met a man who was as fond of virtue as he was of beauty in women.

It is difficult to find anything positive to say about Confucius's view of women. Most references to women in *The Analects* concern the beauty of women as something negative; men pay more attention to female beauty than to virtue. In one statement he links women together with 'small men' as difficult to deal with:

> Women and people of low birth are very hard to deal with. If you are friendly with them, they get out of hand, and if you keep your distance, they resent it.[14]

He was concerned about the plight of the poor, and to extend help to the poor was an essential aspect of goodness, characteristic of a sage:

> Zigong said, If a ruler not only conferred wide benefits upon the common people, but also compassed the salvation of the whole state, what would you say of him? Surely, you would call him Good? The Master said, It would no longer be a matter of 'Good'. He would without doubt be a Divine Sage. Even Yao and Shun could hardly criticize him. As for Goodness — you yourself desire rank and standing. You want to turn your own merits to account; then help others to turn theirs to account — in fact, the ability to take one's own feelings as a guide — that is the sort of thing that lies in the direction of goodness.[15]

In view of his focus on the human being as capable of cultivating himself and improving the world we may speak about Confucius as a humanist and about Confucianism as a type of humanism.

---

[13] Ibid., 15:31.
[14] Ibid., 17:25.
[15] Ibid., 6:28.

Feelings and desires

As we shall see later, feelings, and especially desires, were looked upon with scepticism by many later Confucians, who considered desires gone astray as the source of all evil. Interestingly, Confucius seems to have had a high regard for feelings. He said: 'To prefer it is better than only to know it. To delight in it is better than merely to prefer it.'[16]

Discussing goodness he even says that only the person who is good 'knows how to love people and hate people'. This view of feelings as close to the basis of morality is especially interesting in view of the sceptical attitude to feelings that we meet with in later Confucian thought.

As for desires, Confucius does praise people who have freed themselves from desires. But it seems that for him one of the fundamental aims of personal cultivation and education was to bridge the gap between ethical demand and spontaneous desires, i.e. to desire spontaneously what is good:

> At fifteen I set my heart upon learning. At thirty I had planted my feet firm upon the ground. At forty, I no longer suffered from perplexities. At fifty, I knew what were the biddings of Heaven. At sixty, I heard them with docile ear. At seventy, I could follow the dictates of my own heart; for what I desried no longer overstepped the boundaries of right.[17]

Study

Confucius considered study as crucial in developing one's human potential to the utmost, and it is quite symptomatic that the first sentence in the Analects reads: 'The Master said, To learn and at due times to repeat what one has learnt, is that not after all a pleasure?'[18] The focus on the importance of study, in particular study of the

---

[16] Ibid., 6:18.
[17] Ibid., 2:4.
[18] Ibid., 1:1

ancient texts, has indeed remained characteristic of Confucian thought, and Chinese culture, throughout the centuries.

Confucius lamented what he saw as the decay of his time and he placed his hope for improvement on the human beings whose natural endowment gives them moral capacity. It is true that he saw morality as basically somehow rooted in Heaven, but he considered it man's duty to realize his capacity and model himself after Heaven, achieve the unity of heaven and man – a key notion in all Confucian thought – and so improve the world.

Again, in this perspective we may indeed speak about the humanism of Confucius.

Confucius the political philosopher

Confucius felt that the Way – *Dao* – that had been realized in the early Zhou as well as in the early stages of the two preceding dynasties Shang and Xia no longer prevailed in his own time. Therefore, his main concern was to point out the way to the revival of Dao, to renewed peace and harmony in the world. Thus, we may classify him as a political philosopher more than anything else. However, as a political philosopher he was convinced that the improvement of society has to begin with the self-cultivation of the individual human being. Therefore, we may say that his political philosophy was based upon his humanism.

What then characterized the Dao – the 'system' or the 'order' would perhaps be terms that we would use today – that Confucius wanted to see reinstituted?

i. Society as an organism

Confucius looked upon the human world, what we would call society, as an *organism*. In this organism there were different roles to be performed, roles that were determined by Heaven and which often were defined in relation to other roles: there were rulers and subjects, fathers and sons, husbands and wives etc. In order for the organism to function properly it was vital that each member fulfilled his or her role correctly. Let us turn to *The Analects* again:

> Duke Jing of Qi asked Master Kong about government. Master Kong replied saying, Let the prince be a prince, the minister a minister, the father a father and the son a son. The Duke said, How true! For indeed when the prince is not a prince, the minister not a minister, the father not a father, the son not a son, one may have a dish of millet in front of one and yet not know if one will live to eat it.[19]

ii. Hierarchy

Within the organism relationships are mainly *hierarchical*. But we should keep in mind that in the view of Confucius man must not be reduced to these roles. And he was very much aware that in the course of somebody's life a person will perform different roles: a man will begin as a son, become a subject but also a father and perhaps even a ruler. Still, one cannot get away from the fact that Confucius's conception of the ideal social order is fundamentally hierarchical. Confucius himself saw obedience as an important virtue:

> Meng Yizi asked about the treatment of parents. The Master said, Never disobey. When Fan Chi was driving his carriage for him, the Master said, 'Meng asked me about the treatment of parents and I said, Never disobey! Fan Chi said, 'In what sense did you mean it?' The Master said, While they are alive, serve them according to ritual. When they die, bury them according to ritual and sacrifice to them according to ritual.[20]

After Confucius this aspect of Confucian thought became even more emphasized, particularly in Confucianism as a state philosophy, which placed extreme emphasis on obedience as a virtue in the family and in society.

In Confucius' thought we may discern two kinds of hierarchy, one that we may call 'functional' and another one that we may call

---

[19] Ibid., 12:11.
[20] Ibid., 2:5.

'spiritual', and the relationship between the two is worth thinking about. Functional hierarchy has to do with the heavenly decreed roles in society, for example the relationship between father and son, which is hierarchical no matter what the spiritual qualities of the specific father and son. The other one is a hierarchy of spiritual enlightenment or value: there is 'the sage' (*shengren* 聖人), there is 'the superior man' or 'the gentleman' (*junzi* 君子), there are 'the small people' (*xiaoren* 小人) etc. Confucius seems to have been of the opinion that the higher the position in society, the higher the demand for spiritual enlightenment in the person who performs the role. In principle spiritual enlightenment, even to the point of becoming a sage, was possible for anyone no matter where in society he was born. To attain enlightenment was the purpose of 'self-cultivation' (*xiuji* 修己), which was at the core of the Confucian moral-spiritual praxis. Still it is difficult to escape the impression that Confucius considered large categories of people, including all women and most common people to be destined to remain in subordinate roles.

Confucius seems to have regarded the family, and the relations within the family, as a microcosm of society at large. That is to say, the relationships in society should be modelled on the ideal relationships in the family. He quotes *The Classic of Poetry* and says: 'Inside the family there is the serving of one's father; outside, there is the serving of one's lord.'[21]

iii. Ritual and music

One of the key concepts in Confucius' vision of the good society is 'rites' or 'ritual' (*li* 禮) , often also translated as 'propriety'. But this word is easily misunderstood. Originally, it no doubt referred to precise religious and social rites and what we would call 'good manners'. However, in Confucius it acquired a much broader meaning than this and may, in the words of Benjamin Schwartz, be taken to refer to 'all those "objective" prescriptions of behaviour,

---

[21] Ibid., 17:9; trans. D.C. Lau, *Confucius: The Analects*, Hong Kong: The Chinese University Press, 1992, p. 175.

whether involving rites, ceremony, manners, or general deportment, that bind human beings and the spirits together in networks of interacting roles within the family, within human society, and with the numinous world beyond'.[22] In fact, we may go one step further and agree with Arthur Waley that Confucius was concerned not so much 'with the details of ritual' as with 'morality'. Waley makes an important point when he writes:

> The Confucius of the *Analects* is not much concerned with the details of ritual, either public or domestic. Correct observance of small social rites, what we call 'good manners,' belongs, of course, equally to the Chinese and to our conception of the gentleman, as does also the insistence upon 'giving a fair chance' both to one's competitors in sports and to one's victims in the chase. But the actual text of the *Analects* is concerned with the general principles of conduct, with morality rather than manners [. . .].[23]

However, we should not go from one extreme to another. Even if Confucius was not primarily concerned with the observance of specific rites and good manners, this does not mean that these had no importance for him. The rites that Confucius does refer to cover a wide spectrum, from sacrifices to one's ancestors to the details of social etiquette. Closely related to the notion of rites was the concept of 'music' (*yue* 樂), which also embraces dance. In the words of A.C. Graham, *yue* was 'primarily the music and dance of sacred rites' and 'correspondingly, ceremony [i.e. *li*] is continuous with music in being conducted with style like an artistic performance'.[24]

iv. Rule by the good example

When the world was organized according to the Way that Confucius wanted to revive, the supreme ruler under Heaven would be a sage-king who would rule not by decrees, using carrots and

---

[22] Benjamin Schwartz, *The World of Thought in Ancient China*, Cambridge, Mass. and London: The Belknap Press of Harvard University Press, 1985, p. 67.
[23] Waley, p. 55.
[24] A.C.Graham, *Disputers of the Tao*, p. 11.

sticks, but by his own good example, as the legendary sage-kings Yao and Shun had done. Confucius even suggests that Shun ruled by doing nothing, which may sound more Daoist than Confucian:

> Among those that 'ruled by inactivity' surely Shun may be counted. For what action did he take? He merely placed himself gravely and reverently with his face due south; that was all.[25]

The importance of the good example should permeate society, from the sage-king down through the hierarchy. Confucius' belief in the power of the good example was great. He said:

> The essence of the gentleman is that of wind; the essence of small men is that of grass. And when a wind passes over the grass, it cannot choose but bend.[26]

But we must keep in mind that in the view of Confucius there were hardly any superior men or gentlemen to be seen under Heaven.

The notion of 'good example' is basically moral, and in the perspective of Confucius high moral standards are infinitely more important than competence in practical matters:

> Fan Chi asked the Master to teach him about farming. The Master said, You had much better consult some old farmer. He asked to be taught about gardening. The Master said, You had much better go to some old vegetable-gardener. When Fan Chi had gone out, the Master said, Fan is no gentleman! If those above them love ritual, then among the common people none will dare to be disrespectful. If those above them love right, then among the common people, none will dare to be disobedient. If those above them love good faith, then among the common people none will dare depart from the facts. If a gentleman is like that, the common people will flock to him from all sides with their babies strapped to their backs. What need has he to practice farming?[27]

Placing moral qualities above competence in practical matters has remained a central feature of Chinese élite culture, well into the twentieth century.

---

[25] *The Analects*, 15:5.
[26] Ibid., 12:19.
[27] Ibid., 13:4.

v. The power of words

In the Chinese language the words for 'govern' (*zheng* 政) and 'correct' (*zheng* 正) are, and were in Confucius' time, homonyms. Confucius also derived the meaning of 'to govern' from 'to be correct': 'To govern is to be correct. If you give a lead in being correct, who would dare to be incorrect?'[28]

This explanation fits well in with the notion of the importance of words being correct, which was also considered very important in governing:

> Zilu said, If the prince of Wei were waiting for you to come and administer his country for him, what would be your first measure? The Master said, It would certainly be to correct language. Zilu said, Can I have heard you aright? Surely what you say has nothing to do with the matter. Why should language be corrected? The Master said, You! How boorish you are! A gentleman, when things he does not understand are mentioned, should maintain an attitude of reserve. If language is incorrect, then what is said does not concord with what was meant; and if what is said does not concord with what was meant, then what is to be done cannot be effected. If what is to be done cannot be effected, then rites and music will not flourish. If rites and music do not flourish, then mutilations and lesser punishments will go astray. And if mutilations and lesser punishments go astray, then the people have nowhere to put hand or foot.
>
> Therefore the gentleman uses only such language as is proper for speech, and only speaks of what it would be proper to carry into effect. The gentleman, in what he says, leaves nothing to mere chance.[29]

The preoccupation to the point of obsession with 'correct words' seems to have remained a salient feature of Chinese high culture up until our own times; not least we find it among the Chinese communists.[30]

In his political thinking, Confucius was primarily concerned with reestablishing the lost Dao, but he also discussed quite interestingly

---

[28] Ibid., 12:17; trans D.C. Lau, modif.
[29] Ibid., 13:3.
[30] Cf. Michael Schoenhals, *Doing Things with Words in Chinese Politics: Five Studies*, Berkeley: Center for Chinese Studies, Institute of East Asian Studies, University of California, 1992.

how an individual human being should relate to regimes of different moral qualities. He once said:

> When the Way prevails under Heaven, then show yourself; when it does not prevail, then hide. When the Way prevails in your own land, count it as a disgrace to be needy and obscure; when the Way does not prevail in your land, then count it a disgrace to be rich and honoured.[31]

This is a statement that people in our time have often found reason to go back to and to ponder.

The ideas of Confucius as we meet them in *The Analects* may at first glance appear unsystematic and even contradictory, but the more we study the text the more convinced do we become that they express a coherent vision of the human predicament. Confucius may have been a transmitter rather than a creator, but he is the first thinker we know about who gave shape to some of the basic ideas of Confucianism and, therefore, it is reasonable to look upon him as the most important founding father of the Confucian tradition, much of which has taken the form of exegesis and interpretation of his ideas. The next truly important thinker in tradition, whom we may also think of as a founding father of Confucianism was Meng Zi, or as he is generally referred to in the Western world, Mencius.

Further reading

Historical background

Hsu, Cho-yun. *Ancient China in Transition: An Analysis of Social Mobility, 722–222 B.C.* Stanford: Stanford University Press, 1965.

Loewe, Michael and Edward L. Shaughnessy. *The Cambridge History of Ancient China: From the Origins of Civilization to 221 B.C.* Cambridge, UK; New York: Cambridge University Press, 1999.

General studies of Chinese thought from ca. 500 to ca. 200 BC

Graham, A.C. *Disputers of the Tao: Philosophical Argument in Ancient China.* La Salle, Illinois: Open Court, 1989.

Schwartz, Benjamin I. *The World of Thought in Ancient China.* Cambridge, Mass. and London, England: The Belknap Press of Harvard University Press, 1985.

---

[31] *The Analects*, 8:13.

Translations of *The Analects.*
Ames, Roger T. and Henry Rosemont, Jr. *The Analects of Confucius.* A philosoph-
ical translation by Roger T. Ames, Henry Rosemont, Jr. New York: Ballantine
Pub. Group, 1998.
Chan, Wing-tsit. *A Source Book in Chinese Philosophy.* Princeton: Princeton
University Press, 1969. Partial translation, pp. 14–48.
Dawson, Raymond. *The Analects.* Translated by Raymond Dawson. Oxford and
New York: Oxford University Press, 1993.
Giles, Lionel. *The Analects of Confucius.* Translated from the Chinese, with an introd.
and notes, by Lionel Giles. Illustrated with paintings by Tseng Yu-ho. 1970.
Hinton, David. *The Analects.* Washington, D.C.: Counterpoint, 1998.
Huang, Chichung. *The Analects of Confucius. A literal translation with an introduction
and notes by Chichung Huang.* New York: Oxford University Press, 1997.
Lau, D.C. *The Analects.* Translated by D.C. Lau. Hong Kong: Chinese University
Press, 1992.
Legge, James. *The Analects of Confucius.* In Vol. 2 of *The Chinese Classics.* With a
translation, critical and exegetical notes, prolegomena, and copious indexes by
James Legge. Taipei: SMC Pub., 1991. First edition Oxford University Press in
1893.
Leys, Simon. *The Analects of Confucius.* Translation and notes by Simon Leys.
New York: W.W. Norton, 1997.
Li, David H. *The Analects of Confucius.* A new-millennium translation, translated
and annotated by David H. Li. Bethesda, Md.: Premier Pub., 1999.
Pound, Ezra. *Confucian Analects. Translated by Ezra Pound.* New York, N.Y.:
Kasper & Horton: Gotham Book Mart [distributor], 1951. The ingenious poet's
rendering is fascinating but totally unreliable as a translation.
Soothill, Edward. *The Analects.* Translation from the Chinese by William Edward
Soothill. New York: Dover Publications, 1995. This classical translation was first
published in 1910.
Waley, Arthur. *The Analects. Translated by Arthur Waley, with an introduction by Sarah
Allan. Uniform Title.* New York: Knopf, 2000.

Studies of Confucius' thinking
Carew-Miller, Anna. *Confucius: Great Chinese philosopher.* Philadelphia: Mason
Crest Publishers, 2003
Creel, H.G. *Confucius and the Chinese Way.* New York: Harper, 1960. (Originally
published in 1949 under the title *Confucius, the Man and the Myth.*)
Fingarette, Herbert. *Confucius: the Secular as Sacred.* Prospect Heights, Ill.: Waveland
Press, 1998.
Hall, David L. and Roger T. Ames. *Thinking through Confucius.* Albany: State
University of New York Press, 1987.

Other
Chan, Wing-tsit. 'On Translating Certain Chinese Philosophical Terms.' In
A Source Book in Chinese Philosophy, Princeton: Princeton University Press,
1969, pp. 783–791.
Schoenhals, Michael. *Doing Things with Words in Chinese Politics: Five Studies.*
Berkeley: Center for Chinese Studies, Institute of East Asian Studies, University
of California, 1992.

3

MENCIUS

The man

Born a little more than a century after the death of Confucius, Mencius (ca. 371– ca. 289 BC) stands out as a founding father of Confucianism, next in importance only to Confucius himself.

Mencius is the Latinized form of Meng Zi 孟子, Master Meng, whose Chinese name was Meng Ke 孟軻. He was born in the small ancient state of Zou in modern Shandong province, close to Confucius's home state Lu. Just like Confucius he devoted his life to teaching and, especially, to trying to convince state leaders to adopt his teaching as a means of achieving peace and order under Heaven. Some forty years, beginning about the year 354, he spent travelling, visiting different states.

Very little is known about Mencius' family and private life, but he is said to have been the student of a pupil of Confucius's grandson Zisi 子思. By referring to Confucius as 'the greatest sage' and by engaging in debates with the followers of other philosophical schools, as well as by developing his own philosophical ideas, he contributed decisively to shaping the form of early Confucian thought and laying the groundwork for centuries of Confucian discussions.

By far the most important source for our knowledge about the ideas of Mencius is the book bearing his name, the *Meng Zi* or *Mencius*. Just like *The Analects*, this book consists of the recording of Mencius' discussions with disciples and political leaders. The authorship and dating of the book are still open to debate, but there seems to be no doubt that it reflects the ideas, or body of doctrines, of one man. In comparison with Confucius in *The Analects*, Mencius engages in longer, more analytical and coherent arguments than Confucius whose statements are rather epigrammatic. Mencius can be characterized as a creative follower of Confucius. That is, he built his own doctrines on the teaching of Confucius which he developed. In particular, he went beyond Confucius in declaring unequivocally that human nature is good, the doctrine which more than any other has come to be associated with his name.

Using the categories of scholarship in our times, it seems natural to place the core ideas of Mencius in the three areas of psychology, moral philosophy and political philosophy.

The psychologist

Mencius held a very optimistic view of human nature. While he did not claim that all people are equally talented, he did believe that everyone has the potential for sagehood; the sages Yao and Shun 'were the same as other men'. All men have the capacity to become a Yao or a Shun.

In fact, potential is a key word in trying to understand Mencius' view of human beings. More than anything else he is associated with the notion of 'the goodness of human nature' (*xingshanlun* 性善論). No doubt, he was as aware as anyone else of the evil in the world and saw that people caused each other much harm. This was what he most of all wanted to rectify. But he insisted that human beings have the capacity for goodness. In modern terms we could say that he was convinced that the capacity for empathy is an innate quality characteristic of human beings.

But how can we know that the capacity for empathy is innate if people actually behave as if they were not concerned with the well-being of others? Mencius formulated an argument that has become classical:

My reason for saying that no man is devoid of a heart sensitive to the suffering of others is this. Suppose a man were, all of a sudden, to see a young child on the verge of falling into a well. He would certainly be moved to compassion, not because he wanted to get in the good graces of the parents, nor because he wished to win the praise of his fellow villagers or friends, nor yet because he disliked the cry of the child. From this it can be seen that whoever is devoid of the heart of compassion is not human, whoever is devoid of the heart of shame is not human, whoever is devoid of the heart of courtesy and modesty is not human, and whoever is devoid of the heart of right and wrong is not human.[1]

In all its simplicity this argument appears very forceful, for who can conceive of anyone not feeling the impulse to rush forward and rescue an infant about to fall into a well? Of course, it is quite conceivable that an infant would not be rescued in such a situation, just as it happens that people in our time are left seriously hurt in the busy streets of big cities without anyone lifting a finger to help. But how could the impulse to help not be present?

This is also the essence of Mencius' notion of the goodness of human nature. Innate in the human 'heart' – which in Confucian discourse is the locus of feelings as well as intellect and which is therefore often translated as 'mind-and-heart' – Mencius found 'compassion' (*ceyin* 惻隱), 'shame and dislike'(*xiuwu* 羞惡), 'courtesy and modesty' (*cirang* 辭讓), and the sense of 'right and wrong'(*shifei* 是非) which he called the 'four beginnings' or 'germs' (*siduan* 四端) of 'goodness' (*ren* 仁), 'righteousness' (*yi* 義), 'propriety' (*li* 禮) and 'wisdom' (*zhi* 智) respectively. Thus, when these germs of goodness are realized man's innate capacity for goodness is realized in his or her behaviour.[2]

Thus, according to Mencius the potential or capacity for goodness and moral behaviour is innate in humans; it is innate and endowed by Heaven, for goodness is somehow inherent in the universe. If humans realize their moral potential, they become at one with Heaven.[3] This notion we may characterize as an example of a religious, or even mystical, streak in Mencius.

---

[1] D.C. Lau, Mencius, *Mencius. A Bilingual Edition*, Hong Kong: Chinese University Press, 2003, 2A:6, p. 73.
[2] See *Mencius*, 2A:6.
[3] Cf. *Mencius*, 7 *passim*.

A characteristic feature of human beings, and also an aspect of the goodness of human nature, is that what is good and right is pleasing to human beings. Just as we take delight in beautiful sounds and sights we also approve of what is good and right:

> All mouths have the same preferences in taste, all ears in sound, all eyes in colour. Is there with regard to the hearts only nothing which they all approve of? That which all hearts approve of is called 'principles' [*li* 理]. The sages were only first to grasp that which all hearts approve of.[4]

Since Mencius is of the opinion that all humans are able to be good but actually often act otherwise, it is not surprising that the question how to translate this potential for goodness into actuality becomes a central concern for him. The concept 'principle' (*li* 理) is not used very often in pre-Qin Confucian texts but became, as we shall see, the key notion in Neo-Confucianism during the Song dynasty. For the Neo-Confucians the passage just quoted became then a real *locus classicus*.

Mencius' approach to this problem sheds interesting light on his view of the psychology of man, but also leads on to the realm of political philosophy which we will deal with after a discussion of his moral philosophy. Suffice it here to say that his general answer is that in order for the germs of goodness to grow and to develop, material and spiritual nourishment is essential. Just like the playwright Berthold Brecht in the twentieth century, Mencius argued that if hungry and lacking basic welfare, men cannot be expected to care about what is good and right, or in Brecht's words: 'Erst kommt das Fressen und dann die Moral': 'In good years most of the young people behave well. In bad years most of them abandon themselves to evil.'[5]

Only 'the gentleman' – that is he who is more fully developed than ordinary people – can stick to what is good and right even under difficult material conditions:

> Only a Gentleman can have a constant heart in spite of a lack of constant means of support. The people, on the other hand, will not have

---

[4] Ibid., 6A:7; writer's translation.
[5] Ibid., 6A:7; trans. Chan, *A Source Book in Chinese Philosophy*, p. 55.

constant hearts if they are without constant means. Lacking constant hearts, they will go astray and fall into excesses, stopping at nothing.[6]

Of course, moral cultivation by means of study is also crucially important for making possible the translation of moral potentiality into actuality: 'Learn widely and go into what you have learned in detail so that in the end you can return to the essential.'[7]

He even goes so far as saying that even if well-fed, warmly clothed and comfortably lodged people will become 'almost like animals' if they are not educated:

> This is the way of the common people: once they have a full belly and warm clothes on their backs they degenerate to the level of animals if they are allowed to lead idle lives, without education.[8]

The moral philosopher

Mencius anchors his moral philosophy in his conception of human beings as potential sages. It is thus our duty to develop as fully as possible our moral potential. But in this perspective Mencius is acutely aware of the dialectic between inner and outer: the individual human beings have their duties and capacities but they are also constrained by external circumstances. This means that man should cultivate himself but he should also engage in bringing about a social order conducive to personal development. Individual morality and politics form a polarity with two mutually interdependent poles.

Mencius insists that moral action is determined by moral purposes – what he refers to as 'goodness' (ren 仁) and 'righteousness' (yi 義) – not by considerations of 'profit' or 'benefit' (li 利). The first lines of the book bearing his name spell out this message:

> Mencius went to see King Hui of Liang. 'You, Sir', said the King, 'have come all this distance, thinking nothing of a thousand li. You must surely have some way of profiting my state?'

---

[6] Ibid., 1A: 7; trans. Lau, p. 23.
[7] Ibid., 4B:15; trans. Lau, p. 177.
[8] Ibid., 3A:4; trans. Lau, p. 115.

'Your Majesty', answered Mencius. 'What is the point of mentioning the word "profit"? All that matters is that there should be goodness and righteousness.'[9]

But while he emphasizes that moral behaviour is determined by goodness and righteousness rather than by profitable or useful consequences, he is also convinced that such behaviour will result in the best consequences.

Interesting in this regard is his notion that the universal norms of moral behaviour must sometimes be modified according to the specific circumstances prevailing. For example, a man and a woman should ordinarily not touch each other, but yet he characterizes the man who does not stretch out his hand to help a woman who is drowning as a brute:

> Chunyu Kun said, 'Is it prescribed by the rites that, in giving and receiving, man and woman should not touch each other?'
> 'It is', said Mencius.
> 'When one's sister-in-law is drowning, does one stretch out a hand to help her?'
> 'Not to help a sister-in-law who is drowning is to be a brute. It is prescribed by the rites that, in giving and receiving, man and woman should not touch each other, but in stretching out a helping hand to the drowning sister-in-law one uses one's discretion.'[10]

With reference to his insistence that human behaviour should be motivated in terms of goodness and righteousness rather than profit, Mencius is often described as anti-utilitarian. No doubt, he has contributed to setting a tone of anti-utilitarianism in the Confucian tradition.

However, if we look closely at what Mencius had to say, we will find that neither did he show any lack of concern with the consequences of action, nor did he condemn pleasure or even the search for pleasure.

As for his view of motives and consequences, Mencius seems to have been of the opinion that goodness and righteousness as

---

[9] Ibid., 1A:1; trans. Lau, p. 3 modif.
[10] Ibid., 4A:17; trans. Lau, p. 163–4, modif.

intrinsic and unquestionable values should guide our actions and that behaviour so motivated will also yield the best results.

In the final analysis, his teaching was predicated upon the assumption that if goodness and righteousness were translated into behaviour, the world would become a better place and human beings would lead better and happier lives.

As for pleasure, it is clear that Mencius thought of it as such as something good rather than bad. He did argue for the limitations of 'desires', probably associating desires with selfishness, but he was certainly not opposed to trying to enjoy life. What did concern him was the unequal distribution of pleasure. He criticized leaders he met for indulging in pleasures that they did not allow their subordinates to enjoy.

Once in a conversation with Mencius, King Xuan of Qi tried to explain why he was unable to implement a truly good government in his state. He said: 'I have a weakness. I am fond of money.' Mencius replied:

> You may be fond of money, but so long as you share this fondness with the people, how can it interfere with your becoming a true King?[11]

Then King Xuan continued to say that he had another weakness: 'I am fond of women.' But again Mencius did not think this in itself was a problem:

> You may be fond of women, but so long as you share this fondness with the people, how can it interfere with your becoming a true King?[12]

Mencius furthermore approved of King Xuan's fondness for music, not even the respectable music of the ancient kings but popular music, and made a comment which we may read as a general statement of his view of pleasure: 'Now if you shared your enjoyment with the people, you would be a true King.'[13]

Thus, we may conclude that Mencius saw pleasure in itself as something good but that he was of the opinion that it must be

---

[11] Ibid., 1B:5; trans. Lau, p. 39.
[12] Ibid.
[13] Ibid., 1B:1.

evenly distributed. If this is true we may even somewhat provocatively say that Mencius shared some of the views of the most typical advocate of classical utilitarianism in Europe, Jeremy Bentham, who wanted to see maximum pleasure for a maximum number of people.[14]

In discussing moral behaviour Mencius proceeded from the famous 'five relationships' (*wu lun* 五倫) as a kind of microcosm:

> Love between father and son, duty between ruler and subject, distinction between husband and wife, precedence of the old over the young, and faith between friends.[15]

Except that between friends, these relationships are all hierarchical in nature. It seems clear that Mencius himself distinguished between the individual human beings and the roles that they performed. As individuals he considered all humans equal in that we are endowed with the capacity to develop into sages, but in performing our roles in the five relationships we are part of a hierarchical organism. In later Confucian discourse these relationships have also often been used to legitimize a hierarchical social structure.

The political philosopher

Just like Confucius, Mencius believed that in ancient times order and harmony had prevailed in the world and saw it as his main task to point out the way to renewed order and harmony. For decades he travelled around visiting state leaders offering them his recipe to achieve this task, a recipe that may be summed up by the notion of the 'Kingly Way' (*wangdao* 王道).

If Mencius impresses us with the wisdom of some of his psychological insight and the depth of his moral understanding, it is difficult not to consider some of his fundamental ideas in the realm of politics as rather unrealistic.

---

[14] Concerning utilitarianism, see Frederick Rosen, *Classical Utilitarianism from Hume to Mill.* London: Routledge, 2003.
[15] Ibid., 3A:4; trans. Lau, p. 115–117.

Basically, Mencius believed that the leader who could rule by his example and practise 'good governance' (*ren zheng* 仁政) would be recognized as the true King under Heaven and thus in possession of the Mandate of Heaven. Mencius said to King Xuan of Qi:

> Now if you should practise good governance of your state, then all those in the Empire who seek office would wish to find a place at your court, all tillers of land to till the land in outlying parts of your realm, all merchants to enjoy the refuge of your market-place, all travellers to go by way of your roads and all those who hate their rulers to lay their complaints before you. This being so, who can stop you from becoming a true King?[16]

And what does it mean to practise 'good governance'? The most striking features of his explication of this notion is the emphasis he places on, first, securing good material and spiritual conditions for the people and, second, on the duty of the ruler to share the conditions of the people. He continued to tell King Xuan of Qi:

> The people [. . .] will not have constant hearts if they are without constant means. Lacking constant hearts, they will go astray and fall into excesses, stopping at nothing. To punish them after they have fallen foul of the law is to set a trap for the people. How can a benevolent man in authority allow himself to set a trap for the people? Hence when determining what means of support the people should have, a clear-sighted ruler ensures that these are sufficient, on the one hand, for the care of parents, and, on the other hand, for the support of wife and children, so that the people always have sufficient food in good years and escape starvation in bad; only then does he drive them towards goodness; in this way the people find it easy to follow him.[17]

And he said:

> If you wish to put this [good governance] into practice, why not go back to fundamentals? If the mulberry is planted in every homestead of five *mu* of land, then those who are fifty can wear silk;

---

[16] Ibid., 1A:7; trans. Lau, p. 23 modif.
[17] Ibid.

if chickens, pigs and dogs do not miss their breeding season, then those who are seventy can eat meat; if each lot of a hundred *mu* is not deprived of labour during the busy seasons, then families with several mouths to feed will not go hungry. Exercise due care over the education provided by the village schools, and discipline the people by teaching them duties proper to sons and younger brothers, and those whose heads have turned grey will not be carrying loads on the roads. When the aged wear silk and eat meat and the masses are neither cold nor hungry, it is impossible for their prince not to be a true King.[18]

Securing decent living conditions for the people was the duty of the ruler. If he failed to do so he lost the Mandate of Heaven and the people had the right to rebel. Under certain circumstances Mencius even found it acceptable to kill a tyrant:

King Xuan of Qi asked, 'Is it true that Tang banished Jie and King Wu marched against Zhou?'

'It is so recorded', answered Mencius.

'Is regicide permissible?'

'A man who mutilates goodness is a mutilator, while one who cripples righteousness is a crippler. He who is both a mutilator and a crippler is an "outcast". I have indeed heard of the punishment of the "outcast Zhou", but I have not heard of any regicide.'[19]

In this we may see an embryo of democratic thinking, and also the justification for overthrowing an unjust ruler – even though by means that we may find questionable. In Chinese history this strain in Mencius' thought has been used by rebels and people in opposition as ideological justification and by the same token it has sometimes made him unpopular with rulers. A well-known example is how the first emperor of the Ming dynasty (1368–1644) after reading a chapter in the Mencius became so angry that he ordered the sacrifices to Mencius in the Confucian temple to be suspended.

---

[18] Ibid.
[19] Ibid., 1B:8; trans. Lau, p. 43.

Further reading

Historical background
See suggestions at the end of Chapter 1.

Translations of Mencius
Chan, Wing-tsit. *A Source Book in Chinese Philosophy*. Princeton: Princeton University Press, 1969. Partial translation, pp. 49–83.
Dobson, W.A.C.H. *Mencius: A New Translation Arranged and Annotated for the General Reader*. Toronto: University of Toronto Press, 1963.
Hinton, David. *Mencius*. Washington, D.C.: Counterpoint, 1998.
Lau, D.C. *Mencius. A Bilingual Edition*. Hong Kong: Chinese University Press, 2003. 3rd rev. ed.
Legge, James. *The Mencius*. In Vol 2 of *The Chinese Classics*. With a translation, critical and exegetical notes, prolegomena, and copious indexes. Five volumes. Taipei: SMC Pub., 1991.

Studies of Mencius
Behuniak, James. *Mencius on Becoming Human*. Albany: State University of New York Press, 2004.
Chan, A.K, *Mencius: Contexts and Interpretations*. Honolulu: University of Hawai'i Press, 2002.
Graham, A.C. 'The Background of the Mencian Theory of Human Nature.' In A.C. Graham. *Studies in Chinese Philosophy and Philosophical Literature*. Albany, N.Y.: State University Of New York Press, 1990, pp. 7–66.
Huang, C. *Mencian Hermeneutics: A History of Interpretations in China*. New Brunswick, USA, and London, UK: Translation Publishers, 2001.
Liu, Xiusheng, *Mencius, Hume and the Foundations of Ethics*. Aldershot, Hampshire, England and Burlington, VT, USA: Ashgate, 2003.
Liu, Xiusheng and Ivanhoe, Philip J. eds. *Essays on the Moral Philosophy of Meng Zi*. Indianapolis/Cambridge: Hackett Publishing Company, 2002.
Richards, I.A. *Mencius on the Mind: Experiments in Multiple Definition*, Richmond, Surrey: Curzon, 1997 (This classical study by the famous literary scholar I.A. Richards was first published in 1932).
Verwilghen, Albert Felix. *Mencius: The Man and His Ideas*. New York: St John's University Press, 1967.
Yearley, L.H. *Mencius and Aquinas: Theories of Virtue and Conceptions of Courage*. Albany: State University of New York Press, 1990.

Other
Rosen, Frederick. *Classical Utilitarianism from Hume to Mill*. London: Routledge, 2003.

4

XUN ZI

While Mencius based his moral reasoning on the assumption that man's most fundamental inclinations and impulses are good, his contemporary Xun Zi took the diametrically opposed view and argued that man is by nature evil.

Xun Zi 荀子 – Master Xun – whose real name was Xun Kuang 荀况 came from the state of Zhao in present-day Hebei and Shanxi province. We do not know the dates of his birth and death, but there is reason to believe that his active period fell somewhere within the period 298 to 238 BC. Thus he was a contemporary of Mencius, but there is no evidence to suggest that the two ever met.

At the age of fifty Xun Zi went to the state of Qi in present-day Shandong and Hebei provinces, where many leading scholars of the time congregated. Later, he went to the southern state of Chu, where he worked as an official for a time and then spent his last years teaching.

Unlike *The Analects of Confucius* and the *Mencius*, the book that bears Xun Zi's name is made up of self-contained essays.

Among Xun Zi's disciples we find Han Fei Zi 韓非子 (d. 233 BC) and Li Si 李斯 (d. 208 BC), who both became ministers during the brief Qin Dynasty and who were typical representatives of the school of Legalism in Chinese philosophy, which was used as an ideological pillar of autocratic rule in the Qin Dynasty (221–207 BC).

Xun Zi was very important for the emergence of Legalism but also for Confucianism in the Han Dynasty. In its role as state philosophy during the Han, Confucianism incorporated much of the authoritarianism of Legalism which can partly be traced back to Xun Zi.

However, Xun Zi never became part of the Confucian canon and his view of human nature was considered heterodox. From the end of the Han Dynasty until the nineteenth century not very many works were devoted to him and his ideas.

Yet in terms of intellectual brilliance and originality, there is no doubt that Xun Zi is one of the giants of Chinese intellectual history. His view of language as a system of signs assigned certain meaning by arbitrary conventions seems amazingly modern. Consider for example, the following passage from the chapter 'Rectifying Names' in the *Xun Zi*:

> Names have no intrinsic appropriateness. One agrees to use a certain name and issues an order to that effect, and if the agreement is abided by and becomes a matter of custom, then the name may be said to be appropriate, but if people do not abide by the agreement then the names cease to be appropriate. Names have no intrinsic reality.[1]

Xun Zi had an acute sense of the importance of language for political rule, and in particular of assigning meanings to words as an essential aspect of exercising political power. In the chapter from which we just quoted, we may also read:

> When the sage-kings instituted names, the names were fixed and the actualities distinguished. The sage-kings' principles were carried out and their wills understood. [. . .] Since the people dared not rely on strange terms created to confuse correct terms, they single-mindedly followed the law and carefully obeyed orders. In this way, the traces of their accomplishments spread. The spreading of traces and the achievement of results are the highest point of good government. This is the result of careful abiding by the conventional meaning of names.
>
> Now the sage-kings are dead and the guarding of names has become lax, strange terms have arisen, and names and actualities have been confused. As the standard of right and wrong is not clear, even the guardian of law and the teachers of natural principles are in a state of confusion. Should a true king appear, he would certainly retain some old names and create new ones.[2]

---

[1] Trans. Burton Watson, *Xun Zi. Basic Writings*, New York: Columbia University Press, 2003, p. 148.
[2] Trans. Chan, *A Source Book in Chinese Philosophy*, pp. 124–125.

Xun Zi was probably the one in ancient China who formulated the most advanced ideas in logic. In a recent study of language and logic in China, the chapter from which the above two quotations are taken is characterized as 'the most coherent and sustained discursive survey of the problems of logic that has come down to us from ancient Chinese times'.[3]

Xun Zi's emphasis on the importance of objective facts, as well as his sharp sense of logic and intellectual rigour, clearly demonstrate Xun Zi's scientific spirit. In the wake of the demise of the Chinese empire as well as in more recent times, many leading intellectuals have drawn inspiration from his thinking.

The evil of human nature

By nature man is selfish and seeks only profit and gain, says Xun Zi. The rites, or ritual principles, and righteousness are needed to civilize man, and these qualities are not inherent in human nature but the product of sages:

> Therefore, in ancient times the sages, realizing that man's nature is evil, that it is prejudiced and not upright, irresponsible and lacking in order, for this reason established the authority of the ruler to control it, elucidated ritual principles to transform it, set up laws and standards to correct it, and meted out strict punishments to restrain it. As a result, all the world achieved order and conformed to goodness. Such is the orderly government of the sage kings and the transforming power of ritual principles.[4]

Interestingly, Xun Zi argues that everyone possesses the faculty to understand the ritual principles and righteousness, even to become a sage. This shows that he actually shares some essential common ground with Mencius, whose theory of innate goodness he explicitly rejected.

---

[3] Christoph Harbsmeier, 'Language and Logic',Vol. 7 of Joseph Needham, *Science and Civilisation in China*, Cambridge: Cambridge University Press, 1998, p. 321.
[4] Burton Watson, *Xun Zi. Basic Writings*, pp. 166–167.

But Xun Zi argues that 'to find it practically possible or impossible to do something and to be capable or incapable of doing something are two entirely different things'. Perhaps Xun Zi's idea was that in addition to being in possession of the capacity to act as a sage one must also want to do so and circumstances must allow one to do so:

> The petty man is capable of becoming a gentleman, yet he is not willing to do so; the gentleman is capable of becoming a petty man, but yet he is not willing to do so. The petty man and the gentleman are perfectly capable of changing places; the fact that they do not actually do so is what I mean when I say that they are capable of doing so but they cannot be made to do so. Hence it is correct to say that the man in the street is capable of becoming a Yu but it is not necessarily correct to say that he will in fact find it possible to do so. [. . .] A person with two feet is theoretically capable of walking to every corner of the earth, although in fact no one has ever found it possible to do so.[5]

Then why do certain people want to do what is good and right and others not? Xun Zi does not really answer this question.

Intellect and morality

The different perspectives of Mencius and Xun Zi express a difference in emphasis that was to become even more prominent with the emergence of Neo-Confucianism in the Song Dynasty, a difference which has to do with the role assigned to the intellect and to study of matters of fact, on the one hand, and the cultivation of and reliance on one's moral instincts, on the other hand.

In the perspective of Mencius, man is born with the correct moral instincts which are a kind of emotions, the most fundamental one being compassion. Mencius would probably have agreed that without emotions there could be no sense of what is morally good and bad. The purpose of study, which must always be guided by

---

[5] Ibid., p. 171.

moral standards, was for Mencius ultimately to cultivate these innate sprouts of moral goodness.

In the perspective of Xun Zi a different picture emerges. Behaviour guided by natural desires and emotions will be marked by greed and contentiousness, whereas goodness is the result of conscious activity. It is through study that we can understand what are the requirements of ethics.

In other words we may say that whereas for Mencius morality is the basis and the role of intellectual study and reflection is to see to it that the naturally good instincts are properly translated into action, for Xun Zi our natural desires and instincts are evil and goodness must be acquired by study and upheld by rules of ritual, institutions, punishments etc. Consider the following statement by Xun Zi:

> Mencius states that man is capable of learning because his nature is good, but I say that this is wrong. It indicates that he has not really understood man's nature nor distinguished properly between the basic nature and conscious activity. The nature is that given by Heaven; you cannot learn it, you cannot acquire it by effort. Ritual principles, on the other hand, are created by sages; you can learn to apply them, you can work to bring them to completion. That part of man which cannot be learned or acquired by effort is called the nature; that part of him which can be acquired by learning and brought to completion by effort it called conscious activity.[6]

If for Mencius the original and natural germs of goodness form the basis, for Xun Zi the basis is study and reflection; in want of better words we may say that Mencius is the archetype of a moralist whereas Xun Zi is more of an intellectualist.

Significantly, 'humanity' was the central virtue and moral quality for Mencius, whereas 'wisdom' was more important for Xun Zi.

The difference between Mencius and Xun Zi that we are now discussing is also manifested in their respective views of Heaven. For Mencius Heaven seems to be a purposeful entity and a source of

---

[6] Quoted from chapter 23 'Man's Nature is Evil'; ibid., pp. 162–163.

ultimate control of human destiny. Xun Zi's Heaven is more naturalistic, existing independently of man:

> Heaven's ways are constant. It does not prevail because of a sage like Yao; it does not cease to prevail because of a tyrant like Jie.[7]

For Mencius Heaven was sacred, to be emulated and obeyed. In Xun Zi we also meet with the notion that men should try to act in accordance with Heaven, that is according to what we would call the laws of nature. Yet he criticized the tendency to exalt and admire Heaven, bravely introducing the notion that man should control Heaven, i.e. nature:

> Is it better to exalt Heaven and think of it,
> or to nourish its creatures and regulate them?
> Is it better to obey Heaven and sing hymns to it,
> Or to grasp the mandate of Heaven and make use of it?
> Is it better to long for the seasons and wait for them,
> Or to respond to the seasons and exploit them?
> Is it better to wait for things to increase by themselves,
> Or to apply your talents and transform them?
> Is it better to think of things but regard them as outside you,
> Or to control things and not let them slip your grasp?
> Is it better to long for the source from which things are born,
> Or to possess the means to bring them to completion?[8]

Another aspect again of the difference between Xun Zi and Mencius has to do with their respective views of the relative significance of the inner self of the human being and external reality that can be observed. Whereas Mencius tended to emphasize the importance of looking into one's self to understand one's true nature and thereby also becoming at one with Heaven, Xun Zi rather emphasized the importance of studying the external world. In this we can see an example of the polarity of 'inner' and 'outer' that has been very important in the Confucian tradition.[9]

---

[7] Quoted from chapter 17 'Discussing heaven'; trans Watson, p. 83.
[8] Ibid., pp. 90–91.
[9] Cf. Benjamin Schwartz' seminal article 'Some Polarities in Confucian Thought', in David S. Nivison and Arthur F. Wright, eds., *Confucianism in Action*, Stanford: Stanford University Press, 1959, pp. 50–62.

Evidently the difference between Xun Zi and Mencius also becomes manifest in the realm of politics and statecraft. With his optimistic view of human nature, Mencius argued that rule according to the Kingly Way should rely on the ruler's moral example; a true King would not have to resort to coercion, let alone punishments.

Xun Zi was more tough-minded and insisted that coercion and punishments are necessary. In his formulation the ancient sage kings 'set up laws and standards to correct' man's evil nature and 'meted out strict punishments to restrain it'. This stands in sharp contrast to Mencius' notion of good governance.

Xun Zi differed a great deal from Mencius in terms of his conception of man, nature and politics. But these differences should not make us blind to some fundamental commonalities. They shared the belief that man has the capacity to act morally, and they even agreed that it is possible for anyone to become a sage; they both held on to humanity and righteousness as supreme virtues, although for Xun Zi wisdom was perhaps the most important virtue; they both emphasized the importance of education; and they both spoke about the Kingly Way in statecraft as practised by the sage-kings Yao, Shun and Yu, although we may note that for Mencius, Yao and Shun were the most important paragons of virtue, while Xun Zi tended to exalt Yu the most.

In the Confucian tradition Mencius and Xun Zi represent two different poles within one and the same discourse; later discussions have often gravitated towards the one or the other of the poles that they defined.

Further reading

Historical background
See suggestions at the end of chapter 1.

Translations
Chan, Wing-tsit. *A Source Book in Chinese Philosophy*. Princeton: Princeton University Press, 1969. Partial translation, pp. 115–135.
Dubs, Homer D. *The Works of Hsüntze*. London: Arthur Probsthain, 1928. This companion volume to Professor Dubs' study of Xun Zi (see below) contains translation of the most important chapters.

Knoblock, John. *Xun Zi. A Translation and Study of the Complete Works*. Stanford: Stanford University Press, 1988. This is to date the only complete translation into English. The translation as well as the lengthy scholarly introduction are of very high quality.

Watson, Burton. *Xun Zi. Basic Writings*. New York: Columbia University Press, 2003. This volume includes ten chapters in English translation.

Studies of Xun Zi

Dubs, Homer D. *Hsüntze the Moulder of Ancient Confucianism*. London: Arthur Probsthain, 1927.

Cua, A. S. *Ethical Argumentation: a Study in Hsün Tzu's Moral Epistemology*. Honolulu: University of Hawaii Press, 1985.

Idem. *Human Nature, Ritual, and History: Studies in Xun Zi and Chinese philosophy*. Washington, D.C.: The Catholic University of America Press, 2005.

Goldin, Paul Rakita. *Rituals of the Way: the Philosophy of Xun Zi*. Chicago, Ill.: Open Court, 1999.

Kline III, T.C. and Philip J. Ivanhoe eds. *Virtue, Nature, and Moral Agency in the Xun Zi*. Edited, With Introduction, By T.C. Kline III and Philip J. Ivanhoe. Indianapolis: Hackett Pub., 2000.

Knoblock, John. The introduction to his own translation listed above is an excellent introduction to Xun Zi.

Loewe, Michael. 'Hsün tzu 荀子.' In *Early Chinese Texts: A Bibliographical Guide*. pp. 178–188.

Machle, Edward J. *Nature and Heaven in the Xun Zi: A Study of the Tian lun*, Albany: State University of New York Press, 1993.

Sato, Masayuki. *The Confucian Quest for Order: the Origin and Formation of the Political Thought of Xun Zi*. Leiden and Boston: Brill, 2003.

Other

Harbsmeier, Christoph. *Science and Civilization in China: Language and Logic*. Vol. 7 of Needham, Joseph. *Science and Civilisation in China*. Cambridge: Cambridge University Press, 1998.

Schwartz, Benjamin. 'Some Polarities in Confucian Thought.' In David S. Nivison and Arthur F. Wright, eds. *Confucianism in Action*. Stanford: Stanford University Press, 1959, pp. 50–62.

5

CONFUCIANISM BECOMES STATE PHILOSOPHY

After the fall of the Qin Dynasty, Liu Bang 劉邦, a minor Qin official of peasant origin who had become a rebel, in 202 ascended the throne as Emperor Gao 高帝 of the Han Dynasty and ruled until his death in 195 BC. But for a short interregnum (AD 9–23) when the reformer and 'usurper' Wang Mang 王莽 set up the 'New' Xin Dynasty, the Han Dynasty was to last until AD 220.[1]

The administration of the Han Empire required a large bureaucracy, and so the social class of literati, or scholar-officials, which was to play a crucial role as a bureaucratic pillar of the imperial order for the next two thousand years, now evolved, steeped in Confucian thought.

During the early Han Dynasty Confucianism became the official state ideology. To begin with Emperor Gao 高帝 was negatively disposed towards the Confucians. But a younger brother of his, to whom he was very close, had had a Confucian education. Moreover, the Confucians, who had been persecuted by the Qin emperor, supported the new Han Dynasty and sought to gain the favour of the new rulers. One of these, a scholar by the name of Lu Jia 陸賈 (216-ca. 272 BC), exasperated Emperor Gao by constantly quoting *The Classic of Poetry* and *The Classic of Documents*. It is recorded that he was once cut short by the emperor who said: 'You

---

[1] The Xin Dynasty was not accepted as in possession of the Mandate of Heaven by the later historiography, which divided the Han Dynasties into two parts, the Former, or Western Han, and the Later, or Eastern Han, each with its own dynastic history.

fool, I have conquered the empire on horseback, what use have I for your classics?' But then Lu Jia replied: 'Yes, Sire, you have conquered the empire on horseback, but can you govern it on horseback?'[2] In order to govern it, it was necessary, Lu Jia argued, to learn from the examples of ancient rulers, and so the study of the classical texts was imperative. These words seem to have made some impression on the emperor who asked Lu Jia to write a book about Confucianism. This book – entitled *New Words* (*Xinyu* 新語) – was praised by the emperor.

So although he first showed antipathy to the Confucians, Emperor Gao later favoured them and gave them high positions. Under the next two rulers – Emperor Hui 惠帝 (reigned 195–188 BC) and the infamous Empress Dowager Lü 呂后 – the *de facto* ruler 188–180 BC although never formally proclaimed empress in her own right – Confucianism suffered some setbacks.

However, during the reign of Emperor Wen 文帝 (180–157 BC) Confucianism became a very influential school of thought. This was probably partly due to the influence that the famous eclectic scholar Jia Yi 賈誼 (200–168 BC) exerted on the emperor.

When Emperor Wu 武帝 (reigned 141–87 BC) ascended to the throne, he was from early age favourably inclined towards Confucianism. But Empress Dowager Lü, who was a Daoist, and other opponents to Confucianism were still quite powerful, and for some time there were very serious controversies between the different cliques surrounding the emperor. These philosophical controversies were part of a fierce power struggle with ideological overtones. For some time Emperor Wu wavered, but in 135 BC, a few months after the death of the Empress Dowager, he sided with the Confucians and appointed 'scholars of wide learning' – *boshi* 博士 – who specialized in each of the five Confucian classics.[3] Later, he appointed several hundred Confucians as officials and he dismissed

---

[2] This episode was recorded by Sima Qian 司馬遷 in *The Records of the Grand Historian* (*Shiji* 史記), Book 37. The quotation here is taken from Hu Shi, 'The Establishment of Confucianism as a State Religion During the Han Dynasty', *Journal of the North China Branch of the Royal Asiatic Society* LX, 1929, p. 24.
[3] See Homer H. Dubs, 'The Victory of Han Confucianism', in Homer H. Dubs, *The History of the Former Han Dynasty*, Baltimore: Waverly Press, 1944, p. 345.

numerous Daoists. Nevertheless, some Daoists retained important posts. Among them were the famous historians Sima Tan and Sima Qian who served as Grand Astrologers.

In 124 BC Emperor Wu set up an Imperial University, where the 'Doctors', and fifty carefully appointed disciples, taught. It educated specially selected students in the Confucian classics, who upon graduation after one year were given important positions as officials in the imperial bureaucracy. This was the beginning of an enormously important feature of imperial China: the meritocracy exercised by scholar-officials who had gained their merits in Confucian studies:

> So in 125 BC the Prime Minister, Gongsun Hong, proposed to the Emperor Wudi that in the future all those who could pass an examination in one of the Confucian Classics, should be employed in the various government offices, in the provinces as well as in the Capital City. In all cases, priority should be given to those who read most. This was the beginning of the system of civil service examinations, which, gradually improved and modified, has remained in force for two thousand years. It was the most effective means of popularizing the knowledge of the Confucian Classics, because in later ages the classical examination practically furnished the only channel of civic advancement to all who were not born great. The government had only to announce the standard requirements for the examinations, and all the people who had some ambition for their sons would manage in every possible way to give them an education in the knowledge of the classics and in the ability of writing expository essays on them. In this way, the Confucian Classics, sometimes chiefly the pre-Confucian texts as mentioned above [i.e. the Five Classics], and sometimes the post-Confucian texts (in particular the so-called *Four Books*), have remained the principal text-books in all Chinese schools for the whole period of twenty centuries ever since the time of the Emperor Wu.[4]

During the reign of Emperor Wu, Dong Zhongshu 董仲舒 (ca. 179–ca. 104 BC), the most prominent Confucian during the early Han dynasty, sent three memorials to the emperor, in which he argued

---

[4] Hu Shi, pp. 27–28, transcriptions modif.

for the importance of unity, not only politically but also philosophically and ideologically. He wrote:

> The principle of Great Unification in the *Spring and Autumn Annals* is a permanent warp passing through the universe, and an expression of what is proper extending from the past to the present. But the teachers of today have diverse Ways, men have diverse doctrines, and each of the philosophic schools has its own particular position and differs in the ideas which it teaches. Hence it is that the rulers possess nothing whereby they may effect general unification. [. . .] All not within the field of the Six Classics should be cut short and not allowed to progress further.[5]

Emperor Wu approved of these memorials and declared that Confucianism would be the state philosophy. This focus on the importance of unity was not new; it was embedded in the notion of the Son of Heaven ruling all under Heaven. But it was only when a unified empire was created – first in the Qin and then in the Han Dynasty – that the unification of thought became a core government policy.

We should also observe a difference between the Qin and the Han, which provides us with an illuminating perspective on later Chinese history. While the Qin prohibited all schools of thought except Legalism and even sought to annihilate the texts of other schools, the Han was content to favour one school – Confucianism – as orthodox while still allowing the other schools to continue to exist. The infamous edict of 213 BC ordering the burning of books said:

> All histories not kept in the Imperial archives should be burned; all books outside the Imperial Doctorate College should be delivered to the local magistrates to be burned in their presence. Only books on medicine, divination and agriculture are exempt from this order. All who dare to hold open discussion on the forbidden books are liable to capital punishment. All who uphold the ancients to criticize the present regime should be punished by death.[6]

---

[5] *History of the Han Dynasty* (*Hanshu* 漢書), chapter 56; trans. Fung Yu-lan, *A Short History of Chinese Philosophy*, p, 205, modif.
[6] *The Records of the Grand Historian*, Book 6; here quoted from Hu Shi, pp. 20–21.

This we may see as signifying a difference between the totalitarian rule of the Qin and the 'merely' autocratic rule of the Han. In later Chinese history we find both varieties.

While Emperor Wu favoured the Confucians, he does not personally seem to have been a pure Confucian but rather an ideological eclectic. In a manner that anticipated the autocratic behaviour of many ostensibly Confucian emperors in Chinese history, he did not hesitate to intervene in disregard of Confucian principles when his scholar-officials made decisions that he disliked.

During the reign of Emperor Xuan 宣帝 (reigned 74–49 BC), the position of Confucianism was further strengthened. On his orders more than twenty scholars, who formed a kind of Confucian Council, spent three years studying and comparing different versions of the Confucian classics. In 51 BC this Confucian council sent a memorial to the Emperor informing him of their conclusions. Emperor Xuan ratified the memorial, codifying certain texts as authentic and correct.

This imperial sanction of the correct version of the classics anticipated the focus throughout Chinese history on Confucianism as ideological orthodoxy. Governance was, if not determined by, at least legitimized in the name of ideological orthodoxy, and the emperor was the arbiter of the orthodoxy and its interpretation. The emperor combined the roles of supreme political leader and ultimate spiritual and intellectual authority.

The reign of Emperor Yuan 元帝 (49–33 BC), who succeeded Emperor Xuan, then marked, in the words of one specialist on this period of Chinese history, the 'final victory of Confucianism'.[7] But the process of Confucianization continued and throughout the Han dynasty Confucianism remained state philosophy.

In the Han Dynasty the cult of the person of Confucius became important, which makes it quite reasonable to talk about Confucianism becoming a 'state religion' during this time.[8]

---

[7] Dubs, p. 351.
[8] This was, as we have seen, the expression used by Hu Shi, one of the most prominent intellectuals in twentieth-century China, in the title of his article describing how Confucianism became state orthodoxy: 'The Establishment of Confucianism as A State Religion During the Han Dynasty'.

One may ask why Confucianism of all philosophical schools became state philosophy, and this is also a question that many scholars have addressed. China's most famous philosopher in the twentieth century, Feng Youlan, finds the main answer to be the competence in the field of statecraft and administration that the Confucians had accumulated over the years:

> Hence when, after the Qin and Han unifications, it was necessary to draw up in final form the new institutions that were to be used in government and society, the services of Confucianists were found necessary for their organization. For it was these Confucianists who were versed in the old records and regulations, and who possessed records of every new form of political and social institution that had appeared since the time of Confucius downwards.[9]

It has also been pointed out that the Confucian 'aristocratic' ethics, which meant that the ruler should be good to his people and that the subjects should be 'filial', loyal and decorous to their ruler, was especially suited to be the official ideology of the imperial government of an agricultural state.[10]

Eclecticism

As state philosophy Confucianism became rather different from the ideas that we found in the three founding fathers that we have discussed. It combined elements from several pre-Qin traditions into an eclectic whole, exceedingly complicated and abstruse.

Elements from Legalism were brought into the new ideology in order to make it more effective as a tool in the hands of the leadership, which needed ideological legitimacy for its authoritarian rule.

Divination, especially as described and taught in *The Classic of Changes*, which now became a Confucian Classic, came into the foreground, and to the original hexagrams of this book were added

---

[9] Fung Yu-lan, *A History of Chinese Philosophy*, Vol. 1, pp. 405–6.
[10] Dubs, p. 351.

ten appendices, which set forth a method of controlling events by means of a mystical science of numbers.

Another element from non-Confucian pre-Qin thought which became very basic to early Han Confucianism was the notion that all things can be characterized in terms of either the positive and active male principle *yang* 陽 or the negative and passive female principle *yin* 陰. These ideas originated in the Yin-Yang School of pre-Qin times.[11]

Again, another element, which came to play a key role in the new ideology, was the notion of 'five elements' – 'five phases', 'five agents' or 'five forces' are probably translations closer to the original *wu xing* 五行 – water, fire, wood, metal and earth. This notion also went back to the Yin-Yang School.

This eclectic amalgamation of various pre-Qin strands of thought, which we know as the Confucianism of the Former Han dynasty, laid great emphasis on the relationship between Heaven and man and focused on assumed correspondences between phenomena in the natural and the human worlds. Natural phenomena were seen as omens of events in the human world.

Han Confucianism became, in the words of Hu Shi 胡適, 'a great synthetic religion into which were fused all the elements of popular superstition and state worship, rationalized somewhat in order to eliminate a few of the most untenable elements, and thinly covered up under the disguise of Confucian and Pre-Confucian Classics in order to make them appear respectable and authoritative.'[12]

Dong Zhongshu and the Confucian orthodoxy

As we have already seen, the famous scholar Dong Zhongshu played an important role in convincing Emperor Wu to adopt Confucianism as state philosophy. According to his biography in the

---

[11] Concerning the Yin-Yang School, see Fung Yu-lan, *A History of Chinese Philosophy*, 1, pp. 159–169.
[12] See Hu Shi, 'The Establishment of Confucianism as a State Religion during the Han Dynasty', pp. 34–5.

official dynastic history, many scholars of the time regarded him as their teacher – a very high honour in traditional Chinese culture. He was so serious in his study that for three years he allegedly did not even look out into his garden.

For Dong Zhongshu, as for other Confucians, unity was a major value. The political goal was that a sage-king should become the Son of Heaven ruling all under Heaven. No boundaries would prevail, and life would be harmonious with no strife and conflicts between different people and cliques. Learning – what we would call philosophy and ideology – should ultimately serve this purpose of creating, or rather recreating, an order of unity and harmony.

But Dong Zhongshu was not content just to argue for the importance of working towards these goals. He also set about the task of systematizing Confucian thought so that it would legitimize and promote, as convincingly and effectively as possible, this cause of fostering unity in the world. In doing so he was in fact a great synthesizer forging elements from different strands of Confucian thought as well as from other schools of thought into a unified whole.

His efforts resulted in the book *Luxuriant Dew from the Spring and Autumn Annals* (*Chunqiu fanlu* 春秋繁露). The authenticity of the version of this work that has been preserved is open to doubt, and this, no doubt, makes it difficult to discuss his ideas.[13] But our knowledge about Dong Zhongshu is not confined to the content of the *Luxuriant Dew from the Spring and Autumn Annals*. For example, we can also read his biography in the official *History of the Han Dynasty* (*Hanshu* 漢書), and there can hardly be any doubt that he was an important figure in his time. Also the ideas that we find in the extant *Luxuriant Dew from the Spring and Autumn Annals* seem to be congruent with the intellectual climate of that time as we know it also from other sources.

Therefore, as long as no evidence to the contrary has been presented, it seems sensible to continue to use *Luxuriant Dew from*

---

[13] Professor Göran Malmqvist is convinced, on the basis of linguistic evidence, that most parts of the extant version cannot have been written as early as during the Former Han Dynasty.

the Spring and Autumn Annals as a source for knowledge about the ideas of Dong Zhongshu, bearing in mind that this source is not quite reliable.

Dong emphasized the interconnectedness between Heaven, Man and Earth. In his view we may find ten constituent entities in the universe: Heaven, Earth, *yin* and *yang*, the five elements and human beings. *Yin* and *yang* are the manifestations of the 'ether' (*qi* 氣) which fills up the universe, and so humans are constantly immersed in them:

> Within the universe there exist the ethers of the yin and yang. Men are constantly immersed in them, just as fish are constantly immersed in water. The difference between the Yin and Yang ethers and water is that water is visible, whereas the ethers are invisible.[14]

The notions of *yin* and *yang*, Dong had picked up from the Yin-Yang School of pre-Qin thought. The same is true of the five elements, although from the beginning these go back to another current of thought than the twin notions of *yin* and *yang*. The earliest known mention of the five elements is in the chapter 'The Great Norm' of *The Classic of Documents*. There they are given in the order 'water' (*shui* 水), 'fire' (*huo* 火), 'wood' (*mu* 木), 'metal' (*jin* 金) and 'earth' (*tu* 土); Dong presented them in another order as 'wood', 'fire', 'earth', 'metal' and 'water'.

In Dong's explanation each of the five elements produces the next one and overcomes the next one again, so that wood produces fire and overcomes soil etc. So we may speak about two processes of mutual 'production' (*sheng* 生) and 'overcoming' (*sheng* 勝) respectively. Wood, fire, metal and water preside over the four directions of the compass and the four seasons respectively: wood over the east and spring, fire over the south and summer, metal over the west and autumn, water over the north and winter. Soil presides over the centre and assists all other elements. The alternation of the seasons Dong explains in terms of the operations of *yin* and *yang*:

> The constant principle of the universe is the succession of the Yin and Yang. The Yang is Heaven's virtuous power, while the Yin is its

---

[14] *Chunqiu fanlu*, chapter 81; trans. Fung Yu-lan, *A Short History of Chinese Philosophy*, p. 193.

punishment. . . . In the course of Heaven, there are three seasons [spring, summer and autumn] of formation and growth, and one season [winter] of mourning and death.[15]

Heaven trusts *yang* but not *yin* since 'it likes virtue but not punishment'.[16] For Dong, Heaven, just like man, has its own feelings of joy and anger and a mind, which experiences sadness and pleasure. Therefore, in kind 'Heaven and man are one'.[17]

Heaven, earth and man are 'the origins of all things': 'Heaven gives them birth, Earth gives them nourishment, and man gives them perfection.'[18] How then can men achieve this perfection? Dong's answer is through 'ritual' (*li* 禮) and 'music' (*yue* 樂). Without human effort in applying ritual and music, the universe will suffer imperfection:

> [Heaven, Earth and Man] are related to each other like the hands and feet; united they give the finished physical form, so that no one of them may be dispensed with.[19]

We may thus see how the search for unity, on a grand scale, permeates Dong Zhongshu's thought.

In humans Dong found both 'nature' (*xing* 性) and 'feelings' (*qing* 情), which correspond to the *yang* and *yin* of Heaven. Human nature is the source of 'goodness' (*ren* 仁), whereas 'feelings' may give rise to 'covetousness' (*tan* 貪).[20] In this regard Dong's position represents a step away from the basically positive evaluations of feelings and desires that we found in Mencius and in the direction of the critical attitude to feelings, and even more to desires, that we will meet in Neo-Confucianism.

For Dong the role of *yin* and *yang* in the universe tells us that the social structure must be organized in a hierarchic manner:

> In all things there must be correlates. Thus if there is the upper, there must be the lower. If there is the left, there must be the right. . . . If

---

[15] Ibid, chapter 49, trans. Fung, p. 194 modif.
[16] Ibid., chapter 47.
[17] Ibid., chapter 41.
[18] Ibid., chapter 19; trans. Fung. p. 194.
[19] Ibid., chapter 19; trans Fung, p. 195.
[20] Ibid., chapter 35.

there is cold, there must be heat. If there is day, there must be night. These are all correlates. The Yin is the correlate of the Yang, the wife of the husband, the subject of the sovereign. There is nothing that does not have a correlate, and in each correlation there is the Yin and Yang. Thus the relationship between sovereign and subject, father and son, husband and wife, are all derived from the principles of the Yin and Yang. The sovereign is Yang, the subject is Yin; the father is Yang, the son is Yin; the husband is Yang, the wife is Yin . . . The three cords of the Way of the King may be sought in Heaven.[21]

As we may see from this quotation, Dong Zhongshu simplified 'the five relationships' that Mencius had referred to, into 'three cords', or 'bonds' (*san gang* 三綱). It is probably significant that he removed the relationship between brothers, the only egalitarian relationship in Mencius' version. Dong linked the three cords with the 'five constant virtues' (*wu chang* 五常): 'goodness' (*ren* 仁), 'righteousness' (*yi* 義), 'propriety' or 'conduct in accordance with the rites' (*li* 禮), 'wisdom' (*zhi* 智) and 'good faith' (*xin* 信).

Together the two notions of three cords and five constant virtues were combined to form the notion of 'cord-constants' (*gangchang* 綱常), which refers to morality or moral laws in general.

It was the task of each and everyone to conform to the requirements associated with the three cords and to seek to realize the five virtues. But Dong Zhongshu realized that not everybody was able to do that. Therefore, governance should be designed to help people in this regard:

Heaven has produced men with natures that contain the basic stuff of goodness but are not able to be good in themselves. Therefore heaven has established for them [the institution of] the king to make them good. This is the purpose of Heaven.[22]

And the King should adopt four ways of governance: goodness, rewards, punishments and executions. These different ways he found corresponding to the four seasons of spring, summer, autumn and winter respectively.

---

[21] Ibid., chapter 53; trans Fung, pp. 196–7.
[22] Ibid., chapter 35; trans. Fung, pp. 197–8.

For Dong, the four seasons even offer a pattern for the organization of the Government. So we can see that he really goes to extremes in emphasizing the organic unity within not only society, but in the whole universe.

Dong articulated a vision of historical development that may appear peculiar. The succession of dynasties, in Dong's view, takes place in accordance with the 'Three Reigns': the Black, White and Red Reign, each one of which has its own system of government. In the preceding history Dong found that the Xia Dynasty had represented the Black, the Shang the White and the Zhou the Red Reign. Thereby one cycle of historical development had been completed, and after the Zhou this was to be repeated. The three reigns are not identical. A new ruler brings about some institutional changes, he moves the capital. Yet the fundamental principles – the Way 道 – are the same. In essence, the reigns do not differ:

> Therefore [the founder of a new dynasty] must shift his place of residence, assume a new title, change the beginning of the year and alter the colour of the clothing – all for no other reason than that he dares not but obey the will of Heaven and make clear the manifestation [of the mandate it has conferred] on him. But as to the great bonds of human relationships and as to morality, government, moral institutions, customs and the meaning of words, these remain wholly as they were before. For why, indeed, should they be changed? Therefore, the king of a new dynasty has the reputation of changing his institutions, but does not as a matter of fact alter the basic principles.[23]

When a new king founds a dynasty he has the Mandate of Heaven to do so. But it is to be noted that in Dong's conception all dynasties were doomed to lose the mandate sooner or later. It was not in the power of humans to transcend this cyclical development and create a dynasty that would eternally be in possession of the Mandate of Heaven.

Throughout the history of Imperial China the notion of the Mandate of Heaven remained immensely important. It legitimized the imperial rule, but it also placed some limits on it. It cautioned

---

[23] Ibid., chapter 1; trans. Fung, *A History of Chinese Philosophy*, Vol. 2, p. 62.

the rulers to be alert to expressions of Heaven's pleasure or displeasure. In Chinese history natural phenomena such as floods and earthquakes were taken as manifestations of Heaven's displeasure and did indeed make emperors uneasy and caused them to examine themselves and the policies of their government. Also the notion that the time of any dynasty was limited inculcated in the élite the notion that when time is up, a dynasty much be prepared to yield and hand over power to a new dynasty.

Dong Zhongshu held that neither the Qin nor the Han Dynasty was the legitimate successor to the Zhou. Instead Confucius (!) had received the Mandate of Heaven and he represented the Black Reign. Dong and his followers picked up Mencius' idea that *The Spring and Autumn Annals* was an important political work that Confucius had written exercising his right as new King and Son of Heaven. This peculiar idea undoubtedly served to promote the cult of Confucius in the Han Dynasty.

During the Han Dynasty there emerged a number of 'apocryphal' writings, referred to in Chinese as *wei shu* 緯書, the dating of which is in many cases rather uncertain.[24] In these we may find references to Confucius as a man possessing 'superhuman' powers; for example, he was said to have performed miracles. He was also referred to as the son of a god.

Dong Zhongshu divided the Spring and Autumn period into three phases: (1) that which Confucius had heard of through transmitted records, (2) that which he had heard elder living contemporaries tell him about and (3) his own age.

This theory of three stages can also be found in the *Gongyang Commentary* and during the Later Han Dynasty it was elaborated upon by He Xiu 何休 (AD 129–182). According to He, the *Spring and Autumn Annals* records how Confucius transformed the age of decay and disorder into that of 'approaching peace' and finally into that of 'universal peace'. This conception of historical stages is interesting in that it suggests a notion of progress towards a Utopian stage of 'universal peace', whereas notions in pre-modern China of historical

---

[24] The word *wei* 緯 was used in juxtaposition to classic, since the Chinese word for 'classic' – *jing* 經 – literally means 'warp' of a fabric, while *wei* means 'woof'.

stages have generally placed the ideal, model stage of culture and social organization at the beginning of history. This idea is, of course, utterly strange in that Confucius lived only during the final of these three supposed phases.

In the chapter 'Evolution of the Rites' (*Liyun* 禮運) in the *Classic of Rites* (*Liji* 禮記), we may find a notion of historical stages which is rather similar. Yet it differs from He Xiu's notion of progress towards 'universal peace' in locating the stage of 'Great Unity' (*Datong* 大同) at the beginning of history.

Dong Zhongshu's and He Xiu's writings about the Mandate of Heaven and historical stages offer another example of the tension between meaning and function in Confucianism. On the one hand, we can study these writings as attempts to understand and clarify history, and in this vein we may ask ourselves to what extent their ideas seem tenable, valid, fruitful etc. On the other hand, we should also see these writings in the context of the ideological and political realities of the Han Dynasty.

The Han Dynasty introduced a new order as compared to the preceding Qin, let alone the period before the first real unification of the Chinese empire. As state philosophy, Confucianism should legitimate the changes that the Han introduced, but it should also serve the stability of the new order by anchoring it in constant, universally valid principles.

Notions of a lost stage of peace, harmony and happiness are perhaps 'normal' integral parts of premodern cultures, just as the shift of focus from the paradise lost, or the decay of Great Unity, towards a future Utopia of affluence, which will allow for the realization of freedom, equality and brotherhood, are characteristic of the emergence of modernity. But we can also see that the distance from lost paradise to future Utopia is short. In Confucian thought the age of the sage-kings was held up as a model to emulate, and so Yao and Shun and Great Unity could in fact be used to point out a road of change. As we shall see, this became very obvious in the nineteenth and the twentieth centuries when some Confucians tried to use Confucianism to promote modernization. Likewise in European thought, it is quite obvious that the Christian notion of the Garden of Eden has indeed inspired many future Utopias.

Old and new texts

The title of his book – *Luxuriant Dew from the Spring and Autumn Annals* – shows that Dong Zhongshu assigned great importance to the *Spring and Autumn Annals*. For his interpretation of this work he used mainly the *Gongyang Commentary*. This brings us to the *problematique* surrounding the New Text School and the Old Text School.

As we know, in their efforts to institute Legalism as the one and only ideology, the rulers of the Qin Dynasty organized the burning of the writings of other schools of thought. In order to root out Confucianism they even buried a number of Confucian scholars alive.

As a result, when Confucianism was rehabilitated in the Han Dynasty and studies of the Confucian classics were to be resumed, old copies of these texts were very difficult to find. During the early Han there existed for several of the classics different versions that had been copied recently. The *Gongyang* and *Guliang* Commentaries on the *Spring and Autumn Annals*, which played such a very important role in early Han Confucianism, were such texts that were written in the script used at that time, and so obviously not copies that had been preserved since pre-Qin times.

However, during the Han there also emerged classical texts written in the pre-Qin script. One such text was a version of *The Classic of Documents*, another was the *Zuozhuan* Commentary on *The Spring and Autumn Annals*. These and other classical texts which emerged in the Han Dynasty written in the classical script have come to be collectively referred to as the Old Texts (*guwen* 古文) in opposition to the New Texts (*jinwen* 今文) that Dong Zhongshu and others used.

These two sets of texts have been at the core of the controversy between the Old Text School and the New Text School, which first erupted in the Han Dynasty, then remained very much in the background throughout the centuries until the eighteenth and nineteenth centuries when it came to the surface again. Then the adherents to the New Text School maintained that the Old Texts had been forged by Liu Xin 劉歆 (ca. 46 BC – ca. AD 23), an astrologer and librarian at the court.

From the beginning the controversy between these two schools of thought has concerned ideas as much as authenticity as such. The Old Text School rose in opposition to what they considered fantastic and supernatural ideas propagated by the New Text School describing Confucius as an 'uncrowned king' (*su wang* 素王) and semi-God and emphasizing the importance of prognostication etc.

In spirit the Old Text School is much closer to the pre-Qin Confucianism that we may find in, for example, *The Analects*. But when it comes to the authenticity of the different texts, the picture is quite complex. There seems to be almost universal agreement in the scholarly world that the Old Text version of *The Classic of Documents* must be a forgery. On the other hand, as the Swedish sinologist Bernhard Karlgren and others have shown, the *Zuozhuan* Commentary, no matter when the copy presented during the Former Han Dynasty was actually written, is definitely a text that goes back to pre-Qin times.[25]

From abstruse speculation to common sense

While the New Text School was dominant during the greater part of the Early Han Dynasty, the Old Text School came to dominate during the Later Han, and this led to a dissolution of the eclecticism of the Early Han.

Philosophically the two interesting early representatives of the Old Text School were Yang Xiong 楊雄 (53 BC – AD 18) and Wang Chong 王充 (AD 27 – ca. 100).

Yang Xiong tried to divorce his interpretation from the cluster of ideas associated with *yin* and *yang* and the five elements. On the other hand, he was himself deeply influenced by Daoism, and some scholars believe that his writings – *The Great Mystery* (*Taixuan* 太玄) and *The Model Sayings* (*Fayan* 法言) – were quite important in paving the way for a true Daoist revival in the period that followed after the fall of the Han Dynasty.

---

[25] Bernhard Karlgren, 'On the Authenticity and Nature of the Tso Chuan', in *Göteborgs Högskolas årsskrift* XXXII, No. 3, 1926, pp. 1–65.

Wang Chong appears as one of the most profoundly critical spirits in Chinese history. In his great work *Critical Essays* (*Lunheng* 論衡), he directed vitriolic criticism at what he felt were superstitious beliefs about correspondences which prevailed at the time.

In certain ways one may even think that Wang Chong anticipated some of the core ideas of the European Enlightenment. For example, he argued for the importance of independent judgement and emphasized that one should not only quote from the classics but also express one's own ideas. He also argued that his own time was as important to study as the ancient antiquity, and he even seems to have cast doubt on the historicity of some of the legends about the age of the sage kings:

> Narrators of events like to exalt antiquity and disparage the present; they esteem what they know through hearsay and slight what they themselves see.[26]

Not even the very notion of a golden past to be emulated seems to escape his scepticism:

> As far as the actual transformations effected by virtue are concerned, the Zhou [Dynasty] cannot equal the Han, whereas if we speak about fortunate omens and presages, the Han excels the Zhou.[27]

The search for truth permeated his analyses in *Critical Essays*. In his own words he was motivated by his 'hatred of fictions and falsehood'. He demands that every doctrine must have a factual basis:

> In things there is nothing more clarifying than having an example, and in argument there is nothing more decisive than having evidence.[28]

Wang Chong makes interesting comments, mostly critical, on many different subjects. On the whole he impresses the modern reader with his independent and critical judgement and his rational and

---

[26] Quoted from Alfred Forke trans., Wang Ch'ung [Wang Chong], *Lun-Heng*, 2 Vols., New York: Paragon Book Gallery, 1962, p. 158, modif.
[27] Ibid., p. 159.
[28] Ibid., p. 160.

logical reasoning, avoiding to express beliefs that cannot be based on facts. Yet in spite of his repeated attacks on the superstitious nature of the beliefs of the Yin–Yang School, even he himself cited favourable 'omens' which he thought had been manifested during the Han dynasty without any real factual support. 'This demonstrates', in the words of Feng Youlan, 'how powerful was the prevailing ideology of his age – so powerful, indeed, that even such an exceptional person as himself could sometimes hardly tear himself from its grasp'.[29]

During the history of the Chinese empire Wang Chong was generally not considered a very important figure. His writings were probably far too critical, and not sufficiently constructive, to give him a place among the canonical writers. After the fall of the empire, however, many critical minds have drawn inspiration from his writings.

After the collapse of the Han Dynasty in AD 220, Confucianism lost its central position in Chinese culture for the next few centuries. However, in the Tang Dynasty (618–907) the revival of Confucianism began, which would lead to the establishment of the Neo-Confucian Schools of thought which represent a peak in the development of Confucianism. This will be the subject of the next chapter in this brief overview of Confucian thought.

Further reading

Historical background

Bauer, Wolfgang. *China and the Search for Happiness: Recurring Themes in Four ThousandYears of Chinese Cultural History*. New York: The Seabury Press, 1976.

Bielenstein, Hans. *The Bureaucracy of Han Times*. Taipei: Rainbow Bridge Book Co., 1983.

Twitchett, Denis and Michael Loewe eds. *The Cambridge History of China*. Vol I: *The Ch'in and the Han Empires 221 B.C. – A.D. 220*, Cambridge: Cambridge University Press, 1986.

Overview of Han Confucianism

Fung, Yu-lan [Feng Youlan]. *A History of Chinese Philosophy*. Princeton: Princeton University Press, 1953. pp. 1–68.

---

[29] Fung, *A History of Chinese Philosophy*, Vol. 2, p. 167.

Idem. *A Short History of Chinese Philosophy.* New York: Free Press, 1997 [1st ed. 1948]. Chapters 16–18.

Han Confucianism becoming state orthodoxy

Dubs, Homer H. 'The Victory of Han Confucianism.' In Homer H. Dubs. *The History of the Former Han Dynasty.* Baltimore: Waverly Press, 1944, pp. 341–355.
Hu Shih. 'The Establishment of Confucianism as a State Religion During the Han Dynasty.' *Journal of the North China Branch of the Royal Asiatic Society* LX, 1929, pp. 21–41.

Studies of individual Han Confucians
Dong Zhongshu
Fung Yu-lan. *A History of Chinese Philosophy,* 2, chapter 2.
Idem. *A Short History of Chinese Philosophy,* chapter 17.

Jia Yi
Svarverud, Rune. *Methods of the Way: Early Chinese Ethical Thought,* Leiden and Boston: Brill, 1998. Contains a partial translation of *Xinshu* 新書 (New writings).

Lu Jia
Ku, Mei-kai. *A Chinese Mirror for Magistrates.* Canberra: Faculty of Asian Studies Monographs, Australian National University, 1988. Contains a complete translation of Lu's *New Words* (*Xinyu* 新語).

Wang Chong
Alfred Forke trans. Wang Ch'ung [Wang Chong]. *Lun-Heng.* Translated from the Chinese and annotated by Alfred Forke. 2 Vols., New York: Paragon Book Gallery, 1962. First published 1907–1911. This is a complete translation of Wang Chong's *Critical Essays.*

Yang Xiong
Knechtges, David R. *The Han shu Biography of Yang Xiong (53 B.C.–A.D. 18.* translated and annotated by David R. Knechtges. Calligraphy by Eva Yuen-wah Chung. [Tempe]: Center for Asian Studies, 1982.

Other
Ho, Ping-ti. *The Ladder of Success in Imperial China: Aspects of social Mobility, 1368–1911.* New York: Columbia University Press, 1962.
Karlgren, Bernhard. 'On the Authenticity and Nature of the Tso Chuan.' In *Göteborgs Högskolas årsskrift* XXXII, No. 3, 1926. pp. 1–65.
Miyazaki, Ichisada. *China's Examination Hell: the Civil Service Examinations of Imperial China,* New Haven: Yale University Press, 1981.

6

THE NEO-CONFUCIAN REVIVAL

Historical background

After the fall of the Han Dynasty in AD 220, China entered a period of political division that was to last for almost four centuries until the Sui Dynasty was set up in 581. This was a period of impressive intellectual vitality and pluralism during which Buddhism and Daoism became dominant intellectual currents. The impact of Buddhism, which had come to China from India already during the first century AD, if not earlier, extended far beyond the realm of thought as such. During this time of political division, Confucianism almost fell into oblivion, and those scholars who continued to study the Confucian classics were deeply tinged with Buddhism and Daoism.

In the Sui and the Tang Dynasties China became again a unified empire, and Chinese society underwent some very fundamental changes. Following the collapse of the Han Dynasty Chinese society was dominated by a number of aristocratic families and groups, among which the imperial family was the foremost. These families also dominated the bureaucracy. New officials were recruited on the basis of descent and social standing rather than on scholarly merits.

The unification under the Sui and Tang changed this situation, and over time, the aristocracy declined in power. Officials were to an increasing extent recruited by examinations and in office came to represent the ruling dynasty rather than their own families and clans. The emperor and the imperial family were no longer the first among equals but occupied an absolutely unique position in society, high up and above everyone else, and gradually acquired despotic powers.

This is in broad outline the content of a widely held thesis about fundamental structural changes of the political order that took place during the Sui and, especially, the Tang Dynasties. This thesis was first presented by the Japanese historian Naitō Torajirō 內籐虎次郎 on the eve of World War I.[1]

While Naito's hypothesis may still be seen as providing a general perspective on this period, later scholars have accumulated much more knowledge than Naito – who was as much a journalist as a scholar – had at his disposal. Indeed, an exceedingly complex picture is now emerging of economic, social, institutional and political change, a picture which includes some contradictory trends.

For example, examinations did come to play a significant role for the recruitment of officials but other avenues into the bureaucracy remained open, and some new ones were even introduced, so that experts estimate that during the late Tang not more than ten per cent of officials were actually recruited by means of examinations.

Similarly, it is certainly true that in a broad perspective the unification of the empire and the concentration of power in the hands of the emperor is one salient feature of this long stretch of history comprising the Sui and Tang Dynasties. However, this should not obscure the fact that in the wake of the rebellion of An Lushan 安祿山 in 755, which in many respects stands out as a pivotal point for some of the processes of transformation that characterize the period, the administration of the empire was decentralized and the power of the emperor was weakened. In the ninth century massive discontent then led to social unrest and rebellions, which led to the fragmentation of China and the eventual demise of the empire in 907.

Yet, to quote Professor Denis Twitchett:

. . . political division, in short now came to be thought of as a temporary disturbance of the natural order of things, that would in due

---

[1] Concerning Naito's hypothesis, see Hisayuki Miyakawa, 'An Outline of the Naito Hypothesis and its Effects on Japanese Studies of China', *Far Eastern Quarterly*, 14:4, 1955, pp. 533–552.

time be brought to an end by the rise of a new centralized regime.
[. . .] The Sui and T'ang thus finally established the idea of the
integrity of China as the territory of a single unified empire.[2]

About half a century after the collapse of the Tang, China became
united under a new centralized regime when the Song Dynasty was
established in 960. In many ways, the Song Dynasty was a flourish-
ing period in Chinese history. An élite culture developed and
reached a high level of sophistication. We can see this in scholarship
and in the arts, especially in painting. Academies were set up, book
printing developed and expanded greatly. The civil service examination system became a much more significant part of the elaborate government structure than before. Material production also
developed. Yet although the Song has even been described as
'China's greatest age', this was also a period when tribes from Inner
Asia gained ground in northern China and gradually came to constitute an increasingly serious threat to the Chinese state.[3] In 1126
the Tungusic Jürchen tribes from Manchuria forced the Song to
abandon their capital at Kaifeng in Henan province and move it to
the southern city of Hangzhou in southern China. So from that
time what had been the northern part of the Song Dynasty came
to belong to the Jin Dynasty (1115–1234).

In Chinese history the year 1126, therefore, marks the demarcation between Northern and Southern Song. Culturally, the Jürchen
invaders became quite absorbed by Chinese culture, however. For
example, they organized examinations on the Confucian classics for
their own people and produced at least 5000 metropolitan degree
holders.

However, the rule of the Jin would not last long. The Mongols
were advancing and extinguished the Jin in 1234, and in 1279 they
defeated the Southern Song and established the Yuan dynasty,
which would last until 1368.

---

[2] Denis Twitchett, 'Introduction' to *The Cambridge History of China*, Vol 3 *Sui and T'ang China,
589–906*, Part I, London, New York and Melbourne, 1979, p. 7.
[3] The American China scholar John King Fairbank referred to the Song as 'China's greatest
age'; see his *China: A New History*, Cambridge, Mass. and London: Harvard University Press,
1992, p. 88.

The Confucian revival began in the Tang dynasty and culminated in the Song. In the Yuan dynasty the Neo-Confucianism of Zhu Xi – the School of Principle – became state orthodoxy, a position it would retain until the abolition of the examination system in 1905.

In the early Tang attempts were made to redefine an orthodox Confucian orthodoxy. The second emperor Taizong 太宗 (reigned 626–649) assigned a team of scholars led by Kong Yingda 孔穎達 (574–648) to select the most accurate commentaries on the Confucian classics and add subcommentaries that would serve to codify the Confucian orthodoxy. The commentaries bearing Kong Yingda's name have remained very important up until our own days. But the Confucian orthodoxy was not really enforced; in fact, Buddhism and Daoism continued to develop and flourish.

The British sinologist T.H. Barrett has in a few words captured some essential aspects of the intellectual climate of the early Tang:

> Despite some measures taken to achieve intellectual unification in the early Tang, its founding rulers appear to have been much more cautious about imposing an ideological conformity on their subjects than some of their immediate predecessors in North China. In general, they presided over a cosmopolitan empire as tolerant of religious and philosophical plurality as it was of ethnic diversity. The average member of the Chinese intellectual élite, if he was not actually numbered among the Buddhist or Taoist clergy, probably had a smattering of both Buddhism and Taoism. He would certainly have looked to one or the other religion, if not both, to satisfy any inner promptings he might have felt towards self-cultivation. Confucianism he would have been thoroughly familiar with, but would have only thought of as providing solutions to purely secular problems, and probably not the only acceptable solutions, at that.[4]

In the eighth century Emperor Xuanzong 玄宗 (reigned 712–756) turned to Daoism which he used to prop up his absolute monarchy. Examinations on Daoist texts now provided an avenue into the bureaucracy, in basically the same way as we are used to associating with the examinations focusing on the Confucian canon.

---

[4] T.H. Barrett, *Li Ao: Buddhist, Taoist, or Neo-Confucian*, Oxford and New York: Oxford University Press, 1992, p. 16.

But Xuanzong's dream of consolidating a Daoist empire was brought to an abrupt end by the rebellion of An Lushan. It is a historical irony that this general of mixed Turkish and Sogdian descent, illiterate in Chinese, thereby became in the apt words of Professor Barrett 'a most unlikely godfather of Neo-Confucianism'.[5]

Taoism and Buddhism did of course survive the uprising, but in its wake scholars gradually began to perceive the social unrest as a serious threat to Chinese culture and so felt a need to return to the early sources and to rid China of extraneous corrupting influences. In this way, we may see how An Lushan paved the way for a Confucian revival.

Two precursors

The Confucian revival began in the Tang when some important commentaries on the classics were written and when the two scholars Han Yu 韓愈 (768–824) and Li Ao 李翱 (770s–840s) made important contributions towards pointing out a new direction for the Confucian movement.

In Han Yu's and Li Ao's time China was still more Buddhist than Confucian. But it was the conviction of these two scholars that it was necessary to cleanse the empire of the corrupting influence of foreign creeds such as Buddhism and erroneous indigenous teachings such as Daoism. To begin with they may have been rather lonely voices, but gradually more and more people began to think in a similar vein. This was partly because of the influence that they exerted but also because this time was somehow ripe for these ideas.

In his essay 'On the Origin of Dao' (*Yuan Dao* 原道), which has been enormously influential in Chinese history, Han Yu established an orthodox line of succession within the Confucian tradition:

What Dao is this? It is what I call Dao, not what the Daoists and Buddhists have called Dao. Yao passed it on to Shun, Shun to Yu, Yu to Tang, Tang to King Wen, King Wu and the Duke of Zhou; then

---

[5] Barrett, p. 18.

these passed it on to Confucius, who passed it on to Mencius. But after the death of Mencius it was not passed on. Xun Zi and Yang Xiong

Excerpted it but not its essence,
Discussed it but not in detail.
Before the Duke of Zhou
Our sages were kings,
And things got done.
After the Duke of Zhou
Our sages were subjects
And long theory won.

This being so, what can be done? Block them or nothing will flow; stop them or nothing will move. Make men of these people, burn their books, make homes of their dwellings, make clear the way of the former kings to guide them, and 'the widowers, the widows, the orphans, the childless, and the diseased all shall have care.' This can be done.[6]

From these words we can see how essential Han Yu felt it was to restore Confucianism. It has been pointed out that 'perhaps at no other time did the Confucian tradition come closer to extinction as a meaningful force in Chinese history' than when Han Yu took it upon himself to work for its restoration.[7] Seen in this light, the significance of Han Yu's contribution as a transmitter – very much in the vein of Confucius himself – can hardly be overestimated.

The passage just quoted expresses Han Yu's faith in what he felt was the orthodox Confucian tradition, but it also reveals his uncompromising rejection of Confucian heterodoxy: 'Block them or nothing will flow; stop them or nothing will move. Make men of these people, burn their books.' It is often said that syncretism and tolerance are characteristics of Chinese traditional thought. It is

---

[6] 'Essentials of the Moral Way', trans. Charles Hartman, in *Sources of Chinese Tradition*, Vol. 1: From Earliest Times to 1600, pp. 569–573. Here and below I quote Hartman's translation with some minor modifications, mainly to maintain a uniform use of Chinese terms and of transcriptions. Hartman translates *Yuan Dao* as 'Essentials of the Moral Way'. In the text here I adopt the more conventional 'On the Origin of Dao'.

[7] Charles Hartman, *Han Yu and the T'ang Search for Unity*. Princeton, New Jersey: Princeton University Press, 1986, p. 5.

pointed out that one and the same person could be Confucian in office and Daoist at home. This is not wrong, but it should not obscure the fact that the notion of orthodoxy was also very important in traditional China.

The focus on orthodoxy goes hand in hand with the lack of tolerance. It is characteristic how Han Yu issues a warning against the widespread influence of barbarians in Tang society:

> When Confucius wrote *The Spring and Autumn Annals*, if the enfeoffed lords followed the usage of the barbarians, he treated them as barbarians. If they progressed to the level of the central states, then he treated them as central states. The classic says: 'The barbarians with their rulers are not the equal of all Xia without them.' The Ode says: 'The Rong and Di barbarians, them he withstood; Jing and Shu, those he repressed.
>
> Yet today we elevate barbarian practices and place them above the teachings of our former kings. How long will it be before we ourselves have all become barbarians?[8]

Han Yu was extremely critical not only of heterodox forms of Confucian thought but also of other currents of thought such as Buddhism, Daoism and the teachings of the pre-Qin thinkers Mo Zi and Yang Zhu:

> After the traditions of the Zhou dynasty declined and Confucius passed away, there was the burning of the books in Qin and the rise of Daoism in the Han and of Buddhism in the Jin, Wei, Liang, and Sui dynasties. During these times those who spoke of humaneness and rightness, of the Way and its power, were either followers of Yang Zhu or Mo Zi, Lao Zi or Buddha. To adopt one of these one had to reject the others; so when believers took these men as their masters and followed them they despised and defamed Confucius. And those of later ages who might wish to hear the teachings on humaneness and rightness, the Way and its power, had no one to listen to.
>
> The followers of Lao Zi and Buddha both maintained that Confucius had been a disciple of their masters. And the followers of Confucius grew so accustomed to hearing these theories that they

---

[8] *Sources of Chinese Tradition*, Vol. 1, p. 572.

began to enjoy such calumnies and belittled themselves, acknowledging that the Master himself had indeed taken Lao Zi or the Buddha as his master. They not only said such things but also recorded them in their books. Those of later ages who might have wished to hear of the teachings on humaneness and rightness, the Way and its power, had no one from whom to seek them.[9]

Han Yu attaches great importance to the five human relationships that Mencius had discussed, adding to these the relationship between teacher and student, and so laments that Buddhist tendency to disregard these relationships and instead direct people's attention away from mundane affairs:

> But now the Buddhist doctrine maintains that one must reject the relationship between ruler and minister, do away with father and son and forbid the Way that enables us to live and to grow together – all this in order to seek what they call purity and *nirvana*. It is fortunate for them that these doctrines emerged after the Xia, Shang, and Zhou dynasties and so were not discredited by the ancient sages and by Confucius. It is equally unfortunate for us that they did not emerge before that time and so could have been corrected by the same sage.[10]

Han Yu is no less relentless in his criticism of Daoism:

> The titles of emperor and of king are different, yet they are sages for the same reason. To wear linen in summer and fur in winter, to drink when thirsty and to eat when hungry – in both cases the concern is different, yet the logic is the same. But now the Daoists advocate 'doing nothing' as in high antiquity. Such is akin to criticizing a man who wears furs in winter by asserting that is easier to make linen, or akin to criticizing a man who eats when he is hungry by asserting that it is easier to take a drink.[11]

Han Yu's essay on the origin of Dao or the Way has been very significant both in focusing on the importance of defining orthodoxy

---

[9] Ibid.
[10] Ibid., p. 571.
[11] Ibid., pp. 57–1–572.

and in elevating the position of Mencius and his ideas in the Confucian tradition. Apart from this essay, Han Yu also wrote many other pieces that were significant as part of the emerging Confucian revival. One example is his essay 'An Inquiry on Human Nature' (*Yuan xing* 原性).

A younger friend of Han Yu, and also his student, Li Ao is most famous for his *Book on Returning to One's True Nature* (*Fuxing shu* 復性書), in which he discussed such themes as 'human nature', 'feelings', 'decree', 'the sage', 'self-cultivation' etc. and anticipated some typically Neo-Confucian philosophical jargon.

His explanations of these notions make use of Buddhist and Daoist terminology, and he has often been described as heavily influenced by Buddhism. While it would be wrong to deny all Buddhist influence, it seems more important to recognize that Li Ao's major objective was indeed, just like in Han Yu's case, to return to Confucianism and to get away from the heterodox teachings of the Buddhists and the Daoists.[12]

In his essay he makes a radical distinction between true human nature as good, and feelings as the source of delusion:

> That whereby a man may be a sage is his true nature; that whereby he may be deluded as to this nature is emotion. Joy, anger, sorrow, fear, love, hate, and desire – these seven are the workings of emotion. When the emotions have become darkened, nature is hidden, but this is through no shortcoming of the nature: these seven follow one another in constant succession, so that the nature cannot achieve its fullness.[13]

He elaborates on these concepts and says:

> The nature is the decree of Heaven: the sage is he who obtains it and is not deluded. The emotions are the movements of the nature: common folk are those who drown in them and are unable to know their basis.[14]

---

[12] The British sinologist T.H. Barrett has shown this in his seminal study *Li Ao: Buddhist, Taoist, or Neo-Confucian*, Oxford and New York: Oxford University Press, 1992.
[13] *Book on Returning to One's True Nature*, 1.1; trans. Barrett, p. 94.
[14] Ibid., 2.1, p. 97.

He develops this line of thought *in extremis* by saying that a sage never really activates his emotions:

> Is the sage without emotions? The sage is absolutely still and without movement, arrives without travelling, shows his spirit-like power through not speaking, and gives light without shining. His conduct aligns him, with Heaven and Earth, and his transformations correspond to match those of the forces of yin and yang. Although he has emotions, he never has emotions.[15]

At the same time it is important for Li to point out that everybody is in possession of true human nature, although it may become beclouded by emotions:

> So, then, do common folk not have this nature? The nature of common folk is not different from that of the sage. However, they are darkened by the emotions and under successive attack from them, and this goes on for ever, so that even to the end of their lives they do not themselves view their true natures.[16]

In this way Li Ao could support Mencius in his insistence that every one of us has the potential to become a sage.

We should take note of this very critical view of what feelings might do. Often in the Confucian tradition, scholars have been careful to distinguish clearly between feelings and desires, considering desires more problematic than feelings. For Li Ao this distinction does not seem to be important. In this regard his view is similar to Buddhism. We cannot with certainty conclude that Li himself was directly influenced by Buddhism in this regard, for there were other Confucians who also shared these views, but be that as it may the increasingly critical judgement of desires and feelings within Confucianism at this time cannot be understood if we leave out the influence of Buddhism and Daoism.

However, the most interesting aspect of Li Ao's ideas was probably his emphasis on the individual human being's capacity to 'return to his or her true nature' (*fu xing* 復性). Li Ao does not express his views

---

[15] Ibid., 2.2, p. 97.
[16] Ibid., 2.3, p. 99.

very clearly in this regard, but it is possible to interpret him as asserting a moral and intellectual autonomy which enables the individual human being to understand the Way by means of introspection and self-cultivation, rather than by relying on the authority of the masters. This aspect of his thought anticipates, as we shall see, the ideas of later Neo-Confucians of the so-called School of Mind.[17] But we can also say that this focus on the human capacity to return to her true nature and comprehend the important existential truths was also a return to the fundamental ideas of Mencius.

By bringing new vitality into the Confucian tradition, defining its legacy and points of departure for its future direction, Han Yu and Li Ao were important precursors of the Neo-Confucian movement of the Song Dynasty which would elevate Confucianism to unprecedented heights, in terms of intellectual quality as well as social status.

Neo-Confucianism: synthesis and orthodoxy

The Song Dynasty brought about renewed unity and order after the disorderly last decades of the Tang and the rather chaotic period that followed in the aftermath of its demise. The new dynasty also set the context for the evolution of the major schools of Neo-Confucianism.

When the new Song Dynasty was set up, Confucian scholar-officials found an opportunity to suggest reforms. This is indeed a recurring pattern in Chinese history: the early phase of a dynasty offers opportunities for change and reform. One example in the Song is the famous Prime Minister Fan Zhongyan 范仲淹 (989–1052), who in the words of John King Fairbank:

> . . . pushed a series of reforms in the bureaucracy against favouritism, in the examinations for practicality of subject matter, in land-holding to give local officials a chance to rely on income instead of squeeze, in defence to strengthen local militia.[18]

---

[17] Cf. below pp. 117 ff.
[18] Fairbank, p. 96.

From the point of view of the evolution of Confucian thought it seems especially illuminating to compare the famous radical reformer Wang Anshi 王安石 (1021–81) and the more moderate scholar official-cum-historian Sima Guang 司馬光 (1019–86).

Wang Anshi wanted to create a perfect society modelled on the example of the order that the legendary sage-kings had instituted. There was something absolutist, almost fundamentalist about Wang's outlook. In the legendary antiquity he saw a blueprint for his own reform programme. Sima Guang did not share Wang's fundamentalist inclinations. In particular he turned for guidance not so much to the period of the sage-kings as to the historical period after that. To this end he wrote his monumental *Comprehensive Mirror for Aid in Government* (*Zizhi tongjian* 資治通鑑), which in 294 volumes covered the period 403 BC to AD 949. This work has remained enormously important into modern times.

Wang Anshi brought about a series of radical institutional reforms referred to as 'The New Policies' (*xinfa* 新法), aiming at bringing about the regeneration of a perfect order under Heaven. Wang's reform programme may also be characterized as radical in that he wanted to bring about very thorough changes in the prevailing order, for example create a materially more equal society.

In comparison, Sima Guang's proposals for bureaucratic reform were much more cautious and practical in orientation, aiming at improving the functioning of the existing institutional framework. One may say that Sima was more conservative than Wang in that he was against using the state to bring about a higher degree of material equality. He feared that radical changes in the hierarchical order would lead to the collapse of the state.

Wang Anshi and Sima Guang were both Confucians. Their main concern was to define and assist in applying the principles for this task as well as could possibly be done. In this regard they were both very much preoccupied with history. Wang in a more 'Utopian' sense, identifying in the distant past a blueprint of reform, the implementation of which would result in radical change; Sima in a more cautious and conservative sense in describing the evolution of history up until his own time as a 'comprehensive mirror for aid in government'.

The thinkers who are more archetypically thought of as representing the emergence and development of Neo-Confucian thought, and to whom we shall now turn our attention, all differed from Wang and Sima in that they regarded it as very important to clarify a series of fundamental questions concerning the human predicament by means of a Confucian discourse that was most often interpretive in form but which in fact also moved Confucian thought to a new stage. This is not to say that these scholars were pure intellectuals or even that their main concern was necessarily intellectual. Confucianism was for them, as for other Confucians, both philosophy and moral-spiritual praxis. For the Neo-Confucians we may even say that intellectual inquiry was ultimately a means to realizing one's innate potential and to contributing to creating a better world. Nevertheless, in what follows the main focus will be on their intellectual pursuits.

The term 'Neo-Confucianism' refers broadly to two schools of thought, the School of Principle (*Lixue* 理學) and the School of Mind (*Xinxue* 心學), which developed in the Song dynasty and which would dominate China's intellectual life for many centuries. Thus, this term is really a Western coinage. In Chinese there are different ways of referring to these currents of thought. One way is to refer to the School of Principle and the School of Mind. Another way is to refer to *Song Ming Lixue* 宋明理學, which literally means 'The School of Principle of the Song and the Ming Dynasties', but which in fact often also includes the School of Mind. Another way again is to speak about *Daoxue* 道學, 'The Learning of the Way'. Finally, the word *Songxue* 宋學 'The Learning of the Song' is sometimes also used in a sense that may resemble the notion of Neo-Confucianism. However, we should notice that it differs in two important ways. First, this term refers to Neo-Confucianism during the Song dynasty only, and secondly it may also refer to other aspects of 'learning' during the Song than philosophy.

A unifying characteristic of the different varieties of Neo-Confucian thought was that in one way or another they were all a response to Buddhism and Daoism and expressions of a conscious effort to bring about a Confucian revival.

The Neo-Confucian masters wanted to distinguish themselves from Buddhism and Daoism, and yet their ideas did not escape the influence from these creeds. We may see this in the view of 'desires' (*yu* 欲) as the sources of evil and often also in a rather sceptical view of 'feelings' (*qing* 情): these ideas were the result mainly of Buddhist influence.

We may also see it in the focus on the dichotomy of 'stillness' (*jing* 靜) and 'movement' (*dong* 動), where the former connotes purity and flawlessness while the latter connotes possible problems. Furthermore, in the metaphysical theories that the Neo-Confucian thinkers developed there are also clear traces of influence from Buddhism and Daoism.

Above all, the focus on 'principle' (*li* 理) was very much a result of Buddhist influence. This notion had not been at the core of early Confucianism but became an essential category in Neo-Confucianism.

Thus, Neo-Confucianism can be seen as a synthesis of elements combined from the traditions of classical Confucianism, Buddhism and Daoism. This was part of a project to formulate an all-embracing 'correct' theory of man and the universe, i.e. to re-establish orthodoxy. The need for such a project was, as we have seen, perceived and formulated during the Tang already especially by Han Yu. But it was only during the Song that it was brought to a fruitful completion.

The founders of Neo-Confucianism

The growth of Neo-Confucian thought in the Song dynasty is associated with a rather small number of highly creative spirits. One may say that they continued where Han Yu and Li Ao had finished. The outstanding figure in bringing the project to completion was without comparison the great scholar and philosopher Zhu Xi 朱熹 (1130–1200), who was a creative synthesizer who managed to forge together ideas formulated by other scholars into a unified whole.

Before turning our attention to Zhu Xi himself we should briefly deal with five other scholars who all contributed decisively to the Neo-Confucian systems of thought.

1. Zhou Dunyi 周敦頤 (1017–73) laid the pattern for metaphysics and ethics of Neo-Confucianism by means of two short treatises. In his most famous and influential essay – *Explanation of the Diagram of the Supreme Ultimate* (*Taiji tu shuo* 太極圖說) – he sought, in the words of his biography in the official Song history, to 'elucidate the origins of "Heavenly Principle" [*tianli* 天理] and probe into the beginning and end of all things'.[19] Some scholars believe that Zhou himself composed the diagram, while others hold that he got it from a Daoist priest. It may also well be that the diagram, as we find it in the works of Zhou, is a revised version of a diagram designed by somebody else. The concept *taiji* most people in the West associate with *Taiji quan*, a form of martial arts. In this context it refers to the origin or basis of everything there is. It has been variously translated as 'Supreme Ultimate', 'Great Ultimate' or, recently, 'Supreme Polarity'.[20]

As the classical statement of Neo-Confucian metaphysics, this essay is worth quoting in full:

> The Ultimate of Non-being [*wuji* 無極] and yet the Supreme Ultimate! When the Supreme Ultimate moves [*dong* 動] it produces *yang*. Having moved to the ultimate, it becomes still [*jing* 靜]. When still, it produces *yin*. Having reached the ultimate of stillness, it moves again. Movement and stillness alternate; each is the root of the other. It divides *yin* and *yang*, and so the two modes [*liang yi* 兩儀] are established.
>
> *Yang* changes and *yin* unites [with *yang*] and so water, fire, wood, metal and earth are produced. When these five forms of ether are harmoniously distributed, the four seasons run their course.
>
> The five elements are one in *yin* and *yang*, *yin* and *yang* are one in the Supreme Ultimate. The Supreme Ultimate is fundamentally the Ultimate of Non-being. When the five elements come into being, each one has its nature [*xing* 性].
>
> The reality of the Ultimate of Non-being and the essence of the two [modes] and five [elements] unite mysteriously and coalesce. 'The Way

---

[19] Quoted from Fung Yu–lan, *A History of Chinese Philosophy*, Vol. 2, p. 435, modif.

[20] Derk Bodde, among many others, uses 'Supreme Ultimate' (e.g. in his translation of Fung Yu-lan's *A History of Chinese Philosophy*, vol. 2, pp. 435–8; Wing-tsit Chan uses 'Great Ultimate' in *A Source Book in Chinese Philosophy*, pp. 463–4; Joseph Adler uses 'Supreme Polarity' in his recent translation in *Sources of Chinese Tradition*, 1, pp. 672–6. In rendering the full text into English, I have drawn on all three translations.

of *qian* 乾 becomes the male element, and the Way of *kun* 坤 principle becomes the female element.'[21] The two ethers [*yin* and *yang*] interact and produce the myriad things. The myriad things produce and reproduce and there is change and transformation without end.

Only man receives them [the five elements] in their highest excellence and so he is the most intelligent. When his bodily form has been produced, his spirit develops consciousness, the five [principles] of nature are aroused by and react to the external world and so good and evil are distinguished and the myriad affairs take place.

The sage regulates them with centrality, correctness, goodness and rightness, and he takes stillness as essential in establishing the ultimate of being human. Thus the sage's 'virtue equals that of Heaven and Earth; his brilliance equals that of the sun and moon; his timeliness equals that of the four seasons; his good and bad fortune equal those of ghosts and spirits.'[22] The superior man cultivates these and has good fortune. The petty man rejects them and has bad fortune.

Therefore [*The Classic of Changes*] says: 'Establishing the Way of Heaven, [the sages] speak of *yin* and *yang*; establishing the Way of Earth [they] speak of being softness [*rou* 柔] and hardness [*gang* 剛]; establishing the Way of Man, they speak of goodness [*ren* 仁] and righteousness [*yi* 義].' It also says: '[The sage] investigates beginnings and follows them to their ends; therefore he understands death and birth.'[23] Great indeed is [the *Classic of*] *Changes*! Herein lies its perfection.

As we shall see, the *Taiji* diagram and Zhou Dunyi's explanation were integrated into Zhu Xi's great synthesis of Neo-Confucian thought, providing the fundament, as it were, for a Neo-Confucian cosmology and metaphysics. In principle, most Neo-Confucians have subscribed to the ideas expressed in this text, but interpretations have varied. In particular, the interpretation of the first sentence – 'The Ultimate of Non-being and yet the Supreme Ultimate!' (*Taiji er wuji* 太極而無極) – has given rise to much controversy over the centuries, both in terms of interpretation and validity. Some scholars have taken this phrase to mean 'The

---

[21] This is a quotation from 'Appended Words' (*Xici* 系辭) 1:1. The *qian* 乾 and the *kun* 坤 are the two first hexagrams in *The Classic of Changes*, symbolizing pure *yang* and pure *yin*, or Heaven and Earth.
[22] 'Commentary on the Words of the Text' (*Wenyan* 文言) under hexagram 1.
[23] 'Explaining the Trigrams' (*Shuo gua* 說卦), 2.

Ultimate of Non-being and then the Supreme Ultimate', which would suggest the idea of 'being' as a creation of 'non-being'. Other scholars have subscribed to this idea philosophically, while others have found it objectionable. Other scholars again have preferred the interpretation 'The Ultimate of Non-being and also the Supreme Ultimate', which would mean that it refers to one entity, difficult or impossible to define precisely, which has these two aspects.

Moreover, the interpretation of this phrase has played an important role in the controversy between the School of Principle and the School of Mind. The followers of the latter have criticized Zhou Dunyi on this point saying that his formulation suggests a bifurcation of reality into two different realms, a dualism to which they have objected. The followers of the School of Principle have, on the other, insisted that the idea is not that there is an Ultimate of Non-being outside the Ultimate of Being but that these two concepts refer to two different modes of reality.

In his second famous essay, *Penetrating The Classic of Changes* (*Tongshu* 通書), Zhou Dunyi's main concern is to discuss what humans can do to cultivate themselves in the direction of attaining sagehood. In this regard, he places great emphasis on getting rid of one's selfish desires and focuses on 'stillness' as the source of clarity or enlightenment. In his own words:

– Can one learn to be a sage?
– Yes, one can.
– Is there anything which is crucial for this?
– Yes, there is.
– May I hear what it is?
– To be one is crucial, to be one and have no desires. Having no desires one will be still and vacuous, and one's movements will be straight. Being still and vacuous one will see clearly. Seeing clearly one will comprehend. One's movements being straight, one will be impartial; being impartial one will be all-embracing. Seeing clearly, comprehending, being impartial and all-embracing – then one is almost a sage![24]

---

[24] *Penetrating The Classic of Changes*, chapter 30.

Many scholars have objected to the central role that Zhou accorded the notion of 'stillness', which may be considered Daoist rather than Confucian. Not least in more modern times this tenet of Zhou's thought, and of other currents of Neo-Confucian thought, too, has been criticized as leading to a passive, non-active attitude harmful to the improvement of the human condition.

2. Shao Yong 邵雍 (1011–77) also formulated a metaphysical theory about the origin of all being and about the laws governing man and nature. In these endeavours he based himself on *The Classic of Changes* and especially on the trigrams and hexagrams. A characteristic feature of his thought is a focus on numbers which, in a sense, he held governed all creatures including men. Shao Yong's most famous work is the *The Book of the Supreme World-Ordering Principles* (*Huangji jingshi* 皇極經世), in which he uses the interplay of *yin* and *yang*, as manifested in the hexagrams of *The Classic of Changes*, to elucidate the cyclical development of the world. Like other Confucians he held that the Golden Age of our world had prevailed more than three thousand years earlier during the reign of the sage-king Yao and that in his own time the world found itself in a period of decline corresponding to the hexagram *bo* 剝.

Another interesting tenet of Shao Yong's thought is related to epistemology or the theory of knowledge. He argues that things should be observed on their own terms and that the observer must avoid letting his personal feelings distort the image of the object he observes:

> To observe things in terms of those things: this is to follow one's nature. But to observe things in terms of the self: this is to follow one's feelings. Human nature is impartial and enlightened; the feelings are partial and blind.[25]

In Shao Yong's view it was characteristic of the sage to be able to deny his ego and 'observe things in terms of those things'.

---

[25] *The Book of the Supreme World-Ordering Principles*, 12b. 2; trans Bodde in Fung Yu-lan, *A History of Chinese Philosophy* Vol. 2, p. 467, modif.

The interest that Shao Yong showed in basic epistemological questions is rather unusual not only in Confucianism but in the Chinese tradition as a whole.

3. Zhang Zai 張載 (1020–77) developed a strikingly mechanistic and monistic conception of nature and man. Zhang was a monist in that he insisted that all that exists is 'ether' (*qi* 氣), which is sometimes also translated as 'matter' or 'material force'. Like Zhou Dunyi and Shao Yong he took his point of departure in *The Classic of Changes*, and specifically in the statement in the Appendices that states: 'In the *Changes* there is the Supreme Ultimate which produces the Two Forms.' For Zhang Zai it is essential that even the Supreme Ultimate is *qi*, ether; for him there is no such thing as the 'Ultimate of Non-being'. The effort to get away from the Daoist and Buddhist notions of 'non-being' as some kind of mysterious entity permeates his work.

Zhang Zai's most famous work is his *Correcting Ignorance* (*Zhengmeng* 正蒙), and one chapter in this work has become very famous in its own right: *The Western Inscription* (*Ximing* 西銘), which was inscribed on the western wall of Zhang's study. In this essay, Zhang argues that since all things in the universe are made of 'ether', humans and all other creatures are really part of one and the same body. We may let Zhang speak for himself:

Heaven is my father and Earth is my mother, and even such a small creature as I finds an intimate place in their midst.

Therefore that which extends throughout the universe I regard as my body and that which directs the universe I consider as my nature.

All people are my brothers and sisters, and all things are my companions.

The great ruler [the emperor] is the eldest son of my parents [Heaven and Earth], and the great ministers are his stewards. Respect the aged – this is the way to treat them as elders should be treated. Show affection towards the orphaned and the weak – this is the way to treat them as the young should be treated. The sage identifies his virtue with that of Heaven and Earth, and the worthy is the best [among the children of Heaven and Earth]. Even those who are tired and infirm, crippled or sick, those who have no brothers or children, wives or husbands, are all my brothers who are in distress and have no one to turn to.

When the time comes, to keep himself from harm – this is the care of a son. To rejoice in Heaven and have no anxiety – this is filiality at its purest.

One who disobeys [the principle of Heaven] violates virtue. One who destroys humanity [*ren*] is a robber. One who promotes evil lacks [moral] capacity. But one who puts his moral nature into practice and brings his physical existence to complete fulfilment can match [Heaven and Earth].

One who knows the principles of transformation will skilfully carry forward the undertakings [of Heaven and Earth], and one who penetrates the spirit to the highest degree will skilfully carry out their will.

Do nothing shameful even in the recesses of your own home and thus bring dishonour to it. Preserve the mind and nourish the nature and thus [serve] them with untiring effort.

The great Yu shunned pleasant wine but attended to the protection and support of his parents. Border Warden Ying cared for the young and thus extended his love to his own kind.

Emperor Shun's merit lay in delighting his parents with unceasing effort, and Shensheng's reverence was demonstrated when he awaited punishment without making an effort to escape.

Zeng Can received his body from his parents and reverently kept it intact throughout life, while [Yu] Boqi vigorously obeyed his father's command.

Wealth, honour, blessing, and benefit are meant for the enrichment of my life, while poverty, humble station, care, and sorrow will be my helpmates to fulfilment.

In life I follow and serve [Heaven and Earth]. In death I will be at peace.[26]

This text, which is here quoted in full in Wing-tsit Chan's translation, is one of the most famous texts of Neo-Confucianism. In modern times, Marxist scholars have praised Zhang Zai for his 'materialism'. Through his insistence that 'ether' is the only thing that really exists Zhang does indeed represent one wing of

---

[26] *The Western Incsription*; trans. Wing-tsit Chan in Wm. Theodore deBary and Irene Bloom Irene eds., *Sources of Chinese Tradition*, Vol. 1, New York: Columbia University Press, 1999, pp. 683–4.

Neo-Confucian thought which one may characterize in terms of monism and materialism.

4. The Cheng brothers, Cheng Hao (程顥, also known as Cheng Mingdao 程明道 1032–85) and Cheng Yi (程頤, also known as Cheng Yichuan 程伊川 1033–1107) were both students of Zhou Dunyi and friends of Zhang Zai.

The Cheng brothers – in Chinese often referred to as 'The Two Cheng' *Er Cheng* 二程 – were the first Confucian philosophers to make 'principle' *li* 理 their major concept. Principle makes every object what it is, but it also runs through all objects and provides unity beyond or underneath the apparent chaotic multiple phenomena. In their search for underlying unity they were no doubt typical of the mainstream of Chinese thought, but their discussion of 'principle' marked the introduction of a new mode of thinking – a new discourse – to deal with the issues involved in this quest. They also elevated the discussion to a higher level of intellectual sophistication.

Their interpretations of the Confucian canon took somewhat different directions and anticipated the opposition between the School of Mind and the School of Principle, which would become clear a century later when the two positions were clearly articulated by Zhu Xi and Lu Xiangshan respectively.

The focus on principle united the two brothers. In the sayings of the two brothers recorded by their disciples, which remain a major source for knowledge of their ideas, it is often not made explicit which one of the two who actually made a specific statement. But although they shared many ideas, one can also say that in their search for unity they explored different paths. Cheng Hao was more of a monist, Cheng Yi more of a dualist. In this regard Cheng Hao's ideas were more 'conventional', more similar to the ideas expressed by Zhou Dunyi and others before; Cheng Yi was more creative in formulating a dualistic tendency which appears new and original. Yet it seems to me that the difference between the two was one of accent rather than essence.

Cheng Hao's view of the oneness of all myriad things was fundamentally based on the assumption of a common source: 'like the underground spring from which the stream flows and divides, or the buried root from which the tree grows and branches out'.[27] He admired Zhang Zai as a monist. But while Zhang was of the opinion that 'ether' – *qi* – is the only thing that *really* exists, and reduced principle to an aspect of ether, Cheng Hao regarded ether as essentially the same as principle since it was constantly produced by principle.

When one first reads about the polarity of monism and dualism in Neo-Confucian thought, one may easily interpret the position of Cheng Hao, and others who focus on 'principle', in terms of the idealism of Berkeley and others in European tradition. But this would probably be a mistake. Cheng Hao did not really deny the reality of 'ether'; to do so was considered to be a Buddhist position, which the Neo-Confucians opposed. It was rather that ether was essentially the same as principle since it was produced by principle. In the words of A.C. Graham:

> But the Neo-Confucians did not criticize sense-perception; their epistemology is 'naïve realism'. Those of them who are monists escape the duality of mind and ether, not by denying the existence of the latter, but by claiming that mind is perpetually becoming ether.[28]

Cheng Yi's philosophical orientation was more dualistic. He tended to juxtapose ether, which is the material which makes up everything, and principle which determines the generic characteristics of the different objects, while at the same time uniting the myriad phenomena. For Cheng Yi, as later for Zhu Xi, principle and ether came to represent two dimensions or realms of reality; the one pure, flawless, good still, the other more or less impure and the source of different kinds of imperfection and evil.

The most important difference between the two is related to the monism–dualism polarity but they also differed in terms of objectivism and subjectivism.

Cheng Hao was quite *subjectivistic* in the sense that he thought that human beings should seek important knowledge within themselves

---

[27] A.C. Graham, *Two Chinese Philosophers*, La Salle, Illinois: Open Court, 1992, p. xix.
[28] Ibid., p. 121.

rather than in the external world. Cheng Yi was more *objectivistic* and directed his attention to the external world as a source for knowledge. It was this difference, more than anything else, that anticipated the difference between the School of Principle and the School of Mind.

The creative synthesizer: Zhu Xi (1130–1200)

Zhu Xi was the creator of the greatest system of thought that has ever come into being in China – the School of Principle – which would become the official ideological orthodoxy for more than five centuries.

The son of a scholar-official, Zhu Xi was born in central Fujian province two decades after the death of Cheng Yi, but the ideas of the Cheng brothers exerted important influence on him.

In his youth Zhu Xi studied Buddhism and Daoism and it was only when he was about thirty years old that he rejected these in favour of Confucianism. Already at the age of nineteen he passed the highest degree of the government examinations, which was quite unusual, and so became a scholar-official. During his life he held several different positions in the government bureaucracy.

It was more important for Zhu Xi to be a scholar and a teacher than to be an official, and during the half century that he lived after gaining his *jinshi* – 'presented scholar' – degree he actually served as a government official only during nine years. During the years 1163–78 he declined all official positions in order to devote his energies to scholarship. In 1179, after assuming the office of prefect of Nankang prefecture in present-day Jiangxi province, he restored the famous White Deer Grotto Academy, beautifully located on the famous Lushan mountain, where many important lectures were given, by Zhu Xi and others. In 1181 he invited his philosophical rival Lu Xiangshan to come to the academy and lecture. Lu's lecture dealt with the relationship between profit and righteousness and it pleased Zhu so much that he had it inscribed on stone. However, he left his office at Nankang the same year as Lu Xiangshan came there to lecture, and after this he held different positions in the bureaucracy until 1195 when he withdrew from office, dissatisfied with the actions of 'wicked officials' of the times.

Zhu had a strained relationship with the leaders of his time. On three occasions he sent memorials to the emperor advocating changes and on three occasions he also had audiences with the emperor. The criticism that he voiced, which was based on his moral convictions, seems on the whole not to have been welcomed by the emperor and his closest aides. For example, in 1180 he infuriated the emperor by sending in a sealed memorial in which he insisted that economic distress, military weakness and political corruption could be removed only if the ruler rectified his mind.

Probably as a result of his daring criticism he was impeached towards the end of his life and government officials criticized his ideas as 'false learning'. Someone even petitioned that he should be executed.

It was only in 1313, during the Mongol Yuan dynasty, that his commentaries on *The Four Books* became by an imperial decree the orthodox interpretation and norm for the civil service examinations, a position they would retain until the abolition of the examination system in 1905. In this sense, Zhu Xi's School of Principle served as state philosophy for nearly six centuries.

Zhu Xi was a synthesizer. In working out his system of ideas he built upon classical texts from the pre-Qin period and managed to unify and reconcile different orientations of Confucian thought from this time. One of his most important works was his edition of *The Four Books – The Great Learning, The Doctrine of the Mean, The Analects* and *Mencius* – entitled *Collected Annotations on the Four Books* (*Sishu jizhu* 四書集注). Another extremely important work was a collection of sayings by the predecessors that we have just mentioned except Shao Yong. This work, entitled *Reflections on Things at Hand* (*Jinsilu* 近思錄) – which in 1175 Zhu Xi compiled together with his friend Lü Zuqian 呂祖謙 (1137–81) – has served for centuries as a compendium of Neo-Confucian thought. To the quotations Zhu added comments with the help of which the ideas expressed by the four thinkers included come out as an expression of a unified vision of man in the universe. This later became the basis for *The Great Collection on Nature and Principle* (*Xingli daquan* 性理大全) published in 1415, which is the most voluminous anthology of texts representing Neo-Confucian thought.

Zhu Xi was a prolific writer and completed almost one hundred works. Apart from his own writings we also have access to a large collection of transcripts of his talks with students and others. Over the years the literature about him has grown to become quite enormous, especially in Chinese but also in Japanese, Korean and Western languages.

To penetrate into all aspects of his thought is, no doubt, a formidable task. Yet what we find reflected in his writings is a very clear mind eager to communicate rather than to mystify.

Two dimensions of reality

Zhu Xi distinguishes two dimensions of reality. On the one hand there is the world of principle and the Way – *li* and *dao* – which exists 'above form' (*xing er shang* 形而上), which has no physical substance and which we cannot perceive by our senses; we may call this the metaphysical world. On the other hand there is the world of ether or physical substance, which exists 'below form' (*xing er xia* 形而下), i.e. where physical objects exist. This we may call the physical world.

These are dimensions of one and the same reality. If we consider an object or a person – be it the computer on which I am now writing or my wife and daughter – they are all ether and principle. Ether is the physical stuff that in different forms constitute all physical things and creatures. The principle in this case are three different principles which make my computer a computer, my wife my wife and my daughter my daughter. In the words of Zhu Xi himself:

> For the bricks of these steps there is the Li of bricks. For the bamboo chair, there is the Li of the bamboo chair. You may say that dried and withered things have no life or vitality, yet among them too, there are none that do not have Li.[29]

---

[29] Original in *Classified Conversations with Master Zhu* (*Zhu Zi yulei* 朱子語類), vol. 4; quoted from Fung Yu-lan, *A Short History of Chinese Philosophy*, p. 296.

He also said:

> In the production of man and things, they must be endowed with principle before they have their nature, and they must be endowed with material force before they have their physical form.[30]

Thus, principle defines the nature of a thing, but differences in the composition of the ether also account for differences between things. Not least are differences in the endowment of ether important in accounting for differences between human beings who all have the same nature.

It is difficult to know exactly how Zhu Xi understood the relationship between the two entities principle and ether in causing the differences between different things. One way of interpreting his view is to say that the different categories of creatures and objects are determined by principle while the differences between creatures or objects within one and the same category are determined by the endowment of ether. But it is not quite evident that Zhu Xi himself would agree completely with this interpretation, since the endowment of ether most certainly also differs from one category to another. In one interesting statement he suggests that in dealing with this question the perspective is important:

> Considering the fact that all things come from one source, we see that their principle is the same but their ether different. Looking at the various substances, we see that their ether is similar but their principle utterly different. The difference in ether is due to the inequality of its purity and impurity, whereas the difference in principle is due to its completeness or partiality.[31]

Zhu Xi often said that ether cannot exist without principle, and principle cannot exist without ether: 'In the universe there has never been any ether without principle or principle without ether.'[32] Yet, using different words, he also often expressed the view

---

[30] *Classified Conversations with Master Zhu*, 49: 5b; trans. Wing-tsit Chan, *A Source Book in Chinese Philosophy*, p. 636.
[31] Ibid., 49: 7a, p. 637 modif.
[32] Ibid., 49: 1a, p. 634, modif.

that principle is somehow primary and ether secondary. Sometimes he even went so far as to say that in the perspective of creation and time principle is prior to ether:

> Before Heaven and Earth existed, there was after all only principle. As there is this principle, therefore there are Heaven and Earth. If there were no principle, there would also be no Heaven and Earth, no man, no things, and in fact, no containing or sustaining (of things by Heaven and Earth) to speak of. As there is principle, there is therefore ether to operate everywhere and nourish and develop all things.[33]

But, above all, Zhu Xi meant that principle is primary vis-à-vis ether in the sense that principle determines the nature of an a creature or a thing.

Zhu Xi said that 'principle is one but its manifestations numerous' (*li yi fen shu* 理一分殊).[34] This means that each object has its own principle, but at the same time all principles unite into one. In Zhu Xi's discourse, the Way generally refers to principle as one.

The concept of 'ether' corresponds rather closely to the European notion of 'matter'. The difference is that while matter, at least traditionally, connotes solidity, something that can be touched, the everyday meaning of ether is 'air' and as a philosophical concept it connotes something ethereal. It therefore seems quite appropriate to translate it into English as 'ether'.[35] Interestingly, in modern physics with the emergence of quantum mechanics it seems that matter has also become less solid, more ethereal.

Sometimes principle seems to come close to the meaning of 'structure', the structure of the universe, and the concept of 'heavenly principle' (*tianli* 天理), may be compared to 'natural law'. But for Zhu Xi values were an aspect of facts, and so principle referred not only to what is but also to what ought to be. Good behaviour for Zhu Xi was, in the final analysis, behaviour in accordance with heavenly principle.

---

[33] Ibid., 49: 3a, p. 635.

[34] Actually Cheng had said this and Zhu Xi quoted him approvingly; cf. Chan, p. 635.

[35] To emphasize the dynamism of the notion of *qi*, Wing-tsit Chan and other scholars have chosen to translate it as 'material force'. This translation no doubt captures an aspect of *qi* that 'ether' does not. On the other hand it seems to me that this translation sounds more specific than the original and becomes as much an explication as a translation.

1. Oracle bones

2. Yao (2337–2285 BC)

3. Shun (2258–2211 BC)

4. Yu (r. 2205–?)

5. Confucius (551–479 BC)

6. Xun Zi (ca. 298–238 BC)

7. Dong Zhongshu (ca. 179–104 BC)

像帝武漢

8. Han Wudi or Emperor Wu of Han
(ca. 179–104 BC)

9. Wang Chong
(27–ca. 100)

26. Bada Shanren (1626–1705)

27. Dai Zhen (1724–77)

28. Wei Yuan (1794–1856)

29. Xue Fucheng (1838–94)

30. Zhang Zhidong (1837–1909)

31. Kang Youwei (1858–1927)

32. Liang Qichao (1873–1929)

33. Zhang Binglin (1868–1936)

34. Zhang Junmai (1886–1969)

35. Hu Shi (1891–1962)

36. Xiong Shili (1885–1968)

37. Liang Shuming (1893–1988)

38. Feng Youlan (1895–1990)

39. Mou Zongsan (1909–95)

40. Tang Junyi (1909–78)

41. Xu Fuguan (1903–82)

Zhu Xi's two-dimensional psychology

The main interest for Zhu Xi, as for other Confucians, was to understand human beings and to prescribe principles for human behaviour, and this was also the motivation behind his impressive construction of a metaphysical foundation for his thinking.

Zhu Xi located man and man's 'heart' (*xin* 心) – or mind – at the intersection of the physical and metaphysical worlds. 'Human nature', which is part of the heart, belongs in the pure and flawless metaphysical world of principle and Dao, while the other part of the heart exists in the physical world and is dominated by desires and feelings.

Thus, that part of man which exists in the metaphysical world is pure and flawless, and in so far as there is evil and bad behaviour the causes must be sought in the physical self, and especially in human desires.

On the basis of classical texts, and in particular the chapter on music in *The Classic of Rites*, Zhu Xi maintains that when still, the pure and flawless human nature prevails. He postulates this state of stillness as in some sense basic or primary. When acted upon, man responds and so his physical self becomes activated, and this is where things may go wrong. In the activating process the desires play a crucial role and feelings are also effects of activated human nature.

For Zhu Xi the major purpose of study and personal cultivation was to see to it that the original metaphysical human nature is correctly translated into behaviour and action when man is acted upon.

In what way can study and self-cultivation help? Zhu Xi was an optimistic intellectualist in that he believed that the most important way of safeguarding that human nature controls our behaviour is study of the world and the classical texts. He was convinced that if man really understands the world and the valid ethical principles, then he will act accordingly. Thus he belongs in that Confucian tradition that we may characterize in terms of giving priority to 'following the path of inquiry and study'.

Zhu Xi's ethics

Zhu Xi's yardstick for measuring the ethical quality of a certain act was principle, or heavenly principle; a good act accords with principle, while a bad or an evil act does not.

How then can we know principle? Zhu Xi's main answer seems to be that we can know principle by studying books and the external reality. But he also says that human nature is principle, which must mean that principle is also present in our minds. As we shall see, his conception of principle has been considered both to be objectivist and subjectivist.

Anyway, Zhu Xi does not provide us with a very clear and satisfactory answer to the question of the criteria of principle.

His ideas could easily be used by those in power to define good and right as they liked. For if the meaning of principle is embedded in the classical and canonical texts, then the power to determine how these texts should be interpreted is the power to decide what is good and right. Once Zhu Xi's ideas were adopted as state philosophy, this power over the interpretation was monopolized by the celestial court.

If, on the other hand, principle is a subjective thing in the human mind, then its definition also becomes subjective, and under autocratic rule that means that the rulers have the power to define principle as they wish.

There is a tendency in Zhu Xi's thought to oppose principle to desires, and then one easily approaches the standpoint that what is principle cannot be desire, and what is desire cannot be principle. As for Zhu Xi himself, he never rejected desires altogether but he was certainly very critical of them and repeatedly emphasized the importance of controlling them strictly.

Zhu Xi realized, of course, that desires are necessary for mankind to reproduce itself, and to that extent he had to accept desires. But to indulge just for the pleasure of it was bad: he found that it was all right to eat and drink to still one's hunger and thirst, but it was wrong to just enjoy delicious tastes.[36]

---

[36] Zhu Xi said: 'To eat and drink is [in accordance with] heavenly principle, to see good taste is human desire.' In *Classified Conversations with Master Zhu*, 14.

An even more extreme example is how he once expressed that he was in agreement with Cheng Yi who had said: 'To die from starvation is a small thing, to lose your integrity is a big thing.'[37] In concrete terms, to lose your integrity – sometimes a word that is better translated as 'chastity' was also used – meant for a widow to remarry. In other words to do so in order to escape death by starvation would be to let desire take precedence over principle.

The dichotomy of principle and desires, or 'heavenly principle' and 'human desires' was indeed very useful as an ideological tool in the hands of the rulers. Popular demands for improved conditions could often be rejected with reference to this opposition: material standard of living was squarely placed in the realm of desires, whereas adherence to principle manifested itself in disinterest in material goods.

A popular formulation of the ethics of the School of Principle was that one should 'preserve heavenly principle and annihilate human desires'.

Zhu Xi's School of Principle constitutes the most impressive system of ideas ever constructed in China and exerted tremendous influence in pre-modern China and other parts of East Asia. Often it served the government as a source of political legitimacy. However, it was also used to criticize the abuse of power.

The School of Mind

With his monism and subjectivism, Cheng Hao anticipated the main ideas that we associate with the School of Mind: the view that all reality is, in the final analysis, principle and that humans should look into themselves, rather than out into the external world, when seeking important knowledge.

As a school of thought, however, the School of Mind emerges in opposition to the philosophical system formulated by Zhu Xi,

---

[37] See *Reflections on Things at Hand*, trans. Wing-tsit Chan, p. 177. Concerning Zhu Xi's view of women, see Wing-tsit Chan, 'Chu His's Treatment of Women', in his volume *Chu His: New Studies*, Honolulu: Hawaii University Press, 1989, pp. 537–47.

and we should regard Zhu Xi's contemporary and friend Lu Xiangshan 陸象山 (1139–93) as its founder. His personal name was Jiuyuan 九淵, but he is now best known under his literary name Lu Xiangshan, which means Lu the Elephant Mountain, which was the name of a mountain in Jiangxi province where he lectured for many years.

For Lu Xiangshan the world was one, there was nothing outside the realm of principle and Dao; likewise there was nothing outside the myriad things. Human knowledge was innate and, therefore, one should seek knowledge in one's self rather than in the external world.

There was no dualism dividing the human heart, or mind. According to Lu Xiangshan 'the mind is principle' (*xin ji li* 心即理), which became the most famous dictum associated with the School of Mind and which stood in opposition to the idea first formulated by Cheng Yi, and then taken up by Zhu Xi, that 'human nature is principle' (*xing ji li* 性即理).

If for Zhu Xi knowledge came before morality, or moral behaviour had to be based on knowledge acquired through 'inquiry and study', it was the other way around for Lu Xiangshan and the other followers of the School of Mind. The search for knowledge, as action, had to proceed on the basis of moral correctness, which was innate. In the history of Chinese thought this has been discussed in terms of the polarity of 'following the path of inquiry and study' (*dao wen xue* 道問學 emphasized by Zhu Xi and his followers, on the one hand, and 'honouring moral nature' (*zun de xing* 尊德性), on the other hand.[38]

Thus, while Zhu Xi and the School of Principle emphasized the importance of gaining knowledge through study of the external world, the scholars representing the School of Mind argued that we have to look inside ourselves for knowledge.

Lu Xiangshan did not write very much, and he articulated several of his most important ideas in discussions with Zhu Xi. The two

---

[38] For an illuminating discussion of this polarity, see Ying-shih Yü 'Morality and Knowledge in Chu Hsi's Philosophical System', in Wing-tsit Chan, ed., *Chu His and Neo-Confucianism*, Honolulu: University of Hawaii Press, 1986, pp. 228–54.

men met for the first time in 1175 at Goose Lake Temple on Goose Lake Mountain in Jiangxi province. In their discussion Zhu Xi insisted that seeking extensive knowledge was essential for becoming virtuous, whereas Lu Xiangshan held that the discovery of one's original mind must come first.

Later, the two exchanged nine letters in which they discussed philosophical questions. This discussion centred on the interpretation of Zhou Dunyi's *Explanation of the Diagram of the Supreme Ultimate*. Lu Xiangshan was against the use of the concept 'The Ultimate of Non-being' together with 'The Great Ultimate', since he felt that this suggested a dualism which he could not accept. In these letters the discussion is then widened and clearly illustrates the important differences between in terms of monism-dualism and subjectivism-objectivism that we have already briefly touched upon.

The most famous representative of the School of Mind was Wang Yangming 王陽明 (1472–1529), who lived in the Ming dynasty, three centuries after Zhu Xi and Lu Xiangshan.

Wang Yangming grew up in a scholarly family in Zhejiang province in Eastern China. In 1499 he himself passed the highest degree in the imperial examinations – the *jinshi* – and after this he served as a government official in many different positions. In 1506 he spoke up for two censors who had been put into prison for revealing a corruption scandal involving a powerful eunuch, and as a result Wang Yangming got into serious trouble himself. He was sentenced to forty strokes of the bamboo and then banished to the distant province of Guizhou, where he spent three years with the Miao people. In 1510 he was rehabilitated – even granted an audience with the emperor – and in the following years served as an official in Beijing and Nanjing. During the years 1516–19 he successfully carried out orders to suppress some rebellions in southern China. He now gained fame both for his administrative skills and for his military strategy. But at this time he had also developed his philosophical ideas and now received an increasing number of students who sought his advice and guidance. In 1529 he was recalled from retirement to suppress a rebellion in Guangxi province. He was successful in completing this task, but then asked to be relieved of his duties because of ill health. Soon thereafter, on his way home, he died at the age of fifty-seven. He was denied the usual honours because he had left his post without permission and also because he had taught what was labelled 'false learning'. However, almost forty years later in 1567 he was posthumously rehabilitated and thereafter even offered sacrifices in the Confucian Temples.

The most important source at our disposal for knowledge about Wang Yangming's ideas is a collection which exists in a complete English translation by Wing-tsit Chan under the title *Instructions for Practical Living and Other Neo-Confucian Writings by Wang yang-ming* (*Chuanxilu* 傳習錄). The main part of this collection contains recorded conversations with Wang Yangming in which he articulates his ideas.

In 1489, as a very young man, Wang Yangming met an old scholar who talked to him about Zhu Xi's idea of 'investigating things and thereby extend one's knowledge' (*gewu zhizhi* 格物致知) as an important means of self-cultivation and approaching sagehood. So he and a friend tried to pursue this path of learning but without success:

> People merely say that in the investigation of things we must follow Zhu Xi, but when have they carried it out in practice? I have carried it out earnestly and definitely. In my early years my friend Qian and I discussed the idea that to become a sage or a worthy one must investigate all things in the world. But how can someone have such tremendous energy? I therefore pointed to the bamboos in front of the pavilion and told him to investigate them and see. Day and night, Mr Qian went ahead trying to investigate to the utmost the principles in the bamboos. He exhausted his mind and thoughts and on the third day he was tired out and fell ill. At first, I said it was because his energy and strength were insufficient. Therefore, I myself went to try to investigate to the utmost. From morning till night, I was unable to find the principles of the bamboos. On the seventh day I also fell ill because I thought too hard. In consequence we sighed to each other and said that it was impossible to be a sage or a worthy, for we do not have the tremendous energy to investigate that they have.[39]

---

[39] Quoted from Wing-tsit Chan, *A Source Book in Chinese Philosophy*, p. 689.

Almost twenty years later, in 1508, he finally gained enlightenment and understood the basic principle that was to guide him through the rest of his life:

> After I had lived with the barbarian for three years [i.e. when he was banished to Guizhou and lived with the Miao people], I understood what all this meant and realized that there is really nothing in the things in the world to investigate, that the effort to investigate things is only to be carried out in and with reference to one's body and mind, and that if one firmly believes that everyone can become a sage, one will naturally be able to take up the task of investigating things.[40]

Zhu Xi had based himself on *The Great Learning* when he argued that the way to extend one's knowledge is to investigate things. Now in a way that is characteristic for discussions within a system of ideas which is considered as an intellectual orthodoxy, Wang Yangming would and could not reject the wording in *The Great Learning*, which was really a sacred text, but instead chose to reinterpret the classical formulation. While Zhu Xi had interpreted *ge wu* 格物 as 'to reach and investigate things', Wang Yangming argued that it meant 'to rectify' oneself and 'to eliminate what is incorrect in the mind so as to preserve the correctness of its original substance'. This interpretation could then serve his conviction that in order to be able really to 'extend one's knowledge', it is necessary first to have a correct heart, or to put it in words that we would be more used to, one must first see to it that one's own position or perspective is correct. In particular, he meant that it was decisive that one's outlook reflected one's 'innate knowledge of the good' (*liang zhi* 良知), a notion which he derived from Mencius.

It is difficult to accept Wang's reinterpretation of *ge wu* in *The Great Learning* as philologically correct, and from Wang's own writings we may get the impression that philological accuracy was a much lesser concern for him than philosophical truth. If we assume that he was in no doubt that the sacred texts were absolutely true, then we may also conclude that it would have been foreign to him

---

[40] Ibid.

as to others operating within the Confucian hermeneutical tradition to question the truth of any proposition in these texts. The task was instead to clarify, to find the interpretation that brought out the inherent wisdom and truth. In this particular case this would mean that he felt that he had found an interpretation of a few words in the *Great Learning* which was in complete accord with the spirit and essence of Confucianism.

Wang was anxious to preserve unity and avoid dualism, or fragmentation, in his conception of man and the world. And the unifying factor was the subjectivity of the self with its innate knowledge of the good. As humans we should bring out our sense of what is good and act on this basis; in Wang's words we should 'extend our knowledge of the good' (*zhi liangzhi* 致良知). He saw knowledge as the beginning of action and action as the completion of knowledge. This is his doctrine of the unity of knowledge and action which has attracted quite a lot of attention and been very influential in later Confucianism:

> Only after one has experienced pain can one know pain. The same is true of cold and hunger. How can knowledge and action be separated? This is the original substance of knowledge and action, which have not been separated by selfish desires. In teaching people, the Sage insisted that only this can be called knowledge. Otherwise this is not yet knowledge. This is serious and practical business. [. . .] But people today distinguish between knowledge and action and pursue them separately, believing that one must know before one can act. They will discuss and learn the business of knowledge first, they say, and wait till they truly know before they put their knowledge into practice. Consequently, to the last day of life they will never act and also will never know. This doctrine of knowledge first and action later is not a minor disease and it did not come about only yesterday. My present advocacy of the unity of knowledge and action is precisely the medicine for that disease.[41]

Wang Yangming has become one of the most influential thinkers in the Confucian tradition, not least in periods of drastic social and

---

[41] Ibid., p. 11–12.

political change. One reason for this is probably his emphasis on action. But more fundamentally I believe that the explanation of the appeal of his ideas should be sought in his subjectivity. As ideological orthodoxy the ideas of the School of Principle seemed to leave no or little room for the individual to articulate his own beliefs. According to the orthodoxy knowledge should be based on study, and while in theory the 'investigation of things' should be an important way to knowledge, in fact this investigation became more or less equated with the study of the classical books which had to be interpreted in accordance with the orthodoxy. In this intellectual universe, by insisting that humans must look into themselves and identify that innate knowledge of the good which we all possess, Wang Yangming seemed to open up space for the individual human beings to think for themselves. In this sense, his ideas have been shown to have the potential to serve as an instrument of liberation from the shackles of the authoritarian restraints imposed by ideological orthodoxy.

This aspect of Wang Yangming's thought became especially clear among his followers in the so-called Taizhou School. This school got its name from one of its leaders, Wang Yangming's disciple Wang Gen 王艮 (1483–1540), who came from the city of Taizhou in Jiangsu province.

According to the followers of the Taizhou School Zhu Xi's School of Principle had become a tool of oppression and stifled the minds of its followers. Those who had the authority to define the orthodox interpretation of the classics, also had the power to define rather arbitrarily what is good and what is bad, what is right and what is wrong. The Taizhou scholars, on the other hand, wanted an end to this oppression and argued that individual people had the capacity to and should define the true values.

Wang Gen stands out as quite unusual in the Confucian tradition by addressing so-called ordinary people as much as scholars. Himself the son of a salt-maker, he never sought the status of a scholar-official. The idea that any person has the potential to become a sage stood very much at the centre of his thought. He articulated an amazingly modern view of the importance of the individual human being. He recognized the independence and moral authority of every individual and so inferred that in order to bring about an ideal social order all men must actively participate. In his most famous essay, 'Clear Wisdom and Self-Preservation' (*Mingzhe baoshen lun* 明哲保身論), he wrote:

> Clear wisdom is innate knowing. To clarify wisdom and preserve the self is innate knowing and innate ability. It is what is called 'to know without deliberating and to know how without learning how'. All men possess these faculties. The sage and I are the same. Those who know how to preserve the self will love the self like a treasure. If I can love the self, I cannot but love other people; if I can love other people, they will surely love me; and if they love me my self will be preserved. [. . .]
> If I only know how to preserve my self and do not know how to love other men, then I will surely seek only to satisfy my self, pursue my own selfish gain, and harm others, whereupon they will retaliate and my self can no longer be preserved. [. . .] If I only know how to love others and do not know how to love my self, then it will come to my body being cooked alive or the flesh being sliced off my own thighs, or to throwing away my life and killing my self, and then my self cannot be preserved. And if my self cannot be preserved, with what shall I preserve my prince and father?[42]

A later follower of Wang Yangming, who is often associated with the Taizhou School, was Li Zhi 李贄 (1527–1602), one of the greatest heretics and iconoclasts in Chinese history. Li Zhi grew up in Quanzhou in Fujian province. Quanzhou had been an important port and trade centre with a somewhat cosmopolitan atmosphere, but the seclusion policy of the Ming dynasty had in Li's time largely cut it off from foreign trade. Students of his thought have found that commercial atmosphere was still reflected in Li's writings 'by his frequent use of the language of the market-place and by his aggressive, hard-driven mentality'.[43]

Li Zhi found it difficult to comply with the demands placed on a scholar-official. He did pass the intermediate imperial examination and became a *juren* – provincial graduate – and held different posi-

---

[42] Quoted from *Sources of Chinese Tradition*, p. 862.
[43] Ibid., p. 865.

tions in the imperial bureaucracy for more than thirty years. He often came into conflict with his superiors but also found much time to pursue his own studies, searching for the truth. He did not want to join any group or school, but he did appreciate the writings of Wang Yangming and the members of the Taizhou School. In 1588 he shaved off his hair and became a Buddhist monk. This decision reflected his interest in Buddhism but also his wish to gain more personal freedom than the life of an official permitted. Two years later, in 1590, he published his work *Books to Burn* (*Fenshu* 焚書), which contained letters essays, prefaces and poems expressing his unconventional views and challenging many established truths. His iconoclastic ideas as well as his highly unconventional life-style evoked fierce criticism. Among other things he was accused of social and sexual misconduct. In 1600 he published a big work entitled *Books to Hide* (*Cangshu* 藏書), in which he castigated among other things conventional Confucian views of history. As a result the local authorities incited a mob to burn down the house where he was living in the Buddhist temple compound, and so he began to spend his life moving from one friend to another. In 1602 a court in Beijing charged him with a long list of crimes and ordered his arrest and the burning of his books. In prison he then slashed his throat and so ended his own life.

Li Zhi was a firm believer in the innate goodness of human beings. But he found that this goodness only rarely found expression in the society that surrounded him. He therefore combined his scathing criticism of the hypocrisy of the prevailing culture with a plea for the immediate and direct expression of the innate goodness. He argued for the importance of preserving one's 'child's heart' (*tongxin* 童心) or as it has been translated more freely into English one's 'childlike mind':

> Once people's minds have been given over to received opinions and moral principles, what they have to say is all about these things, and would not naturally come from their childlike minds. No matter how clever the words, what have they to do with oneself? What else can there be but phony men speaking phony words, doing phony things, writing phony writings? Once the men become phonies, everything becomes phony. Thereafter, if one speaks phony talk to the phonies,

the phonies are pleased; if one does phony things as the phonies do, the phonies are pleased; and if one discourses with the phonies through phony writings, the phonies are pleased. Everything is phony, and everyone is pleased.[44]

Li Zhi opposed a core tenet of Neo-Confucian ethics, the rejection on moral grounds of 'gain' or 'profit' as a determining factor behind human behaviour, and he made an effort to show that his affirmation of 'gain' was not in opposition to the ideas of Confucius himself:

> Confucius said: 'The humane person first faces the difficulties and only later thinks of the rewards' [Analects, 6:20]. He speaks of facing the difficulties first, after which one could expect some reward. He does not say there should be no seeking for reward at all [. . .].
> Thus if you wish to be true to moral principle, there must be some thought of gain. If there is no thought of gain, there can be no 'being true'. If the Way is to be made manifest, one's own success must thereby be accomplished. If there is no consideration of one's success, how can the Way ever be made manifest? Now if someone says that in the learning of the Sage, there is not self-interestedness, and thus no such aim could be allowed, how could anyone aim to achieve sagehood?[45]

In opposition to the Neo-Confucian ideological orthodoxy, Li Zhi affirmed:

> . . . the desire for goods, for sexual satisfaction, for study, for personal advancement, for the accumulation of wealth; the seeking out of the proper geomantic (fengshui) that will bring blessings to their children – all the things that are productive and sustain life in the world, everything that is loved and practised in common by the people, and what they know and say in common.[46]

Both in describing 'gain' as a necessary and respectable motive of human behaviour and in affirming the fulfilment of human desires

---

[44] *Books to Burn*, 3:97; trans. Wing-tsit Chan in *Sources of Chinese Tradition*, pp. 867–868.
[45] *Books to Hide*, 32:544; trans Wing-tsit Chan, *Sources of Chinese Tradition*, p. 872.
[46] Ibid.

as being ethical and fully in accord with the common good, Li Zhi challenged central tenets of the Neo-Confucian orthodoxy. No doubt in both these regards the orthodox strict denials of important aspects of human well-being were not only absurd in themselves but also stood in sharp contrast to the actual behaviour of many guardians of this morality who themselves did not forsake either material gain nor the satisfaction of sensual desires.

Tradition and principle

In this chapter we have seen how the origins of Neo-Confucian thought may be traced back to the attempt on the part of a few scholars in the Tang Dynasty to revive the Confucian tradition and define the transmission of orthodox thought from the time of the ancient sages. During the Song Dynasty Confucian thought developed and became much richer and varied than ever before. In the Yuan dynasty, Zhu Xi's School of Principle was elevated to the position of state orthodoxy which it was going to retain until the early twentieth century, but throughout this long stretch of history there was, in fact, considerable diversity within the Confucian tradition.

Tradition, and the definition of the correct tradition, remained a central concern for the Confucians but, as the American scholar Peter Bohl has shown in his interesting study of intellectual transitions in Tang and Song China, one may nevertheless discern an interesting change in the view of tradition. While for Han Yu in the Tang it was obvious that the ancient tradition provided the models for his own time, scholars in the Song Dynasty came to focus more on the possibility and importance to discover 'principle' themselves, either by 'investigation of things' or by looking into themselves. Certainly for all Confucians, the legendary sages and Confucius continued to be paragons of virtue who should be emulated, but with the emergence of the Neo-Confucians we may nevertheless discern a shift of focus in the direction of emphasizing the subjective role of one's contemporaries in discovering what is right and wrong. This became especially obvious in Wang Yangming and his followers.

Further reading

1. Historical background

Miyakawa, Hisayuki. 'An Outline of the Naito Hypothesis and its Effects on Japanese Studies of China.' *Far Eastern Quarterly*, 14:4, 1955, pp. 533–52.

Pulleyblank, Edwin G. *The Background of the Rebellion of An Lu-shan*. London and New York: Oxford University Press, 1955.

Twitchett, Denis. 'Introduction.' *The Cambridge History of China*, Vol 3 *Sui and T'ang China, 589–906*, Part I, London, New York and Melbourne, 1979. pp. 1–47.

2. The rise and unfolding of Neo-Confucianism

Bol, Peter. *'This Culture of Ours': Intellectual Transitions in T'ang and Sung China*. Stanford: Stanford University Press, 1992.

Chang, Carson. *The Development of Neo-Confucian Thought*. New York: Bookman Associates, 1957.

De Bary, Wm Theodore. *Learning for One's Self. Essays on the Individual in Neo-Confucian Thought*. New York: Columbia University Press, 1991.

Idem. *The Message of the Mind in Neo-Confucianism*. New York: Columbia University Press, 1989.

Idem. *Neo-Confucian Orthodoxy and the Learning of the Mind-and-Heart*. New York: Columbia University Press, 1981.

De Bary, Wm Theodore. ed. *Self and Society in Ming Thought*. New York: Columbia University Press, 1970.

Idem. *The Unfolding of Neo-Confucianism*. New York: Columbia University Press, 1975.

De Bary, Wm Theodore and John W. Chafee eds. *Neo-Confucian Education: The Formative Stage*. Berkeley: University of California Press, 1989.

De Bary, Wm. Theodore and Irene Bloom eds. *Principle and Practicality: Essays in Neo-Confucianism and Practical Learning*. New York: Columbia University Press, 1979.

Huang, Siu-chi. *Essentials of Neo-Confucianism: Eight Major Philosophers of the Song and Ming periods*. Westport, Conn.: Greenwood Press, 1999.

Liu, James T.C. 'How Did a Neo-Confucian School become the State Orthodoxy?' *Philosophy East and West*, no 23, 1973, pp. 483–505.

3. Individual scholars

Cheng Hao and Cheng Yi

A.C. Graham, A.C. *Two Chinese Philosophers*. La Salle, Illinois: Open Court, 1992. This work is based on Graham's doctoral dissertation from 1953 and was first published as a book in 1958.

Han Yu

Han Yu. 'Essentials of the Moral Way.' Translated by Charles Hartman. In *Sources of Chinese Tradition*, Vol. 1: From Earliest Times to 1600, compiled by Wm Theodore de Bary & Irene Bloom, New York: Columbia University Press, pp. 569–573.

Idem. 'An Inquiry into Human Nature.' Translated by Wing-tsit Chan. In *A Source Book in Chinese Philosophy*, pp. 451–3.

Hartman, Charles. *Han Yü and the T'ang Search for Unity.* Princeton, New Jersey: Princeton University Press, 1986.

Li Ao
Barrett, T.H. *Li Ao: Buddhist, Taoist, or Neo-Confucian.* Oxford and New York: Oxford University Press, 1992. Includes a complete translation of Li Ao's *Book on Returning to One's True Nature.*

Li Zhi
De Bary, Wm Theodore. 'Li Chih: Arch Individualist.' In idem. *Learning for One's Self. Essays on the Individual in Neo-Confucian Thought.* New York: Columbia University Press, 1991, pp. 203–70.

Lu Xiangshan
Huang Siu-chi, *Lu Hsiang-shan: A Twelfth Century Chinese Philosopher.* New Haven, Connecticut: American Oriental Society, 1944.
Idem. *Essentials of Neo-Confucianism: Eight Major Philosophers of the Song and Ming Periods.* Westport, Conn.: Greenwood Press, 1999, pp. 167–88.

Sima Guang
Ming K. Chan, Ming K. 'The Historiography of the Tzu-chih t'ung-chien.' *Monumenta Serica*, 31, 1974–75. pp. 1–38.

Shao Yong
Birdwhistell, Anne D. *Transition to Neo-Confucianism: Shao Yung on Knowledge and Symbols of Reality.* Stanford: Stanford University Press, 1989.
Wyatt, Don J. *The Recluse of Loyang: Shao Yung and the Moral Evolution of Early Sung Thought.* Honolulu: University of Hawai'i Press, 1996. Wyatt argues that the analysis of Birdwhistell and others, according to which Shao Yong differed from the other famous Neo-Confucian thinkers by not focusing on moral issues, is one-sided and misleading.

Wang Anshi
Liu, James T.C. *Reform in Sung China: Wang An-shih (1021–1086) and His New Policies.* Cambridge, Mass.: Harvard University Press, 1959.

Wang Gen
Wm Theodore de Bary. 'Wang Gen and His School.' In idem. *Learning for One's Self. Essays on the Individual in Neo-Confucian Thought.* New York: Columbia University Press, 1991. pp. 155–202.

Wang Yangming
Chan, Wing-tsit. *Instructions for Practical Living and other Neo-Confucian Writings by Wang Yang-ming.* New York and London: Columbia University Press, 1963.
Ching, Julia. *To Acquire Wisdom: The Way of Wang Yang-ming.* New York: Columbia University Press, 1976.
Cua, A. S. *The Unity of Knowledge and Action: A Study in Wang Yang-ming's Moral Psychology.* Honolulu: University Press of Hawaii, 1982.

Ivanhoe, P. J. *Ethics in the Confucian Tradition: The thought of Mencius and Wang Yang-ming.* Atlanta, Ga.: Scholars Press, 1990.

Kim, Heup Youn. *Wang Yang-ming and Karl Barth: a Confucian-Christian Dialogue.* Lanham, Md: University Press of America, 1996.

Tu, Wei-ming. *Neo-Confucian Thought in Action: Wang Yang-ming's Youth (1472–1509).* Berkeley: University of California Press, 1976.

Zhang, Junmai [Carson Chang]. *Wang Yang-ming: Idealist Philosopher of Sixteenth-Century China.* Jamaica, N.Y.: St. John's University Press, 1962.

Zhang Zai

Kasoff, Ira E. *The Thought of Chang Tsai (1020–1077).* Cambridge and New York: Cambridge University Press, 1984.

Zhang Zai. *The Western Incsription.* Translated by Wing-tsit Chan. In Wm. Theodore deBary and Irene Bloom Irene eds. *Sources of Chinese Tradition.*Vol. 1. New York: Columbia University Press, 1999. pp. 683–4.

Zhu Xi

Bruce, J. Percy. *The Philosophy of Human Nature.* London: Probsthain, 1922. Translations from *Collected Writings of Master Zhu (Zhu Zi quanshu* 朱子全書).

Chan, Wing-tsit. *A Source Book in Chinese Philosophy*, pp. 589–653. Translation.

Idem. 'Chu Hsi.' In Herbert Franke, ed. *Sung Biographies*, 1 Wiesbaden: Franz Steiner Verlag, 1976, pp. 282–90.

Idem. *Chu Hsi: Life and Thought.* Hong Kong: The Chinese University Press, 1987.

Idem. ed. *Chu Hsi and Neo-Confucianism.* Honolulu: University of Hawaii Press, 1986. Contains papers presented by distinguished scholars from Asia and the West at an international conference on Zhu Xi held in Honolulu in 1982.

Idem. *Chu Hsi: New Studies.* Honolulu: Hawaii University Press, 1989.

Idem. *Reflections on Things at Hand. The Neo-Confucian Anthology compiled by Chu Hsi and Lü Tsu-ch'ien.* New York and London: Columbia University Press, 1967.

De Bary, Wm. Theodore and Irene Bloom ed. *Sources of Chinese Tradition.* 1 New York: Columbia University Press, 1999, especially pp. 699–714 and 722–54. Translations.

Gardner, Daniel K. *Learning to be a Sage. Selections from the Conversations of Master Chu.* Arranged Topically. Berkeley and Los Angeles: University of California Press, 1990.

Idem. *Zhu Xi's Reading of the Analects: Canon, Commentary, and the Classical Tradition.* New York: Columbia University Press, 2003.

Kim, Yung Sik. *The Natural Philosophy of Chu Hsi (1130–1200).* Philadelphia: American Philosophical Society, 2000.

Schirokauer, Conrad. 'Chu Hsi's Political Career: A Study in Ambivalence.' In Arthur Wright and Denis Twitchett eds., *Confucian Personalities*, Stanford: Stanford University Press, 1962.

Yü, Ying-shih. 'Morality and Knowledge in Chu Hsi's Philosophical System.' In *Chu Hsi and Neo-Confucianism*, pp. 228–54.

7

BACK TO BASICS: FROM PHILOSOPHY TO PHILOLOGY

The Yuan Dynasty and its Mongolian rulers demonstrated their allegiance to Chinese culture as *the* civilization by adopting Neo-Confucianism as state orthodoxy. When the comparatively short-lived Yuan was replaced in 1368 by the Ming Dynasty, which was ethnically Han Chinese, Neo-Confucianism retained this position, although the peasant leader Zhu Yuanzhang 朱元璋 (1328–98; reigned as Ming Taizu 明太祖 1368–98), who became the first Ming emperor, seems to have been rather ignorant about Confucian philosophy.

For example, he was very upset when he discovered the anti-autocratic ideas of Mencius and ordered that all sections containing such ideas be deleted from the book bearing Mencius' name and that the tablet of Mencius be removed from the temple of Confucius.

In the fifteenth century in the reign of the Yongle 永樂 emperor (reigned 1403–25) – a son of Zhu Yuanzhang and the third emperor of the Ming Dynasty – important anthologies of Neo-Confucian works were published.[1] Throughout the Ming dynasty not only the School of Principle but also the School of Mind maintained a very significant position in Chinese society.

---

[1] Three major anthologies or compendia were published dealing with *The Four Books* (*Sishu daquan* 四書大全), *The Five Classics* (*Wujing daquan* 五經大全) and Neo-Confucian writings on human nature and principle respectively (*Xingli daquan* 性理大全); cf. de Bary *Neo-Confucian Orthodoxy and the Learning of the Mind-and-Heart*, pp. 63–4, 164–8.

Barbarians on the throne? The Qing Dynasty and Confucian loyalties

In 1644 the Ming Dynasty was defeated by the expansive Manchus from the northeast. Ideologically, the new dynasty continued to adhere to the teaching of Zhu Xi and the School of Principle, and the Manchu emperors invested much energy into demonstrating the legitimacy of their dynasty in cultural terms.

In the seventeenth, and especially in the eighteenth century, several gigantic cultural projects were undertaken to demonstrate the glorious civilization of the empire. In this context Confucianism was extremely important.

During the reign of the Kangxi 康熙 emperor (reigned 1661–1722), the government paid great attention to legitimizing their rule in Confucian terms. Zhu Xi was elevated to a position even higher than that of Confucius himself, and a famous scholar declared that one only had to read Zhu Xi's writings to reach perfection.[2] Li Guangdi 李光地 (1624–1718), Grand Secretary at the court and a close associate of the Kangxi emperor compiled and published in 1714 the *Complete works of Master Zhu* (*Zhu Zi quanshu zhu* 朱子全書), which at once became a very important edition of Zhu Xi's writings. While the position of Zhu Xi was elevated, Ming Confucianism, with Wang Yangming as the most famous representative, was criticized.

However, the ascent of the Manchus and the establishment of the Qing Dynasty was by no means uncontroversial among the élite of scholars and artists. Some of them remained loyal to Ming and refused to serve the new leaders.

One example is Zhu Da 朱達 or Bada Shanren 八大山人 (ca 1626-ca 1705), one of the greatest painters in Chinese history, who became a monk when the new dynasty was set up but continued throughout his life to express his misgivings about the Manchu rule in his exceedingly original work.

---

[2] The scholar was Lu Longqi 陸隴其 (1630–93). See Zhu Weizheng, *Coming out of the Middle Ages*, p. 123.

Many Confucian scholars accepted the new rulers, whom they served diligently, but others refused to comply. It seems that the complacency and subservience to the new rulers on the part of many Confucians nurtured a feeling among more critically spirited scholars that Neo-Confucianism, whether of the School of Principle or School of Mind type, was to blame for the complacency.

Gu Yanwu, Huang Zongxi, Wang Fuzhi and the rise of Han learning

The great pioneer among the critics of Neo-Confucianism, Gu Yanwu 顧炎武 (1613–82), who never accepted the Manchu rule, thought that the lack of stamina and the unwillingness to oppose openly the new rulers had to do with the introverted tendency of Neo-Confucianism, often more bent on introspection and empty speculation than on solid learning, social involvement and action.

Gu bitterly attacked the subjectivism and introverted orientation of Wang Yangming and his followers. He pointed out a new direction for scholarship, which he argued must not be limited to the study of classical texts. He himself read voraciously in many different fields, including economics and geography, and performed path-breaking studies in phonology. He argued that broad studies should be combined with a sense of shame over remaining injustices in the world. In a letter to a friend he wrote:

> What then do I consider to be the way of the sage? I would say 'extensively studying all learning' and 'in your conduct having a sense of shame'.[3] Everything from your own person up to the whole nation should be a matter of study. In everything from your personal position as a son, a subject, a brother, and a friend to all your comings and goings, your giving and taking, you should have things of which you would be ashamed. This sense of shame before others is a vital matter. It does not mean being ashamed of your clothing or the food you eat,

[3] Quotations from *The Analects* 6:25 and 13:20 respectively.

but ashamed that there should be a single humble man or woman who does not enjoy the blessings that are his or her due.[4]

He required that scholarship must be based on evidence and not degenerate into empty speculation. Criticizing the Neo-Confucian masters of the Song dynasty, he found serious faults with them in these regards and instead pointed to the famous Old Text School scholars of the Han Dynasty and their meticulous, unadorned but solid scholarship as models to be emulated.

The rejection of Song scholarship in favour of Han scholarship marks the beginning of The School of Han Learning. Many famous scholars came after him working in different disciplines, but common to them all was their special respect for the Han commentaries on the Classics and their focus on basing their interpretations of the classics on textual evidence. For this reason today these scholars are also often referred to in terms of 'textual criticism' or 'evidential studies', in Chinese *kaozheng xue* 考證學.

For Gu Yanwu the most important thing was to stand up for what is good and right, not the philosophical notions as such. One example is the high esteem, in which he held his contemporary Huang Zongxi 黃宗羲 (1610–95), who was a follower of Wang Yang-ming's School of Mind, of which Gu was especially critical. Huang was outspoken in his demands on the rulers, and probably directed harsher criticism than any other Confucian against the imperial abuse of power.

In his famous work *Waiting for the Dawn: A Plan for the Prince* (*Mingyi daifang lu* 明夷待訪錄), Huang contrasted the ruler of ancient times, who regarded the people 'all-under-Heaven' as his 'master' and himself their 'tenant', to the ruler of his day, who considered himself master and the people his 'tenants':

> In ancient times all-under-Heaven were considered the master, and the prince was the tenant. The prince spent his whole life working for all-under-Heaven. Now the prince is master, and all-under-Heaven are tenants. That no one can find peace and happiness anywhere is all

---

[4] 'A letter to a Friend Discussing the Pursuit of Learning'; quoted from *Sources of Chinese Tradition*, Vol. II, p. 37.

on account of the prince. In order to get whatever he wants, he maims and slaughters all–under–Heaven and breaks up their families – all for the aggrandizement of one man's future. Without the least feeling of pity, the prince says, 'I am just establishing an estate for my descendants.' Yet when he has established it, the prince still extracts the very marrow from people's bones, and takes away their sons and daughters to serve his own debauchery. It seems entirely proper to him. It is, he says, the interest on his estate. Thus he who does the greatest harm in the world is none other than the prince. If there had been no rulers, each man would have provided for himself and looked to his own interests. How could the institution of rulership have turned out this way?[5]

Although a follower of Wang Yangming, Huang was amazingly 'modern' in emphasizing the need for law and institutional reforms rather than individual virtue. In his own time, Huang's criticism did not reach out to very many people but it is significant that his ideas were taken up by reformers towards the end of the dynasty.

Huang Zongxi's criticism of the prevailing order may be seen as an indirect call for radical reform. Although he couched his criticism in traditionalist terms contrasting the decay of the present against the ideal conditions of the ancient past, it is still tempting to see Huang's democratic perspective of the relationship between rulers and ruled as well as his focus on the political system as anticipating the calls for modernization of the political system. This reminds us that although it was only late in the nineteenth century that radical reforms to modernize China began to take place, nevertheless there were a few individual scholars much earlier than that who harboured reformist ideas.

The European impact on China beginning with the Opium War, and the defeat in the war against Japan in 1894–5, contributed to making the Chinese embark on the road of reform and modernization. However, the idea that reforms were necessary was present earlier – whether or not nourished by earlier European influence. In a short essay written in late 1815 or early 1816 the insightful poet

---

[5] Wm. Theodore. de Bary, *Waiting for the Dawn: A Plan for the Prince. Huang Tsung-hsi's Ming-i-tai-fang lu*, New York: Columbia University Press, 1993, p. 92.

and thinker Gong Zizhen 龔自珍 (1792–1841) wrote: 'Rather than allowing someone in the future to bring about reform, would it not be better to do it ourselves?'[6]

One of the most original thinkers of his day was Wang Fuzhi 王夫之 (1619–93), who was basically a self-taught man. After having fought the Manchus, Wang retired at the age of thirty-three to the mountains of his home province of Hunan where he spent forty years studying and writing. He took a very critical attitude to Neo-Confucian thought and formulated his own interpretation of the Confucian legacy. Linking up with the ideas of Zhang Zai in the Song dynasty, Wang argued that 'principle' and 'ether' are really two aspects of the same reality, principle being the structure or order of ether. But he went even further than Zhang in formulating a monistic position with materialistic overtones. He once said: 'The world consists only of concrete things.'[7] Further, he argued that concrete things change with time, those of today are different from those of yesterday. Basing himself on his ontological materialism he suggested that the past cannot be a model for the present, an amazingly bold not to say sacrilegious thesis in his time. One may easily see the ideas of 'progress' and 'evolution' implicit in his thinking.

In Wang's thought the distinctions between Chinese and barbarians as well as between the gentleman and the mean man seem to be more than a question of already civilized and not yet civilized and a question of already well educated and not yet well educated respectively. In his work 'On reading "A Comprehensive Mirror"' (*Du Tongjian lun* 讀通鑑論), he wrote:

> There are in the world two great lines of demarcation to be drawn: that between Chinese and barbarians and that between the gentleman and the mean man. It is not the case that there was originally no difference between them. Barbarians and Chinese are born (live) in different lands. Since their lands are different, so too are their habits, and consequently all they know and all they do is different. The noble

[6] Quoted from Zhu Weizheng, *Coming out of the Middle Ages*, Armonk, N.Y. and London: M.E. Sharpe, Inc., 1990, p. 9. The whole essay has also been translated in *Sources of Chinese Tradition*, Vol. II, p. 183.
[7] Quoted from Wing-tsit Chan, *A Source Book in Chinese Philosophy*, p. 693.

and the inferior emerge spontaneously among them. It is simply that they are divided by physical frontiers and that their climates are different, and so there must be no confusion. If there is confusion, the destruction of (the order of) the human sector will ensue, and the people of China will suffer from the encroachments of the barbarians and be distressed. If, however, early measures are taken to ward off the barbarians, (the order of) the human sector will thereby be stabilized and human life be protected. This is in accord with Heaven. As for the gentleman and the mean man, they are born of different stock. Since they are born of different stock, their physical substance is different. Since they differ in their physical substance, their habits too are different, and consequently all they know and all they do are different. The clever and the stupid emerge spontaneously among them.[8]

Opposing the Qing Dynasty, Wang used the ethnic argument that the rulers were Manchu and not Han Chinese, thereby deviating from the culturalism that we may identify as part of mainstream Confucianism. He argued that different peoples should live separately, 'ignoring one another like the fish in rivers and lakes'. He emphasized the distinction between 'Chinese' and 'barbarian' as different in a way that tempts people in the modern world to use the word 'race' to characterize this distinction. In his famous *Yellow Book* (*Huangshu* 黃書) he wrote:

Man is like other creatures insofar as he is constituted of *yin* and *yang* and eats and breathes, but he cannot be put in the same category as other creatures. The Chinese are like the barbarians insofar as their general physical characteristics are similar and they are both subject to assemblies and divisions, but the Chinese cannot be put in the same category as the barbarians. Why is this? It is because if man does not draw lines of demarcation in order to set himself apart from other creatures, the order of Heaven is violated; if the Chinese do not draw lines of demarcation in order to set themselves apart from the barbarians, terrestrial order is violated. Heaven and earth regulate mankind through such demarcation, and if men are incapable of drawing the lines of demarcation between different groups, human order is violated.[9]

---

[8] Trans. Ian MacMorran, in *Sources of Chinese Tradition* Vol II, pp. 32–3.
[9] Ibid. pp. 34–5.

Wang was not a famous man in his own lifetime, but he became discovered as it were in the nineteenth century. In the twentieth century, Mao Zedong, who came from the same province as Wang, and other communist leaders eulogized him for his 'materialism' and progressive ideas. This should not detract from his reputation as one of the most interesting thinkers in the Confucian tradition.

From philosophy to philology

Gu Yanwu, Huang Zongxi, and Wang Fuzhi were all scholars with a strong sense of involvement in the social problems of their time, which they tended to regard as rooted in erroneous philosophical thinking.

In order to rectify the philosophical errors that had paved the way for social injustice and political degeneration, Gu Yanwu and Wang Fuzhi rejected Neo-Confucianism, and especially for Gu Yanwu it was crucially important that one's philosophical views should be based on a correct reading of the ancient classics.

To establish the correct reading it was imperative to pay great attention to philology and textual criticism. So for the practitioners of Han Learning, philology – in the spirit of the famous masters of the Han dynasty – was the foundation for philosophy. To tackle philosophical problems without proceeding on the basis of a thorough philological analysis of the classics was to engage in empty speculation.

For Gu Yanwu as a founder of the School of Han Learning, the focus on philology was philosophically motivated, but later representatives of this school often became so immersed in the intricate questions of philological exegesis, that they put the philosophical questions aside, or forgot about them. As a result, what began as a movement to anchor philosophy in philology gradually tended to become merely philology.

The School of Han Learning in the Qing dynasty was extraordinarily important in putting classical scholarship – what we would call classical sinology – on a scientific footing. Even for scholars today working on ancient Chinese texts, the works of the masters of Han learning in the Qing are still obligatory reading; some of them have even remained handbooks that any classical sinologist wants to have on his desk. One example is the critical bibliography *Synopses of All Titles in the Complete Library of the Four Treasuries* (*Siku quanshu zongmu tiyao* 四庫全書總目提要) which was a bi-product of the huge project in the Qianlong 乾隆 era (1736 to 95) to compile *The Complete Library of the Four Treasuries* (*Siku quanshu* 四庫全書). This bibliography contains entries on more than three thousand works copied into the *Four Treasuries* as well as on altogether more than ten thousand works. Other examples are the edition of the classics published in the early nineteenth century by Ruan Yuan 阮元 (1764–1849) under the title *The Thirteen Classics with Annotations and Commentaries* (*Shisanjing zhushu* 十三經注疏) and the collection of explanations by Qing scholars of the classics that he edited under the title *Imperial Qing Exegesis of the Classics* (*Huang Qing jingjie* 皇清經解).

Back to philosophy: Dai Zhen's critique of Neo-Confucianism

The eighteenth century was the heyday of Han Learning. The School of Principle continued to be state orthodoxy in the sense that the imperial examinations were based on this school. But few of the scholarly luminaries of the time were followers of Zhu Xi. There are even reasons to believe that the Qianlong emperor himself was critical of this school. Maybe it retained its orthodox position much out of concern for social stability – rather similar to the position of Marxism in China today.

In some ways one may get the impression that there prevailed a rather high degree of tolerance of different ideological currents during much of the Qing Dynasty and that there was not really all that much emphasis on guarding the orthodoxy. If we look at the entries on Confucian works in the *Synopses of All Titles in the Complete Library of the Four Treasuries,* one does not get the impression that these entries were written to uphold a rigid interpretation of the School of Principle orthodoxy. This is not really very surprising since the editor-in-chief of the huge *Four Treasuries* project – Ji Yun 紀昀 (1724–1805) – and his closest associates were scholars of Han Learning who were generally more interested in scholarly textual criticism than in the big ideological questions.

However, in some ways the dynastic regime was prepared to go to any lengths to uphold its ideological orthodoxy. The *Four Libraries* project was on the one hand a way to demonstrate the dynasty's interest in and support of culture and scholarship. It is the biggest project of its kind ever undertaken. Between 1773 and 1782 more than 300 editors, collators and copyists are said to have catalogued and sorted more than 100,000 manuscripts into the four categories used to classify texts in imperial China: classics, history, philosophers and miscellanea. Out of these 3,460 works, altogether comprising some 800 million characters, were then copied in a uniform script by more than two hundred calligraphers into four full sets.

The purpose of this purportedly largest project of its kind ever was not only to demonstrate the dynasty's interest in culture but also to weed out texts that were considered really harmful. Therefore the project has also been referred to as 'the literary inquisition of Qianlong'.[10] In particular the editors, who were thus also censors, sought meticulously for any trace of criticism of the Manchu rulers, which would absolutely not be tolerated.

One frightening example of what could happen to anyone who criticized the Manchus is the posthumous fate of Lü Liuliang 呂留良 (1629–83) and several of his family members. Lü was a scholar born in the Ming, who never accepted the Manchu rule of China, which began in 1644. He tried to stay away from state affairs in the Qing dynasty and devoted himself, among other things, to editing so called eight-legged essays, a form of essays that aspiring scholars had to master to pass the civil service examinations. In editing these works, he sneaked in critical comments of the Manchus which were

---

[10] Cf. the classical study by L. Carrington Goodrich, *The Literary Inquisition of Ch'ien-lung*, Baltimore: Waverly press, inc., 1935.

discovered fifty years after his death, during the rule of the Yongzheng 雍正 emperor (1723–35). As a result the corpses of both Lü and one of his sons were unearthed and dismembered and their skulls were exposed in public. A son who was still alive was executed as were two of his students who were known to support his views, and more than twenty other people were punished. Fifty years later, in connection with the *Four Treasuries* project all writings by Lü that could be found were burned.

Lü Liuliang was a follower of the School of Principle and as such one of many examples that this school was not only used to legitimize the prevailing rule but also to criticize perceived injustices.

In the eighteenth century only few really interesting philosophical works appeared. No doubt the most interesting philosopher in this period was Dai Zhen 戴震 (1724–77), himself a prominent representative of the School of Han Learning, who wrote on a variety of topics – mathematics, philology, phonology etc. Above all he articulated an extremely interesting critique of Neo-Confucianism.

Dai Zhen was born and grew up in southern Anhui province. In his time this area as part of the lower Yangzi River delta in a broad sense was a centre of commercial activities and what Marxist historians in China have labelled 'capitalist sprouts' (*zibenzhuyi mengya* 資本主義萌芽). In his youth he came in contact with some of the European mathematical knowledge that had been introduced to China by the early Jesuit missionaries, of whom Matteo Ricci (1552–1610) was the most famous. Ricci and his Chinese collaborator Xu Guangqi 徐光啟 (1562–1633) had translated parts of Euclid's Geometry into Chinese. In his youth Dai Zhen studied with a scholar who was probably quite well acquainted with Euclid's work.

The evolution of Dai's ideas should be seen in the perspective of the commercial activities and the rising position of merchants in his native area, on the one hand, and the introduction to China of early modern scientific mode of thinking from Europe.

Although it was not unusual at this time to criticize Neo-Confucian philosophy, yet Dai Zhen's way of doing so was probably quite dangerous because he felt that Zhu Xi's School of

Principle had become a tool of oppression. In a letter written only shortly before his death in 1777 he went so far as to claim that 'principle was used to kill people'.[11]

His most important philosophical treatise, entitled *Evidential Commentary on the Meaning of the Words of Mencius* (*Meng Zi ziyi shuzheng* 孟子字義疏證) appeared only after his death. In this book he argued that 'principle' had ceased to refer to the objective structure of the world and become a subjective notion considered 'as if it were a thing, received from heaven and embodied in the heart'. As a result, anyone with authority could claim that his 'subjective opinions' (*yijian* 意見) were 'principle'.

He believed that the distorted views propounded by the Neo-Confucians could largely be explained in terms of the influence that the Buddhists and the Daoists had exerted on Zhu Xi and other Song Confucians. He maintained that 'principle' as used by Zhu Xi and his followers was another name for the Buddhist concept 'True Emptiness' (*zhen kong* 真空) and the Daoist concept 'True Master' (*zhuzai* 主宰).

He considered the effects of the distortion of Confucianism to be truly disastrous, and he returned to this theme again and again. For example, he wrote:

> A man can have no greater fault than consider himself wise although he is obscured, to give free rein to his opinions and hold on to them as if they constituted principle and righteousness. I am afraid that those who seek principle and righteousness take these to be represented by their opinions – who knows the end of the calamities that this will cause the people?[12]

Dai distinguished two major aspects of human beings, their 'blood-and-ether' (*xueqi* 血氣), or body, and their 'heart-perception' (*xinzhi* 心知) or 'mental faculty'. He held that while it is our 'blood-and-ether' that enables us to discern colours and other properties of the external, objective world, it is our mental faculty that distinguishes

---

[11] 'A letter' ('Yu mou shu' 與某書), in *Dai Zhen ji* 戴震集 (Dai Zhen's collected works), Shanghai: Shanghai guji chubanshe, 1980, pp. 187–8.
[12] *Evidential Commentary*, 1.4.

us from other creatures and enables us to discern 'principles' and to recognize and take pleasure in what is 'necessary', i.e. the ethical aspect of being. For Dai Zhen 'principles' were part of the external, objective world.

In the perspective of the European tradition of David Hume and G. E. Moore, Dai Zhen would be considered to commit the 'naturalistic fallacy' in that he derived what is necessary from what is natural:

> To conform to what is necessary is precisely to fulfil what is natural, and this is what is meant by the ultimate of the natural.[13]

Dai Zhen was a monist in his insistence that there is nothing that exists beyond the empirical world of ether. Accordingly, he disagreed with the dualism which in his view permeated the thought of Zhu Xi and other Neo-Confucian thinkers. He opposed the interpretation of the notions 'above form' and 'below form', which had allowed Zhu Xi to define a number of oppositions between entities of a pure and flawless metaphysical world, on the one hand, and entities of an impure and defective physical world on the other hand. In Dai's interpretation the notions of above and below form both referred to the world of ether, distinguishing the stages before and after ether has been formed into 'objects'.

Dai Zhen criticized the Song philosophers for divorcing 'heavenly principle' from 'human desires':

> When people in ancient times talked about principle, they sought it in man's feelings and desires; when these were made flawless, they considered them as principle. When people nowadays [i.e. Neo-Confucians] speak about principle, they seek it apart from feelings and desires [. . .] This separation of principles and desires serves precisely to turn all people under heaven into deceivers and phonies. How could one fully describe how disastrous [this separation is]? What they call desire is when emperors and kings do their utmost for the people.[14]

---

[13] Ibid. 3.2.1; concerning the 'naturalistic fallacy', see G.E. Moore, *Principa Ethica*, Cambridge: Cambridge University Press, 1966, 1st ed. 1903.
[14] *Evidential Commentary*, 3.5.4

He argued that desires are indeed central to man's moral capacity:

> To desire to preserve and fulfil your own life and also to preserve and
> fulfil the lives of others is humanity. To desire to preserve and fulfil
> your own life to the point of destroying the lives of others without
> any regard is inhumanity. It is true that inhumanity starts when your
> heart desires to preserve and fulfil your own life and that, if this desire
> were eliminated, there would definitely be no inhumanity. But then
> you would also look upon the poverty and hardship of others in the
> world with indifference. You do not necessarily have to preserve and
> fulfil your own life, but then you will not have a feeling for preserv-
> ing and fulfilling the lives of others either.[15]

For Dai Zhen morality was the capacity to feel compassion and
shame. Also, and as importantly, it was the capacity to understand
the order of the objective world.

Thus, he wished to overcome the opposition between principle
and ether as well as between heavenly principle and human desires.
His philosophical thought was a search for unity. The opposition
between principle and ether he sought to overcome by externaliz-
ing the notion of principle to refer to the order of the objective
world. The opposition between heavenly principle and human
desires he sought to overcome by describing desires as essential to
man's capacity to act in accordance with principle.

On the one hand, Dai Zhen argued that our feelings are important in helping us understand moral values. On the other hand, he
also argued that the satisfaction of desires and feelings, to the extent
that it does not encroach on the satisfaction of the feelings and
desires of others, is good and right.

In a way that may remind us of Sigmund Freud and twentieth-
century European psychological theories, Dai Zhen felt that it is
both wrong and impossible to suppress desire. In his work *On the
Origins of Goodness* (*Yuan shan* 原善), he wrote:

> It is futile to try to control a river simply by blocking its passage. If you
> obstruct it on the east, it will flow out from the west; or, worse, it will
> break your dam and create an ungovernable flood. Similarly, if one tries

---

[15] Ibid., 1.10

to control himself or govern others simply by repressing the human desires, he may succeed in quieting them temporarily, but in the end the desires will inevitably outwit all attempts to restrain them.[16]

Dai Zhen was brave in expounding his utilitarian ethics, which indeed stood in sharp contrast to orthodox Neo-Confucianism and which could very well be considered to have potentially destabilizing political implications. However, he was also able to draw support for his view of ethics from early Confucian thought as expounded by Confucius and Mencius. With good reason he reminded his readers:

> Mencius told the rulers of Qi and Liang to 'share their enjoyment with the people', 'reduce punishment and taxation', 'ensure that [the people's means of support] are sufficient for the care of [their] parents, on the one hand, and for the support of wife and children, on the other hand', and to see to it that 'those who stay at home have full granaries and those who go to war have full sacks' and that 'there are neither girls pining for a husband nor men without a wife'. This is what humane rule and the kingly way are like.[17]

The rule of the legendary ancient sages, he characterized in the following words:

> In governing the whole world the sages sympathized with the feelings of the people and satisfied their desires. Thereby the kingly way was completed.[18]

On the one hand, Dai Zhen argued that morality is somehow contained in the order of the external, objective world. By means of his unique nature, man possesses the capacity to understand and even take pleasure in this immanent moral order. But in order to understand the content of morality he must engage in study. This strand in his ethical thought we may characterize as naturalist and intellectualist.

On the other hand, he argued that the satisfaction of desires and the fulfilment of feelings, subject to the so-called measure of the

---

[16] Quoted from Creel, *Chinese Thought from Confucius to Mao Tse-tung*, p. 231
[17] *Evidential Commentary*, 1:10.
[18] Ibid. 3.2.2

self, constitute basic moral values. This strand in his thought we may characterize as utilitarian and hedonist.

Different meanings but similar functions

We have seen earlier how Wang Yangming, and more radically, his followers in the Taizhou group criticized Zhu Xi and the School of Principle for placing principle in an imagined external objective world and so making the definition of principle something objective, thereby denying individual people the space where each and one would have the freedom to find his own definition. This we may call the subjectivistic critique of Zhu Xi.

Now we see how Dai Zhen criticizes Zhu Xi and his school from another direction, arguing that the problem with the Neo-Confucian approach to principle is that principle becomes conceived of as a subjective entity and liable to be defined in accordance with the subjective opinions of the power-holders. This we may call the objectivistic critique of Zhu Xi.

In spite of this basic difference in philosophical orientation, Dai Zhen and the Taizhou School, especially Li Zhi, shared the belief that desires were basically good and also that one's basic desires must be satisfied to be able to do good to others.

We may still say that the Taizhou School and Dai Zhen criticized Zhu Xi from diametrically opposed philosophical positions: while the Taizhou School was subjectivistic Dai Zhen was rather an objectivist. This means that their critique was very different in terms of meaning. Yet in both cases the point was to demonstrate and to criticize that Zhu Xi's philosophy was used as a tool of oppression. In other words, the critique was very similar in terms of function.

It is tempting to see this as the beginnings of a kind of enlightenment thinking. This perspective, which has been adopted by many scholars, is also nourished by the fact that scholars such as Li Zhi and Dai Zhen were living at a time when commerce was developing in China and when the ideas of European science were beginning to be introduced, paradoxically by means of Jesuit missionaries whose relationship with the evolution of science was far from harmonious. As we have seen Li Zhi grew up in the old port of Quanzhou, which had been a centre for commercial activities, and Dai Zhen came from the lower Yangzi River delta which in his time was the economically and probably also intellectually most dynamic area in China.

Further reading

Historical and ideological background

Andrew, Anita M. and John A. Rapp. *Autocracy and China's Rebel Founding Emperors: Comparing Chairman Mao and Ming Taizu.* Lanham, MD: Rowan & Littlefield Publishers, 2000.

De Bary, Wm. Teodore. *Neo-Confucian Orthodoxy and the Learning of the Mind-and-Heart.* New York: Columbia University Press, 1981.

Idem., ed. *Self and Society in Ming Thought.* New York: Columbia University Press, 1970.

Elman, Benjamin. *From Philosophy to Philology: Intellectual and Social Aspects of Change in Late Imperial China.* Cambridge, Mass.: Harvard University Press, 1984.

Guy, R. Kent. *The Emperor's Four Treasuries: Scholars and the State in the Late Ch'ien-lung Era.* Cambridge, Mass.: Harvard University Press, 1987.

Langlois, John D. Jr. 'The *Hung-wu* Reign.' In Frederick W. Mote and Denis Twitchett eds. *The Cambridge History of China.* Vol. 7 *The Ming Dynasty, 1368–1398,* Part I, Cambridge: Cambridge University Press, 1988, pp. 107–181;

Zhu, Weizheng. *Coming out of the Middle Ages.* Armonk, N.Y. and London: M.E. Sharpe, Inc., 1990.

Studies of Individual Scholars

Hummel, Arthur ed. *Eminent Chinese of the Ch'ing Period (1644–1912).* 2 Vols. Washington, D.C.: United States Government Printing Office, 1943–44.

Bada Shanren

Wang Fangyu, Richard M. Barnhart and Judith G. Smith eds. *Master of the Lotus Garden: the Life and Art of Bada Shanren, 1626–1705.* New Haven, Conn.: Yale University Art Gallery : Yale University Press, 1990.

Dai Zhen

Cheng Chung-ying. *Tai Chen's Inquiry into Goodness: A Translation of the Yuan shan, with an Introductory Essay.* Honolulu : East-West Center Press, 1971.

Chin, Ann-ping and Mansfield Freeman. *Tai Chen on Mencius: Explorations in Words and Meaning.* A Translation of the Meng Tzu tzu-i shu-cheng, with a critical introduction by Ann-ping Chin and Mansfield Freeman. New Haven : Yale University Press, 1990.

Ewell, John Woodruff, Jr. *Re-Inventing the Way: Dai Zhen's Evidential Commentary on the Meanings of Terms in Mencius (1777).* Doctoral dissertation in History, University of California at Berkelely, 1990. Ann Arbor: UMI, 1990.

Fang Chao-ying, 'Tai Chen.' In Arthur Hummel ed. *Eminent Chinese of the Ch'ing Period (1644–1912)*. Vol. 2. Washington, D.C.: United States Government Printing Office, 1943, pp. 695–700.

Lodén, Torbjörn. 'Dai Zhen's Evidential Commentary on the Meaning of the Words of Mencius.' *The Bulletin of the Museum of Far Eastern Antiquities*, 60 (1988), pp. 165–313. Complete translation of the *Meng Zi ziyi shuzheng*.

Idem. 'Dai Zhen and the Social Dynamics of Confucian Thought.' *The Stockholm Journal of East Asian Studies*,1, 1988, pp. 26–53.

Nivison, David. 'Two Kinds of "Naturalism": Dai Zhen and Zhang Xuecheng.' In David S. Nivison. *The Ways of Confucianism: Investigations in Chinese Philosophy*. Chicago and LaSalee, Ill.: Open Court, 1996. pp. 261–281.

Yü, Ying-shih. 'Zhang Xuecheng versus Dai Zhen: A Study in Intellectual Challenge and Response in Eighteenth Century China.' In Philip Ivanhoe ed. *Chinese Language, Thought, and Culture: Nivison and His Critics*. Chicago and LaSalle, Ill.: Open Court, 1996, 121–154.

Gu Yanwu
Peterson, Willard. 'The Life of Ku Yen-wu 1613–1682.' *Harvard Journal of Asiatic Studies*, 28, 1968, pp. 114–158.

Huang Zongxi
de Bary, Wm. Theodore. *Waiting for the Dawn: A Plan for the Prince. Huang Tsung-hsi's Ming-i-tai-fang lu*. New York: Columbia University Press, 1993.

Li Guangdi
Fang Chao-ying. 'Li Kuang-ti.' In Arthur Hummel ed. *Eminent Chinese of the Chi'ing Period*. Vol. 1, pp. 473–475.

Ng, On cho. *Cheng-Zhu Confucianism in the Early Qing: Li Guangdi (1642–1718) and Qing Learning*. Albany, N.Y.: State University of New York Press, 2001.

Lü Liuliang
De Bary, Wm Theodore. 'Lü Liu-liang's Radical Orthodoxy.' In idem. *Learning for One's self. Essays on the Individual in Neo-Confucian Thought*. New York: Columbia University Press. pp. 271–363.

Goodrich, Carrington. 'Lü Liu-liang.' In Arthur Hummel, ed. *Eminent Chinese of the Ch'ing Period*. Vol. 1. pp. 551–2.

Wang Fuzhi
Black, Alison Harley. *Man and Nature in the Philosophical Thought of Wang Fu-chih*. Seattle: University of Washington Press, 1989.

McMorran, Ian. *The Passionate Realist: An Introduction to the Life and Political Thought of Wang Fuzhi (1619–1692)*. Hong Kong: Sunshine Book Co., 1992.

Xu Guangqi
Jami, Catherine and Peter Engelfriet and Gregory Blue eds. *Statecraft and Intellectual Renewal in Late Ming China: The Cross-Cultural Synthesis of Xu Guangqi, 1562–1633*. Leiden and Boston: Brill, 2001.

8

CONFUCIANISM AND MODERNIZATION

When Jesuit missionaries came to China for the first time in the late sixteenth century, this was tremendously important for the evolution of cross-cultural contacts and impact between China and Europe. The reports that the Jesuits sent back home stimulated interest in China and gradually had considerable impact on European culture. Towering figures in European culture such as Leibniz and Voltaire were influenced by what they learnt about China, and in the background of the European Enlightenment we may discern notions of China as an enlightened civilization ruled by philosophers. To what extent these notions were accurate is another question.

Similarly, the Jesuits had some impact on Chinese culture. The pioneer Matteo Ricci came to enjoy considerable prestige among the Chinese élite, both for his European learning and for his appreciation of Chinese culture. He played a very important role in introducing not only European theology, but also mathematics and science.

Much research is still needed to fill in the picture of the intercultural influence that the Jesuits transmitted. But we should not rule out the possibility that there is an aspect of European influence in the background of some of the tendencies in the reaction against Neo-Confucianism that we discussed in the last chapter: the respect for empirical facts and critique of empty speculation, the approval of desires and feelings, the critique of autocracy.

Be that as it may, European influence was not a major current in the seventeenth and eighteenth centuries. China was then still 'all under Heaven'; Chinese civilization was civilization as such, and

Confucianism was not one among creeds or ideologies but the essence of civilization. There was no discussion about the validity of Confucianism, the discussion concerned the true interpretation.

This was going to change in the late Qing empire against the background of the confrontation with Western Powers, beginning with the Opium War 1839–42, and the humiliating defeat in the war against Japan 1894–95, which contributed to the crisis of the Chinese empire and its eventual collapse in 1911. In a broad sense, this new phase in China's intellectual history may also be regarded as the beginning of the modern era.

During different periods, China had been at war with neighbours for many centuries and the non-Han Chinese Mongols and Manchus had even occupied the throne of the celestial empire and set up their own dynasties. But these peoples had accepted Confucian Chinese culture as their culture and civilization.

The Europeans were different. When Great Britain confronted China, she posed a threat not only to the Qing Dynasty, which according to the cyclical theory of history was doomed to perish anyway, but to civilization as such. Or to put it in the terms that gradually came to replace the traditional discourse: the British Empire, and other European Powers that came to China, represented another civilization than the Chinese. The Europeans even claimed to represent a more advanced form of civilization.

The defeat in the Opium War and the further humiliations that China suffered in the nineteenth century were therefore perceived as deadly threats to Chinese civilization, threats which made it necessary to re-evaluate the Chinese imperial order and the cultural legacy.

It was against this background that the distinction emerged in Chinese discourse between 'China' and 'Chinese culture'. Up until this time Chinese culture, with Confucianism at the centre, had always been considered part of the definition of China; the notion of a China without Confucian Chinese culture would have been a contradiction in terms. Now scholars began to think that maybe China could be saved only at the expense of parts of Chinese culture. This marks a fundamental change in the position of Confucianism in Chinese society: Confucianism was no longer taken for granted, it was no longer only a question of finding the correct interpretation of Confucianism but rather to determine whether or not to remain Confucian at all or to turn to some other creed or ideology.

The point of departure for the reappraisal of Chinese culture that began in the second half of the nineteenth century was to find the ways and means for the regeneration of a rich and powerful China. The reappraisal passed through different phases and became increasingly radical culminating in the total rejection of Confucianism of the May Fourth New Culture Movement in the early twentieth century.

One response to the European challenge was to explain the strength and success of the foreign Barbarians in terms of Chinese influence. Wei Yuan 魏源 (1794–1856), who in 1844 was the first Chinese writer to publish a thorough description of Western countries in his *Illustrated Gazetteer of Maritime Countries* (*Haiguo tuszhi* 海國圖志), argued that one reason why Europeans had become so successful was that Jesus had got access to the Confucian classics and had them translated into Latin (sic).[1] Another well-known scholar – Xue Fucheng 薛福成 (1838–94) who was Chinese Minister in London in 1890–92 – disagreed with Wei Yuan and argued that Jesus had derived his teaching not from the Confucians but from the ancient philosopher Mo Zi. And another scholar again – Wang Kaiyun 王闓運 (1833–1916) identified Mo Zi with Moses.[2]

Therefore, according to this kind of response to the European threat, what the Chinese needed to do was not to reject the Confucian foundation of their culture but to rectify it and restore it as it once was.

Another response to the European challenge was to distinguish between Chinese and Western culture in terms of 'essence' (*ti* 體) and 'means' (*yong* 用). The idea was that the Chinese should turn to the West to acquire Western technology and practical knowledge

---

[1] See Jerome Ch'en, *China and the West: Society and Culture, 1815–1937*, London: Hutchinson, 1979, p. 65 f. As a matter of fact it is likely that although using the Chinese word for 'Jesus', Wei was actually referring to the Jesuits. Cf. also Wei Yuan, *Illustrated Gazetteer of Maritime Countrie*, chapter 83.
[2] Ch'en, *China and the West: Society and Culture, 1815–1937*, p. 68.

and then use this to uphold the core of Chinese culture. No doubt 'Chinese' in this context referred first and foremost to Confucianism. This idea – which is associated with the formulation of the famous scholar-official Zhang Zhidong 張之洞 (1837–1909) 'Chinese [learning] should be the essence, Western [learning] should be the means' (*zhongxue wei ti, xixue wei yong* 中學為體, 西學為用) – has been recurring again and again in the evolution of modern Chinese culture and is certainly a part of the mind-set of many people in China today.

The New Text School and the projection of European ideas

Another way of responding to the European challenge to Chinese culture was to project some modern European ideas on to classical Chinese texts and the Confucian heritage. Most striking in this regard is how the notion of evolution or progress began to be used in the Confucian discourse.

We have seen how Wang Fuzhi back in the seventeenth century already described the course of history in terms of progress, and in his case one cannot see this as the projection of European evolutionary thought. But in the nineteenth century this clearly was a way on the part of some Confucian scholars to co-opt a European idea associated with the apparent wealth and power of the British Empire as an original and integral part of the Confucian heritage.

This offers an interesting example of the intricate relationship between the meaning and function of ideas. At first, the emergence of the idea of history evolving through different stages can be seen as a natural step on the path pursued by the scholars of Han Learning. When they first went back to the Han commentaries they focused on the texts belonging to the Old Text School, which had dominated scholarship during the later Han dynasty. In spririt the great masters of Han Learning in the Qing were also much closer to the old texts than to the new texts. But having worked on the sources of the Old Text School, which had dominated during the

Late Han Dynasty, it seems quite natural that some of their follow-ers would sooner or later take one step further and begin to study the New Texts associated with Dong Zhongshu and the *Gongyang* and *Guliang* Commentaries, which had dominated during the Former Han dynasty and formed the basis of Confucianism when it first became state orthodoxy.

In the late eighteenth century a few individual scholars started to take an interest in the New Text School and its ideas as reflected especially in *The Gongyang Commentary* on the *Spring and Autumn Annals* and the abstruse *Luxuriant Dew from the Spring and Autumn Annals* attributed to Dong Zhongshu of the Han Dynasty.

Zhuang Cunyu and Liu Fenglu

The pioneers in this regard were Zhuang Cunyu 莊存與 (1719–88) and his grandson Liu Fenglu 劉逢祿 (1776–1829). Zhuang Cunyu represented a lineage in Changzhou in the lower Yangzi River delta which for several centuries had produced important scholar-officials. In the spirit of other prominent members of his lineage, his inter-ests were broad and practical. As a student of Confucian thought his main focus was on governance or 'statecraft' (*jingshi* 經世).

In 1745 Zhuang Cunyu himself ranked number two in the highest imperial examinations. From then until his retirement in 1786 he served in several important functions in the Qing bureau-cracy, for example as the secretary of the Qianlong emperor, Hanlin Academician and Vice President of the Ministry of Rites. As a high-ranking official close to the emperor he upheld the Neo-Confucian orthodoxy. When the authenticity of the old text parts of *The Classic of Documents* was questioned on solid philological grounds, Zhuang argued against removing them, and it seems that his motive for doing so was his concern with political and social sta-bility. It was after retiring from office in 1786 that Zhuang began to study in earnest *The Gongyang Commentary*. The same year a former Manchu guard at the court in Beijing – Heshen 和珅 (1750–99) – rose to the position of grand secretary and president of the min-istries of personnel and finance. Zhuang saw in Heshen a usurper who sought power and influence as a means to build up his private financial and political empire.

Zhuang Cunyu's concerns in this regard may be compared to the scholars of the Donglin Academy (*Donglin shuyuan* 東林書院) in the Ming Dynasty. The Donglin scholars were known for their adherence to the ideas of Zhu Xi and of the School of Principle and for their strict observance of ethical behaviour. They were upset by the rule of terror that a favourite of the emperor's, the illiterate eunuch Wei Zhongxian 魏忠賢 (1568–1628), exercised in the 1620s. These scholars were another example how the teachings of the School of Principle were used as a critical weapon and not only as a tool of oppression.

The results of Zhuang's New Text studies were published only posthumously in the 1820s. In one article entitled 'The Key points of *The Spring and Autumn Annals*' (*Chunqiu yaozhi* 春秋要旨), he wrote:

> A state cannot [survive] without its exalted status and mandate [to rule from Heaven]. Without [the mandate], the ruler is a usurper. According to the meaning articulated by Master Gongyang, there were eight cases in which those who took power were all usurpers. He Xiu recorded it in his commentary. Yes! Yes! The position of ruler is what licentious men use to gain the upper hand. Therefore, the *Annals*, with regard to a time when secret dealings determine life and death, tried mightily to prevent such [usurpation of power].[3]

These words reflected Zhuang Cunyu's interest in New Text Confucianism as a way of criticizing the 'usurpation' of power by corrupt officials. But politically Zhuang was conservative rather than radical, and when he turned to the new texts his aim was to safeguard an order that he saw threatened rather than to argue for reforms. He was certainly not projecting European ideas of evolution on to classical texts in order to promote change and development. But – in the words of the American scholar Benjamin

---

[3] Benjamin Elman, *Classicism, Politics, and Kinship: the Ch'ang-chou School of New Text Confucianism in Late Imperial China*, Berkeley: University of California Press, 1990, p. 115; transcriptions changed in accordance with the Hanyu Pinyin system.

Elman – 'conservatism could have radical implications in a corrupt body of politic rampant with the betrayal of classical ideas'.[4]

Liu Fenglu was his maternal grandfather's most important disciple and represented the culmination of the Changzhou School. With him New Text Confucianism transcended its geographical origins. When in 1805 he sat for the intermediate *juren* degree in the imperial examinations in Beijing, he astonished his examiners by referring to *Gongyang* interpretations of the classics.

As one could expect of someone with his family background, Liu became a scholar-official and served, for example, in the Ministry of Rites. Still, in his own time and unlike his grandfather Zhuang Cunyu, Liu Fenglu was better known as a scholar than as an official.

Liu used the methods of textual criticism developed during the Qing Dynasty to support the *Gongyang* interpretations of the classics, but his main concern was still the 'great meanings' (*dayi* 大義) uncovered by New Text Confucianism. In the words of his imperial biographer as quoted by Elman: 'Liu Fenglu's scholarship endeavoured to penetrate great meanings without overstressing the parsing of sentences and phrases [in the Classics].'[5] In one study Liu set out to demonstrate that the *Zuozhuan* was originally not composed as a commentary on *The Spring and Autumn Annals* but that it was Liu Xin who had turned it into such a commentary.

The New Text studies that Liu published led to much discussion and turned, as we have pointed out, New Text Confucianism into a significant undercurrent of thought in China, not only in Changzhou and the lower Yangzi River delta.

The revival of New Text Confucianism brought about by Zhuang Cunyu and Liu Fenglu should be seen both in the context of the rise of Han Learning in the Qing and as a response to the political environment of the time, especially Heshen's rise to power in the late Qianlong era.

---

[4] Ibid., p. 119.
[5] Elman, p. 224.

Kang Youwei

Neither Zhuang nor Liu tried to use their new texts studies to promote drastic reforms of the prevailing order. In the hands of Liu's students Wei Yuan and Gong Zizhen, New Text Confucianism became more clearly used to promote change. When we come to the late nineteenth century and Kang Youwei 康有為 (1858–1927), one of the most influential thinkers during the last years of the empire, the New Text School played a major role in promoting radical political and social change. Kang anchored his reformist ideas in New Text Confucianism but it does not seem possible to escape the conclusion that both when it comes to his view of history as developing from lower to higher stages and in his formulation of the Utopia of 'Great Unity', Kang's views were also coloured by ideas which came to China from Europe and which attracted increasing attention among Chinese scholars.

Basing himself mainly on the *Gongyang Commentary*, Kang published three books in which he articulated a strikingly heretical interpretation of Confucianism. One of these books was *An Inquiry Into the Classics Forged During the Xin Period* (*Xin xue weijing kao* 新學偽經考), from 1891, in which he tried to prove that the so-called old texts were forgeries by Liu Xin and that it was the New texts that contained authentic Confucian thought.[6]

In his second major work of reform ideology, *Confucius as Reformer* (*Kong Zi gaizhi kao* 孔子改制考) from 1898, he described Confucius not only as the transmitter of ancient wisdom but also as innovator and author of the Confucian classics. He argued that shortly before his death Confucius had received the Mandate of Heaven to devise new institutions for a new dynasty. In his terms, Confucius was a 'sage king' (*sheng wang* 聖王) or an 'uncrowned king' (*su wang* 素王). In Kang's conception Confucianism became a religion with Confucius as its major prophet.

On the basis of his analysis of Confucius as a 'reformer' Kang argued that institutional reforms, and not only moral rectification,

---

[6] The Xin was as we have seen the interregnum between the former and later Han dynasties.

were now also needed. His focus on institutional reform, was extremely important for the ensuing evolution of political thought in China.

According to Kang's interpretation of Confucianism, societies are destined to pass through three developmental stages – or Three Ages (*sanshi* 三世) – in the course of history: beginning with the Age of Disorder (*juluan shi* 據亂世), they pass by the Age of Rising Peace (*shengping shi* 升平時) (in some writings he used the term Small Tranquility [*xiaokang* 小康] to refer to this age) before they ultimately reach the Age of Universal Peace (*taiping shi* 太平世; in some writings he used the term Great Unity [*datong* 大同] to refer to this age).[7] Each of these ages had its appropriate political system: absolute monarchy, constitutional monarchy and republican government respectively. At a time long before 'globalization' was discussed as a concept, Kang's evolutionary perspective was indeed global:

> Confucius was born in the Age of Disorder. Now that communications extend through the great earth and changes have taken place in Europe and America, the world is evolving towards the Age of Order. There will be a day when everything throughout the earth, large or small, far or near, will be like one. There will no longer be any nations, no more racial distinctions, and customs will be everywhere the same. With this uniformity will come the Age of Great Peace. Confucius knew all this in advance.[8]

Today Kang Youwei's most famous work is *The Book of Great Unity* (*Datong shu* 大同書), published only posthumously in 1935. His Great Unity is a radically egalitarian communist Utopia, where state, private property and the family have been abolished. In describing this Utopia Kang does draw on ancient Chinese texts, and in particular the chapter 'Evolution of the Rites' (*Liyun* 禮運) of *The Book of Rites*. Yet there is not doubt that Kang Youwei has been influenced

---

[7] It may be interesting to notice that the term 'Small Tranquility' is now part of the modernization discourse in China. Deng Xiaoping used it in 1979 to set the goal of reaching a per capita GDP of 800 US dollars by the year 2000. Having attained this goal the term is now used to refer to increasing the overall welfare of people in China and by the year 2020 quadruple the GDP of the year 2000.
[8] Quoted from *Sources of Chinese Tradition*, Vol. II, p. 268.

by European and American Utopias, popular at the time, in explaining his great unity. Specialists have especially pointed to the Edward Bellamy's American bestseller *Looking Backward* from 1888 as an important source of inspiration.[9]

Thus, in the case of Kang Youwei we may speak about projecting Western ideas onto Confucianism as a way of handling the challenge and threat that the European Powers posed to China at this time.

For a short time Kang Youwei was the most influential political thinker in China. When serving the young Guangxu 光緒 emperor he drafted the radical programme of the Reform Movement of 1898. However, when in September the empress dowager Cixi 慈禧 (1835–1908) and her entourage staged a coup to abolish the reforms, orders were issued for the arrest of Kang Youwei and his closest associates. Supported by the British, Kang Youwei escaped and was taken to Hong Kong on board a British warship. After that he spent several years in exile, travelling all over the world to Japan, America, Europe, India, Southeast Asia etc. in order to rally support for his reform plans. He returned to China in 1913 and died in 1927 just having celebrated his seventieth birthday. Although in theory opposed to monarchy, he was so critical of the new republic that he argued for a restoration of the Qing Dynasty.

Kang Youwei's reinterpretation of the Confucian legacy met with vehement objections, on scholarly as well as on ideological grounds. In the words of a prominent historian one could say that if his first book caused a hurricane, the second one caused an earthquake.[10] Many scholars in and outside China rejected his basic historical and philological theses that, for example, Confucius had authored the classics and that Liu Xin had forged the ancient text classics.

Implicit in Kang Youwei's vision was a culturalism that found no essential differences based on 'blood' or 'race' between the different peoples or nations of the world. The differences that did exist were

---

[9] See Martin Bernal, *Chinese Socialism to 1907*, Ithaca and London: Cornell University Press, 1976, especially chapter 1, pp. 11–32.
[10] Immanuel Hsü, *The Rise of Modern China*, New York and Oxford: Oxford University Press, 1990, p. 365.

cultural and reflected different degrees of civilization. He regarded culture and civilization as malleable entities which acquire their forms by means of education, reading etc.

Liang Qichao

Kang Youwei's student Liang Qichao 梁啟超 (1873–1929) was one of the most influential intellectuals in twentieth-century China. He published an enormous number of articles, essays and books on Chinese culture and on the world. His collected works are said to contain about ten million words.[11] He spent sixteen years in Japan and travelled extensively in the Western world, and he reported to his Chinese readers about the situation in foreign countries.

Just like his teacher Kang Youwei, he focused on the need for social reform in China and in that context he came to emphasize the importance of developing China into a fully-fledged nation-state. He considered this especially important as a way to meet the threat posed by international imperialism. In order for China to become a nation-state it was necessary to foster a spirit of community and oneness in the national community. In Liang's words, to set up a nation state

> . . . is not merely to have rulers, officials students, farmers, labourers, merchants, and soldiers, but to have ten thousand hands and feet with only one mind, ten thousand ears with one hearing, ten thousand powers with only one purpose of life; then the state is established ten-thousandful strong . . .. When mind touches mind, when power is linked to power, cog to cog, strand around strand, and ten thousand roads meet in one centre, this will be the state.[12]

In Liang's view the Chinese national community would be multi-ethnic, not exclusively Han-Chinese. In this regard he differed from some contemporary revolutionaries who regarded Chinese

---

[11] Yang, Xiao, 'Liang Qichao's Political and Social Philosophy', in Cheng Chung-ying and Nicholas Bunnin eds. *Contemporary Chinese Philosophy*, Oxford: Blackwell, 2002, pp. 17–36.
[12] Quoted from Hao Chang, *Liang Ch'i-ch'ao and Intellectual Transition in China, 1890–1907*, Cambridge, Mass.: Harvard University Press, 1971, p. 100.

nationalism as more immediately anti-Manchu than as opposed to international imperialism. In Liang's view of the nation-state we may see traces of traditional Confucian culturalism in that he saw the future Chinese-nation state as a community held together by common beliefs and attitudes, by culture, rather than by racial or even ethnic bonds.

Liang further argued that a nation-state must be based on 'citizenship', and this category implied for him popular sovereignty. His ideas on the nation-state made him move beyond the idea of government *for* the people, which was important already in classical Confucian thought, to an unequivocal notion of government *by* the people as a prerequisite of the nation-state. In other words, Liang argued that China should become a democratic nation-state. Liang seems to have seen democracy as an important means for building a strong nation-state rather than as an end in itself. This instrumental perspective of democracy exemplifies typically how political thought in China since the collapse of the empire has focused on the task of building a rich and strong Chinese state.

Around the turn of the twentieth century, Liang's thinking underwent some significant changes. For example, in the 1990s, Liang Qichao still regarded the nation-state as a transitory organizational form in the course of social evolution which should exist during the Age of Rising Peace. But later with the advent of the Age of Universal Peace, he at this time felt that the nation-states should dissolve and give way to a universal polity. However, from the early years of the twentieth century Liang no longer viewed the nation-state as merely a transitory form or organization. To turn China into a democratic nation-state remained an urgent task, but once formed Liang now believed that this new China would live on for the foreseeable future.

Earlier Confucian thinkers such as Huang Zongxi may have expressed democratic ideas in embryonic form. But Liang Qichao was probably the first to develop a practical theory for building democracy in China.

For Liang the nation-state was linked with democracy but also with Social Darwinism, another significant tenet of his thought. Liang felt that struggle, and the willingness to struggle, was an important cause behind the progress in the Western world, while the cultural bias against struggle in Chinese tradition was part of the reason for China's relative stagnation. He argued, therefore, that struggle must be accepted as an important dynamic factor in social development. In particular, this perspective of struggle and survival of the fittest characterized Liang's view of international development. In other words, he considered it vitally important to build a powerful Chinese nation-state which could successfully compete with other nations on the world scene.

Ever since the early twentieth century Social Darwinism, and especially the focus on struggle as a major dynamic factor for social and political development, has remained a fundamental strand of thought in China, underlying different currents of ideas.

Liang's focus on building a strong nation-state which could be successful in competing with other nation-states is symptomatic of his collectivistic tendency. His vision gives little room for the individual to maintain a private sphere where no one may interfere. He was not insensitive to the value of individual freedom – he even subscribed to the notion of utilitarianism – but to the extent that there was a conflict between the interest of the nation-state and the individual he felt that the former must prevail.

We should note that after spending nine months in America in 1903, he became more pessimistic about the democratic praxis in the United States and, more importantly, about the possibility of transforming China into a viable and successful democracy in the near future.

Another important aspect of Liang's thinking was his effort to delimit the scope for morality as it were. In education he argued that there should be a differentiation between moral and intellectual education. In his political thinking he moved away from the traditional focus on the 'good governance' towards democracy and, in the words of Professor Chang Hao, a leading specialist on Liang and this period in Chinese intellectual history, 'collective achievement and dynamic growth'.[13]

---

[13] Ibid. p. 298.

As a disciple of Kang Youwei Liang was a Confucian and in the 1890s he wholeheartedly supported Kang's idea of preserving Confucianism as a religious faith. Throughout his life he attached great importance to the importance of faith, as a complement to philosophical reflection and insight, in motivating people to participate in improving the world. However, as he was exposed to Western cultural traditions he became increasingly critical of major tenets of Confucian thought, and in 1902 he wrote a letter to his teacher Kang Youwei in which he advises against continuing to advocate the preservation of Confucianism:

> In the opinion of your disciple [Liang himself] there is nothing more urgent than to change the Chinese mind by introducing new theories. However, in the beginning there is bound to be some destruction. There is much in Confucianism that does not fit the new world. In case one continues to advocate its preservation, that would only mean working against one's own intentions.[14]

Yet Liang remained convinced that faith was extremely important, and so he now turned to Mahayana Buddhism. He found that while the faith of other religions was often based on human superstitions, Buddhist faith was predicated on philosophical enlightenment.

Liang Qichao played a uniquely important role in the process of evolving a new, modern intellectual discourse in China. He popularized Western concepts and modes of analyses to discuss both Western and Chinese culture. His own language was a mixture of classical and modern Chinese, rather easy to read and yet well designed to express what he wanted to express. His *Intellectual Trends in the Ch'ing Period* (original Chinese title *Qingdai xueshu gailun* 清代學術概論) is still widely read by students and scholars not only in China but also in the West.

Liang Qichao took his point of departure in New Text Confucianism, but his main contribution was to open up Chinese culture to new perspectives. He paved the way for deepened dialogue between Confucianism and other spiritual traditions in the world.

---

[14] Ibid. p. 229.

Zhang Binglin

A vitriolic critic of New Text Confucianism and a proponent of an essentialist, anti-Manchu Han-Chinese nationalism, Zhang Binglin 章炳麟 (1868–1936), also known as Zhang Taiyan 章太炎, was in some ways the diametrical opposite of Kang Youwei and Liang Qichao.

No doubt, Zhang Binglin was one of the most erudite and complex Chinese intellectuals of late imperial and early Republican China. As a writer he drew inspiration from the Wei-Jin period between the Han and the Tang dynasties and he showed a predilection for unusual words and obscure allusions. As a result, his writings are often exceedingly difficult to comprehend. In several ways his outlook was paradoxical: he was a revolutionary who rejected the idea of evolution; he was an activist who emphasized the importance of pure and non-utilitarian scholarship; he gave expression to a narrow nationalism, but he was also the first Chinese to reach a deep understanding of the thought of Immanuel Kant.

After three years imprisonment for his anti-Manchu activities he went to Japan in 1906 and gave a talk in which he characterized himself as 'mad' and 'neurotic', but he added that 'it is neurotic people who arrive at profound thoughts that transcend common knowledge'.[15]

Zhang was a follower of the Old Text School and in his classical studies focused on the *Zuozhuan* commentary. In his view Confucius was indeed a transmitter, not a creator, and the first scholar in Chinese history who had set up a private, as opposed to a court-sponsored, school of thought.

As opposed to the views of Kang Youwei and Liang Qichao, Zhang did not consider Confucianism a religion, and he wholeheartedly shared the opinion of the eighteenth-century scholar Zhang Xuecheng 章學誠 (1738–1801) that 'the Six Classics are all history', rather than sacred texts whose contents and truths somehow exist

---

[15] Shimada Kenji, *Pioneer of the Chinese Revolution: Zhang Binglin and Confucianism*, Stanford: Stanford University Press, 1990, p. 29.

beyond time and space. For Zhang Binglin, as it had been for Zhang Xuecheng, this was at the same time a way of criticizing speculative and abstract thought which was not based on evidence and to elevate empirical knowledge of history to the highest level of knowledge.

Zhang distinguished between fact and value, between what is and what ought to be. For him scholarship was a search for truth based on evidence. Thus history should be described as it had actually happened. One should study history in order to know what had happened, whether it had been good or bad, and not necessarily to apply old ideas As the core of the 'national essence' (*guocui* 國粹), history – or the knowledge of history – played an essential role in defining a nation. In response to an open letter in 1907 he wrote:

> If one knows only the 'righteousness' of nationalism without reading any of the histories or classics, one can never attain refined appreciation of antiquity. I believe that nationalism is much like agriculture. If you irrigate it with the people, institutions, geography, and customs recorded in the historical texts, then a thick, luxuriant growth will result. However, if you treat it only as a principle to be esteemed and fail to love the people of the nation, then it will yellow and whither away.[16]

As a Han-Chinese nationalist Zhang was not a Confucian in any exclusive sense, although he did revere Confucius and as a scholar followed the Old Text School. He also embraced Buddhism, and he paid attention to the different schools of thought in pre-China as an important part of the cultural heritage.

Since his early years Zhang was full of hatred for the Manchu rulers as barbaric usurpers. In his article 'Explaining the Republic of China' (*Zhonghua minguo jie* 中華民國解), published in 1907, he wrote:

> During the Han and the period before that, the Chinese did not regard the barbarian tribes as peers and therefore there is no example of barbarians being referred to as men in the records [. . .]
>
> *The Spring and Autumn Annals* cite instances of degrading Xia states to the level of barbarians, but there is no example of barbarian

---

[16] Quoted from Shimada Kenji, p. 61.

states being included among the Xia states. When the Qi state used barbarian rites, there was a record of it being demoted as a barbarian state. In this respect, how could there be a case of regarding the Manchus as Chinese?[17]

Thus, Zhang opposed the culturalist conception of Chineseness as articulated by Kang Youwei and others, according to which in principle anyone who embraced Chinese culture would become Chinese, and emphasized the exclusive national identity of the Han people. For this he drew inspiration from Wang Fuzhi, but he may also have been influenced by European notions of nationalism. However, opposing the culturalism of Kang Youwei and others did not mean that he was willing to divorce traditional Chinese culture from the Chinese identity. According to what we may label his cultural conservatism the Han Chinese had to hold on to Chinese culture.

Zhang's nationalism was at the root of his political radicalism and so distinguished him as a revolutionary from Kang Youwei and Liang Qichao as reformists. For Zhang the Han-Chinese nation must throw off the yoke of the foreign rule exercised by the Manchus, whereas for Kang and Liang one nation and one country could comprise several different ethnic groups.

Yet, Zhang Binglin's writings about nationalism are not free from paradoxes. Often he expresses himself as if the national identity were really anchored in the blood of a people. He does so especially when he argues for the need of the Han-Chinese people to throw off the Manchu yoke, but when he discusses Western culture he appears more willing to accept that identities are malleable and may be acquired.

Wholesale rejection of Confucianism

In the early twentieth century the reappraisal of the Confucian heritage became increasingly radical, and at the time of The New

---

[17] Zhang Taiyan, 'Explaining the Republic of China', *The Stockholm Journal of East Asian Studies*, No. 8, 1997; trans. Pär Cassel.

Culture Movement, which began around 1915 and culminated in the May Fourth Movement of 1919, the radical intelligentsia was ready to reject Confucianism altogether as inimical to progress and incompatible with modernity.

For the iconoclasts of the New Culture Movement Confucianism represented everything backward and outdated in Chinese culture and society: an educational system focusing on ancient texts while neglecting new knowledge, especially in the natural sciences and technology, an oppressive patriarchal family system, an authoritarian political system characterized by arbitrary decision-making rather than the rule of law, etc.

In place of Confucianism the leaders of the New Culture Movement called on Mr Sai (Science) and Mr De (Democracy) to rescue China. The movement was 'scientistic' in spirit looking for scientific solutions to all human and social problems.

Out of The New Culture movement emerged different ideological perspectives, but the radical rejection of Confucianism became mainstream ideology and was especially reinforced by the Communists. One of Mao Zedong's last campaigns was directed against Confucius and the remaining traces of his influence on Chinese culture and society.

New Confucianism

Since the New Culture Movement of the 1910s, Confucianism has lived on in China as an ideological undercurrent overshadowed by the radical rejection of the historical legacy. Of course, one should speak about different Confucian currents rather than one current. The most interesting currents, which also possess the greatest vitality, form what is often referred to as New Confucianism or Modern New Confucianism.

In 1923 there took place an important discussion in China on 'Science and Human Life'. The discussion was triggered by Zhang Junmai 張君勱 (in the West also known as Carsun Chang 1886–1969), a young professor at Qinghua college in Beijing who gave a lecture entitled 'The Philosophy of Life' (*Rensheng guan* 人生觀) in which he argued that a true philosophy of life must have a metaphysical foundation. Zhang felt that Mr Science, to whom the May Fourth radicals had turned for salvation, could not offer a philosophy of life. He argued that a combination of Neo-Confucian thought in the vein of Wang Yangming and the philosophy of intuitionism associated with the French philosopher Henri Bergson, who was very popular at the time, could supplement what science lacked to build a genuine philosophy of life. He found five basic differences between science and a philosophy of life: (i) 'science is objective, whereas a philosophy of life is subjective'; (ii) 'science is controlled by the logical method whereas a philosophy of life arises from intuition'; (iii) 'science proceeds from an analytical method, whereas a philosophy of life proceeds from synthesis'; (iv) 'science follows the law of cause and effect whereas a philosophy of life is based on free will'; (v) 'science arises from the phenomenon of uniformity among objects, whereas a philosophy of life arises from the unity of personality.' On the basis of this analysis he then concluded:

> From the above we can see that the distinguishing points of a philosophy of life are subjectivity, intuitiveness, synthesizing power, free will, and personal unity. Because of these five qualities, the solution of problems pertaining to a philosophy of life cannot be achieved by science, however advanced it may be, but can be achieved only by people themselves.[18]

Zhang Junmai was one of the Confucian voices in the debate, but his arguments also reflected his interest in European philosophy and especially in Kant. This was typical of the 'New Confucians' who emerged in the wake of the New Culture Movement: their interpretation of Confucian thought was more or less influenced by their studies of Western thought.

Some of the prominent May Fourth radicals took up Zhang Junmai's challenge and came out in support of science as the harbinger of solutions to human problems. The leading ideologue of

---

[18] Quoted from Wing-tsit Chan's translation in *Sources of Chinese Tradition*, Vol II, pp. 371–2.

the May Fourth New Culture Movement, Hu Shi 胡適 (1891–1962) set out to present 'an outline of this new philosophy of life':

1. On the basis of our knowledge of astronomy and physics, we should recognize that the world of space is infinitely large.
2. On the basis of our geological and paleontological knowledge, we should recognize that the universe extends over infinite time.
3. On the basis of all our verifiable scientific knowledge, we should recognize that the universe and everything in it follow natural laws of movement and change – 'natural' in the Chinese sense of 'being so of themselves' – and that there is no need for the concept of a supernatural Ruler or Creator.
4. On the basis of the biological sciences, we should recognize the terrific wastefulness and brutality in the struggle for existence in the biological world, and consequently the untenability of the hypothesis of a benevolent Ruler who 'possesses the character of loving life'.
5. On the basis of the biological, physiological, and psychological sciences, we should recognize that man is only one species in the animal kingdom and differs from the other species only in degree but not in kind.
6. On the basis of the knowledge derived from anthropology, sociology, and the biological sciences, we should understand the history and causes of the evolution of living organisms and of human society.
7. On the basis of the biological and psychological sciences, we should recognize that all psychological phenomena are explainable through the law of causality.
8. On the basis of biological and historical knowledge, we should recognize that morality and religion are subject to change and that the causes of such change can be scientifically discovered.
9. On the basis of our newer knowledge of physics and chemistry, we should recognize that matter is not dead or static but living and dynamic.
10. On the basis of biological and sociological knowledge, we should recognize that the individual – the small 'self' – is subject to death and extinction, but humanity – the 'Large Self' – does not die and is immortal and [we] should recognize that to live for the sake of the species and posterity is religion of the highest

kind and that those religions that seek a future life either in Heaven or in the Pure Land are selfish religions.

> This new philosophy of life is a hypothesis founded on the commonly accepted scientific knowledge of the last two or three hundred years. We may confer on it the honourable title of 'scientific philosophy of life'. But to avoid unnecessary controversy, I propose to call it merely 'the naturalistic philosophy of life'.[19]

This passage from Hu Shi's article well reflects the rather extreme 'scientism' prevalent among the May Fourth intelligentsia. One may well surmise that this extremism added fuel to the search among many intellectuals for a third way between the upholders of an ossified Confucian ideology of the past, which had been hopelessly subservient to the dynastic political order, and the materialistic radicalism of the May Fourth iconoclasts, who seemed too one-dimensional. I believe that the notion of such a search captures an important part of the background of the emergence of New Confucianism. Like their May Fourth radical antagonists, the New Confucians did want to see China develop into a modern society, and like the radicals they also felt that China should adopt technology from the Western countries as well as ideas for building a new political system. But unlike the radicals they looked primarily to China's indigenous spiritual traditions, and mainly Confucianism, to articulate their philosophy of life. In a broad sense they operated within the framework of Zhang Zhidong's formula of Chinese learning as essence and Western learning as a means.

First generation of New Confucians

In the first generation of New Confucians we may mention, apart from Zhang Junmai, three seminal thinkers: Xiong Shili 熊十力 (1885–1968), Liang Shuming 梁漱溟 (1893–1988) and Feng Youlan 馮友蘭 (1895–1990).

---

[19] Quoted from Wing-tsit Chan's translation of excerpts from Hu Shi's article 'Science and Philosophy of Life' in *Sources of Chinese Tradition*, Vol. II, pp. 375–377.

Xiong Shili

In his book *The New Doctrine of Mere Consciousnes* (*Xin weishilun* 新唯識論), Xiong Shili gave a systematic presentation of his subjectivistic Confucianism. This book was a Confucian critique of Buddhism but it was still heavily influenced by Buddhist thought; the notion of 'mere consciousness' is indeed Buddhist and the Chinese translation of the Sanskrit word *Vijnanavada*. The first edition of this book, written in classical Chinese, appeared in 1932, and a new and much expanded version written in colloquial Chinese came out in 1944. In 1958–9 he then published two works – *On Original Reality and Function* (*Tiyonglun* 體用論) and *Illuminating the Mind* (*Mingxin pian* 明心篇) – in which he again revised his account of 'mere consciousness'. Like other Confucians Xiong Shili emphasized unity, and a main purpose of his doctrine of mere consciousness was to demonstrate that Confucian ethics and the cultivation of virtue have a solid metaphysical basis. Xiong Shili's writings are not easy to understand but through his students he exercised deep influence over the evolution of New Confucian thought.

Liang Shuming

Liang Shuming is best known for his early comparative study *Eastern and Western Cultures and their Philosophies* (*Dongxi wenhua ji qi zhexue* 東西文化及其哲學) published in 1921. This work became important for the development of New Confucian thought in that Liang here gave a positive interpretation of Confucianism that differed from the radicalism of the May Fourth New Culture Movement and which also suggested that the Confucian tradition has much to offer in terms of ethics as complement to other major spiritual traditions in the world. Throughout his life he was preoccupied with questions relating to the development of China in general and the Chinese rural countryside in particular. His ideas in this field have inspired many followers while they have evoked the antipathy of others. After the founding of the People's Republic of China, he felt that Mao and the communists had betrayed the peasants, placing 'the workers in the ninth Heaven and the peasants in the ninth Hell'. This so infuriated Mao that he told him 'I think you stink' at a meeting in 1953. Mao even honoured him with a furious written attack in an article now included in *Selected Works of Mao Tsetung* and a campaign to criticize Liang's reactionary ideas.[20]

Interestingly, in an interview with an American China scholar in 1983, Liang said that he thought of himself as a Buddhist rather than a Confucian: 'I am a Buddhist first and foremost, no matter if some – like your American colleague Guy Alitto – would call me "the last Confucian".'[21]

Feng Youlan

While Xiong Shili and Liang Shuming drew inspiration from the subjectivism of Wang Yangming and the School of Mind, Feng Youlan 馮友蘭 (1895–1990), China's most famous philosopher in the twentieth century, developed his philosophical ideas on the basis of Zhu Xi's School of Principle.

Feng Youlan received part of his philosophical education in the United States where he attained his doctorate degree in 1923 at Columbia University. During his stay in the West he came into contact with modern Western philosophy and he was especially influenced by the so-called New Realism current of thought of W.P. Montague (1873–1953). In more general terms one may argue that he was impressed by the rigorous methods employed by Western philosophers he came into contact with and which he contrasted with the less precise way of discussing philosophical questions in the Chinese tradition. In terms of themes, or subject-matter, he was still very attached to the Chinese tradition.

---

[20] Concerning Mao and Liang Shuming, see Guy S. Alitto, *The Last Confucian: Liang Shuming and the Chinese Dilemma of Modernity*, Berkeley: University of California Press, 1986, p. 1–3 and pp. 324–30. See also Mao's article ' Criticism of Liang Shu-ming's Reactionary Ideas', in *Selected Works of Mao Tsetung*, Vol. V. Peking: Foreign Languages Press, 1977, pp. 121–130.

[21] Vera Schwarcz, *Time for Telling Truth is Running Out. Conversations with Zhang Shenfu*, New Haven and London: Yale University Press, p. 36.

His attitude in this regard was not uncommon among intellectuals of his generation in China, but he did more than perhaps anyone else to transform it into a philosophical programme which he would exert himself to realize: he wanted to employ modern methods of Western, especially Anglo-Saxon scholarship, to deal with some of the core themes of traditional Chinese, and especially Confucian philosophy. Again, one may hear the echo of the idea of Chinese learning as essence and Western learning as means.

Feng Youlan was a philosopher in his own right but also a historian of Chinese philosophy, and he probably managed to combine these two roles more successfully than anyone else in twentieth-century China. As a philosopher he constructed a system of New Principle Learning (*Xin lixue* 新理學) which he described in six books which he published from 1939 to 1946. Two of these exist in English translation.

Feng's system of New Principle is far too complex to describe, let alone do justice to, in a short introduction to Confucianism. But in order to give the reader some flavour of his philosophy we may briefly look at two tenets of this system. The first one concerns the realm of ontology, or in more everyday language the nature of being. Feng distinguished between three levels or modes of existence, the 'true-and-real', 'the dimension of actuality' and the 'actual things' in the empirical world:

> That which makes a thing be square is 'square'. . . . 'Square' can be not 'actual' (*shi* 實) and yet still be 'true-and-real' (*zhen* 真). If in fact no square thing actually exists, then 'square' is not actual. But if in fact a square thing actually exists, then it must have four corners. An actual and square thing must be dependent on that which makes something square, and cannot escape from it. On this basis we can say that 'square' is true-and-real. If 'square' is not actual but true-and-real, then 'square' is purely true-and-real.
>
> Actual things are stored up (*hanyun* 涵蘊) in the dimension of actuality (*shiji* 實際); the dimension of actuality is stored up in the dimension of truth-and-reality (*zhenji* 真際). Being 'stored up' is equivalent to the relationship expressed in 'if . . . then' statements. If there is an actual thing, there must be the dimension of actuality; if there is the dimension of actuality, there must be the dimension of truth-and-

reality. But the dimension of actuality is there without entailing that any actual thing is there; the dimension of truth-and-reality is there without entailing that there is the dimension of actuality.[22]

'Principle' for Feng is 'true-and-real' but it does not exist in the same way as actual things; using a term which may make us think of Bertrand Russell, he says that principles *qiancun* 潛存, or 'subsist', but the literal meaning of *qiancun* is 'to have the potential to exist', which captures his meaning even better than 'subsist'.

The other tenet of his philosophical system that I would like to draw attention to is his notion of a hierarchy of four 'spiritual realms' (*jingshen jingjie* 精神境界): the 'natural' or the 'spontaneous' (*ziran* 自然), the 'utilitarian' (*gongli* 功利), the 'moral' (*daode* 道德)) and the universal 'Heaven-and-Earth' (*tiandi* 天地) realms. Without making an effort we live our lives within the first two realms, we act spontaneously and we seek what we think benefits ourselves. Through moral and intellectual effort, we may progress to the two higher realms. Reaching the highest realm of Heaven-and-Earth a human being becomes 'naturally in unity with the Great Whole' which Feng says is mystical, 'inconceivable and inexpressible'. Let us again see what Feng himself has to say, in the excellent translation of Lauren Pfister:

> The human within the realm of Heaven and Earth is 'self'-less and yet also has a self . . .. This so-called 'self' has two meanings: that which is 'selfish' and that which is 'sovereign'. The person within the realm of Heaven and Earth is naturally in unity with the Great Whole . . .. The difference between 'self' and 'no self' no longer exists for him. So in referring to a 'self' involved with 'selfishness', he has no 'self'. But because his person is united with the Great Whole, then he can say, 'All things reside in "me".' From the perspective of this natural unity with the Great Whole, it is not the case that the 'self' has been completely extinguished, but rather that the 'self' has been immeasurably

---

[22] The Chinese original can be found in Feng's *New Principle Learning* (*Xin lixue* 新理學), Changsha: Commercial Press, 1939, pp. 22–3; the English translation here is quoted from Lauren Pfister, 'Feng Youlan's New Principle Learning and His Theories of Chinese Philosophy', in Chung-ying Cheng and Nicholas Bunnin, eds. *Contemporary Chinese Philosophy*, p. 170; Chinese characters have been added.

expanded. The 'self' within the immeasurable expansion is the sovereign of the Great Whole. [. . .] The realm of unity with Heaven basically is mysticism. What Buddhist scholars call 'Tathagata' and Daoist scholars call the Way is, according to their own theories, inconceivable and inexpressible. Similarly, what we have called the Great Whole is also, according to our theory, inconceivable and inexpressible.[23]

As a historian of Chinese philosophy, Feng Youlan was a pioneer whose major works still belong to the very best in the field. Generations of Western students and scholars are familiar with his *A History of Chinese Philosophy* in two volumes, beautifully translated by Professor Derk Bodde and published in 1952–3 (the two volumes of the Chinese original had been published in 1931 and 1934 respectively). But already in 1948 he had published *A Short History of Chinese Philosophy*, which he wrote himself in English and which Professor Bodde edited. The author's name in these two cases was written as Fung Yu-lan.

After the founding of the People's Republic of China in 1949, Feng Youlan remained at Peking University as professor of philosophy. He declared that he wanted to support the new regime and also revised his scholarly writings to make them conform to the new ideological demands. After the death of Mao Zedong in 1976 he again began to embrace the major tenets of his New Principle Learning. In the 1980s his complete works were published and before his death he completed a new version of his *History of Chinese Philosophy*. As one of China's most prominent intellectuals, Feng Youlan was active during several decades of China's modern turbulent history. By scrutinizing his work we may better understand how he grappled with the contradictions involved in trying to reconcile values and demands upon himself which were inevitably fraught with tension: deeply committed to the traditional Confucian search for harmony and unity he also wished to promote China's development and modernization. To fulfil his role he seems to have felt that he should be loyal to the political leadership, whether exercised by

---

[23] Chinese original in the *New Treatise on the Nature of Man* (*Xin yuanren* 新原人); quoted from Pfister, p. 173.

Chiang Kai-shek or Mao Zedong. Loyalty to one's prince is of course very much a Confucian virtue. But so is 'dissent', within the framework of loyalty. Striking a reasonable balance between loyalty and dissent is difficult. Perhaps Feng Youlan, who was a truly remarkable scholar and philosopher, is an example of the fact that Confucians have not seldom placed greater emphasis on the duty of loyalty to the ruler than on dissent and criticism as a means of upholding what is true and right.

Second generation of New Confucians

From the beginning the New Confucians shared the belief that there is no fundamental contradiction between Confucianism and the demands of the modern world. Indeed, they argued, modern science and democracy would for the first time in history offer the conditions under which the Confucian ideals may become fully realized. Also Confucianism may promote the growth of China into a modern and affluent society.

These basic standpoints were taken over by the second generation of New Confucians whose most famous representatives were three of Xiong Shili's students: Mou Zongsan 牟宗三 (1909–95), Tang Junyi 唐君毅 (1909–78) and Xu Fuguan 徐復觀 (1903–82).

After the establishment of the People's Republic of China in 1949, it was no longer possible to develop Confucian ideas, let alone propagate, Confucianism in Mainland China. So from the 1950s until the death of Mao Zedong in 1976, Confucianism developed outside the Chinese mainland, in Hong Kong and Taiwan and to some extent in other parts of East and Southeast Asia and in North America. In early January 1958 the three second generation Confucians just mentioned published together with Zhang Junmai a manifesto in Hong Kong and Taipei entitled 'A Manifesto to the World on Chinese Culture' (*Wei Zhongguo wenhua jinggao shijie renshi xuanyan* 為中國文化敬告世界人士宣言), in which they argued that Confucianism constitutes the core of Chinese culture and presents a unique approach to philosophy. They also emphasized that there is no contradiction between Confucianism and science and democracy; that in fact the seeds of democracy, science and technology rooted in Chinese culture could have developed into a modern political system and scientific spirit if properly cultivated. The writers formulated a vision in which the coexistence and interdependence of different cultures would become a major challenge to mankind and they argued that Confucianism could make great contributions to the unity and harmony in the world.

Mou Zongsan

Possibly the intellectually most influential among the second generation of New Confucians, Mou Zongsan, was in his early years a student of logic, and one of his early works was devoted to Russell and Whitehead's *Principia Mathematica* and Wittgenstein's *Tractatus Logico-Philosophicus*.[24] But he soon moved on to Chinese philosophy and to the construction of a philosophical system. His system was a kind of reconstruction of Confucian thought, but he also drew much inspiration from Kant, whom he held in very high esteem. 'Intellectual intuition' is one key concept in Mou's thought which emphasizes the internal subjective experience rather than the external objective evidence. He separates between two kinds of truth, 'extensional' and 'intensional'. The extensional truths are scientific truths, they 'do not belong to the subject and can be objectively asserted'.[25] The concept of intensional truth, which is not easy to understand, rather refers, in the words of one interpreter of his thought, to 'propositional attitudes that belong to the subject'.[26] They are truths not of science but of humanity and culture. To reach the level of intensional truth requires a special kind of mentality. While extensional truths are highly developed in the West, Mou argues, intensional truths are more characteristic of China.

---

[24] *The Model of Logic* (*Luoji dianfan* 邏輯典範), Hong Kong: Commercial Press, 1941.
[25] Mou in *Zhongguo zhexue shijiu jiang* 中國哲學十九講 (Nineteen lectures on Chinese philosophy), Taipei: Student Book Co., p. 21; here quoted from Refeng Tang, 'Mou Zongsan on Intellectual Intuition', in Chung-ying Cheng and Nicholas Bunnin eds., *Contemporary Chinese Philosophy*, p. 341.
[26] Ibid.

Tang Junyi

Mou Zongsan's colleague Tang Junyi reinterpreted Neo-Confucianism in the light of his studies of European philosophy. Like Mou Zongsan his thought was clearly subjectivistic. One of his major concerns was to anchor ethics in a metaphysical reality which he held was immanent in all things in the universe. An important postulate for him was that we must take responsibility for our own life and also assume that we are free subjects; in this we may hear echoes of the philosophy of Kant. He distinguishes between the actual self and the ethical self. Our task is to transcend our actual selves and realize the goodness of our ethical selves:

> One common nature shared by all moral conduct and moral psychology is the self's transcending the limits of the actual self. [. . .]
> What we call Reason [lixing 理性] is the nature that can manifest and follow what is natural. Reason is what the Chinese Confucians call natural reason [xing li 性理]. It is the nature or essence that makes our ethical self, or spiritual self or transcendental self be what it is.[27]

Tang Junyi's emphasis on the tension between the actual and the ethical – which he anchors in the Confucian tradition – may, as the American scholar Thomas Metzger has shown in an important study, be used to question the widely held belief that there is little or no transcendence in Confucian thought and that in Max Weber's words, there is 'no tension between ethical demand and human short-coming'.[28]

Xu Fuguan

Unlike Mou Zongsan and Tang Junyi, the third member of the second generation of New Confucians and the co-signer of the

---

[27] Quoted from Sin Yee Chan, 'Tang Junyi: Moral Idealism and Chinese Culture', in Chung-ying Cheng and Nicholas Bunnin, *Contemporary Chinese Philosophy*, p. 306.
[28] Thomas A. Metzger, *Escape from Predicament: Neo-Confucianism and China's Evolving Political Culture*. New York: Columbia University Press, 1977. Concerning Max Weber, cf below, pp. 179 ff.

1958 Manifesto, Xu Fuguan, never attempted to construct his own philosophical system. His method has rather been described as 'raking the sand in order to find the gold'. In his writings, Xu touched on a great variety of topics, by no means limited to philosophy. Rather than thinking of himself as a pure scholar he placed himself between scholarship and politics. During his career he was a major in the army when in his 40s he decided to resign and then devote himself to cultural work. He was later an editor of a journal as well as a university professor and an independent writer.

Xu Fuguan's writings abound in interesting ideas and formulations that may inspire the reader to follow up what he suggests. One notion that may easily catch our attention is his observation that classical Greek philosophy developed out of a sense of curiosity, whereas early Chinese thought may rather be traced back to a sense of anxiety. One may doubt whether this is really a correct description of historical facts, but the notions of curiosity and anxiety as giving rise to different modes of thought is certainly worth pondering.

In terms of political philosophy, Xu argued with reference to, among other things, the ancient Confucian notion of taking people as the 'root' (*ben* 本) that there is no basic contradiction between Confucianism and democracy. But he felt, in the words of a student of his thought, that the modern Chinese polity has combined the worst parts of Chinese and Western political traditions:

> It took the unlimited political responsibility of the rulers from the Confucian tradition but discarded its moral conscience, and it took the modern Western competition for power but discarded the recognition of basic individual rights.[29]

Xu held that Confucianism and democracy could enrich each other:

> Democracy can obtain a more supreme ground from the revival of the Confucian spirit, and Confucianism can complete its actual

---

[29] Peimin Ni, 'Practical Humanism of Xu Fuguan', in Chung-ying Cheng and Nicholas Bunnin eds. *Contemporary Chinese Philosophy*, p. 297.

objective structure through the establishment of a democratic polity.[30]

He regarded the democratic system as it has evolved in different ways in Western countries as founded on a legal framework, objective and, in a sense, external. What Confucianism could contribute to democracy was therefore, in his view, the idea of the political subjectivity of the people:

> The relationships maintained by legal rights are at best external relations. External relations are not reliable, and they do not allow human nature to develop freely, unless they are grounded on internal relations. To govern by virtue is to establish internal relations between individuals through the moral virtues that everyone possesses, which from the Confucian point of view is the only natural and rational relation.[31]

On the whole, Xu Fuguan comes out in his writings as an openminded and intelligent thinker whose writings are replete with sharp observations and interesting interpretations.

Mao Zedong's death and the dragon economies

According to the radical intelligentsia in China, which in varying degrees possessed a kind of ideological hegemony from about 1920 until the late 1970s, Confucianism was incompatible with modernization and modernity. This negative judgement of Confucianism also dominated among scholars in Western countries. In the early twentieth century, the German sociologist Max Weber, whose studies of the social dynamics of religions have been extremely influential, argued that Confucianism lacked those qualities he had found in Calvinist religion which he

---

[30] Original in Xu Fuguan, *Xueshu yu zhengzhi zhijian* 學術與政治之間 (Between scholarship and politics), Taipei: Student Book Co, 1980, p. 60; here quoted from Peimin Ni, op. cit., p. 297.
[31] Xu Fuguan, op.cit., p. 50; quoted from Peimin Ni, p. 295.

thought had contributed to the growth of capitalism in Europe. Weber wrote:

> A true prophecy creates and systematically orients conduct toward one internal measure of value. In the face of this the 'world' is viewed as material to be fashioned according to the norm. Confucianism in contrast meant adjustment to the outside, to the conditions of the 'world'. [. . .] Completely absent in Confucian ethic was any tension between nature and deity, between ethical demand and human short-coming, consciousness of sin and need for salvation, conduct on earth and compensation in the beyond, religious duty and social political reality. Hence, there was no leverage for influencing conduct through inner forces freed of tradition and convention.[32]

It may well be that Weber's analysis was mistaken both in empirical and theoretical terms. It just does not seem correct to say that Confucianism lacks 'any tension between ethical demand and human short-coming'. Furthermore, we may question whether tension between 'religious duty and social political reality' is necessary for a creed to be able to promote social progress in general or the growth of capitalism in particular.

We may question the validity of Weber's thesis about Confucianism, but it is a fact that he has been influential and probably also reinforced the arguments of the Chinese radicals.

In the late 1970s, and especially in the 1980s, this dominating image of Confucianism as inimical to change and opposed to modernity gave way to an entirely different image of a dynamic ethos which encourages study, hard work and a frugal life-style and which by its focus on the family values promotes social cohesion.

It seems that this breakthrough for a radically more positive appraisal of Confucianism was linked to the successes of the 'dragon economies' – or 'tiger economies' – in East and Southeast Asia: Japan, South Korea, Taiwan, Hong Kong and Singapore. These societies were all considered to be more or less Confucian. In

---

[32] Max Weber, *The Religion of China*, translated by Hans G. Gerth, New York: The Free Press, 1964, pp. 235–236.

Singapore Confucianism was even made official state philosophy, and President Lee Kuan-yew personally did much to promote this new image of Confucianism as an essential ingredient in the emergence of a special kind of East Asian modernity.

It is in this context that we should see the emergence of the notion of 'Asian values' as a set of collective and duty-orientated values as opposed to Western values which are supposed to be more individualistic and emphasize rights at the expense of duties.

However, there were also other factors behind the mainstream reappraisal of Confucianism. One factor was the radical political and ideological changes which followed in mainland China in the wake of the death of Mao Zedong in 1976. It soon became obvious that many people had lost faith in Marxism-Leninism Mao Zedong Thought which had been the ruling ideology for three decades. This loss of faith left behind it a kind of ideological vacuum which made people turn to alternative creeds and ideologies. Some people turned to 'foreign' ideas such as the Christian religion or political democracy, others turned to indigenous traditions such as Buddhism and Daoism and also to Confucianism.

Another factor, which had been a significant part of the motivation behind New Confucianism for a long time, was the perception that modernity as practised in America and Europe had led to a moral crisis. Many people have felt that Confucianism with its emphasis on duty and responsibility would offer an antidote which could help at least Asians avoid this crisis.

Interestingly, we may notice that the Asian economic crisis of the 1990s seemed to make many scholars and journalists more sceptical again as to the modernization dynamism of Confucianism.

Third generation of New Confucians

With the relative intellectual freedom of post-Mao China as opposed to the era when Mao himself was in command, Modern New Confucianism was now allowed. Many intellectuals studied the works of the Confucian scholars, just mentioned, and a third generation of New Confucians – the Harvard professor Tu

Wei-ming 杜維明 (1940-) being one of the most famous names – came to China and attracted large audiences for their lectures.

Since the 1980s New Confucianism has attracted a lot of attention in China. Many scholarly works on New Confucianism have been written by scholars in Mainland China. The works of the Neo-Confucian masters of the first and second generations have been reprinted and circulated in great numbers. And New Confucians of a third generation who are still active have established close contacts with colleagues in Mainland China, where their works are published and where they often go to lecture. The concept of New Confucianism does not have a precise enough definition for us to be able to determine who exactly should be considered a New Confucian. But to the more well-known scholars who should probably be considered to belong to the third generation belong, apart from Tu Wei-ming, among others Professor Liu Shu-hsien 劉述先 (1934-), who has recently retired from a chair in Chinese philosophy at the Chinese University of Hong Kong, Professor Cheng Chung-ying 成中英 (1935-) at the University of Hawaii and Professor Tsai Jen-hou 蔡仁厚 (1930-) in Taiwan. These, and several other scholars, write numerous articles and books both as experts on the history of Chinese thought and as philosophers in their own right.

We can see, therefore, that in the twentieth century, Confucianism was viewed very differently by different groups of people at different times in terms of its relationship to modernization and modernity.

Against this background it is natural to seek for the truth of the matter: how does Confucianism really relate to modernization and modernity, and this is one of the questions that we shall return to briefly in the next and concluding chapter of this book.

Further reading

Historical background

Hsü, Immanuel. *The Rise of Modern China*, New York and Oxford: Oxford University Press, 1990.

Levenson, Joseph Richmond. *Confucian China and Its Modern Fate: A Trilogy*. Berkeley: University of California Press, 1968.

Spence, Jonathan D. *The Search for Modern China*. 2nd ed New York: W.W. Norton, 1999.

Wakeman, Frederic E. *The Great Enterprise: The Manchu Reconstruction of Imperial Order in Seventeenth-Century China*. Berkeley: University of California Press, 1985.

The Donglin Academy

Charles O. Hucker, Charles O. 'The Tung-lin Movement of the Late Ming Period.' In John K. Fairbank, *Chinese Thought and Institution*. Chicago: Chicago University Press, 1957. pp. 132–62.

Busch, Heinrich. 'The Tung-lin Shu-yüan and Its Political and Philosophical Significance.' *Monumenta Serica*, 14, 1949–1955. pp. 1–163.

Intellectual and ideological currents

Bernal, Martin. *Chinese Socialism to 1907*. Ithaca and London: Cornell University Press, 1976.

Chang Hao. 'New Confucianism and the Intellectual Crisis of Modern China.' In Charlotte Furth ed. *The Limits of Change: Essays on Conservative Alternatives in Republican China*. Cambridge, Mass.: Harvard University Press, 1976. pp. 276–302.

Cheng, Chung-ying and Bunnin, Nicholas eds. *Contemporary Chinese Philosophy*. Oxford: Blackwell, 2002.

Chow Tse –tsung. *The May Fourth Movement: Intellectual Revolution in Modern China*. Cambridge, Mass.: Harvard University Press, 1960.

Elman, Benjamin. *Classicism, Politics, and Kinship: the Ch'ang-chou School of New Text Confucianism in Late Imperial China*. Berkeley: University of California Press, 1990.

Goldman, Merle. 'China's Anti-Confucius Campaign, 1973–74.' *China Quarterly*, no 63, 1975. pp. 435–62.

Liang, Ch'i-ch'ao. *Intellectual Trends in the Ch'ing Period*. Cambridge, Mass.: Harvard University Press, 1959. Trans. Immanuel Hsü.

Liu Shu-hsien. *Essentials of Contemporary Neo-Confucian Philosophy*. Westport, Conn.: Praeger, 2003.

Makeham, John ed. *New Confucianism: A Critical Examination*. New York: Palgrave Macmillan, 2003.

Metzger, Thomas A. *Escape from Predicament: Neo-Confucianism and China's Evolving Political Culture*. New York: Columbia University Press, 1977.

Mou Zongsan, Tang Junyi, Xu Fuguan and Zhang Junmai. 'A Manifesto to the World on Chinese Culture' (*Wei Zhongguo wenhua jinggao shijie renshi xuanyan* 為中國文化敬告世界人士宣言). Excerpts in English translation may be found in *Sources of Chinese Tradition*, Vol II, pp. 550–58. An abridged translation was appended to vol. 2 of Carsun Chang, *The Development of Neo-Confucian Thought*, New York: Bookman Associates, 1962, pp. 455–83. A complete translation under the title 'A Manifesto on the Reappraisal of Chinese Culture' was reportedly published in the Taiwan journal Chinese Culture – probably in 1960–1; see John Makeham, 'The Retrospective Creation of New Confucianism', in his *New Confucianism: A Critical Examination*, p. 27 f.

Pusey, James Reeve. *China and Charles Darwin*. Cambridge, Mass.: Harvard University Press, 1983.

Contacts with Europe

Ch'en, Jerome. *China and the West: Society and Culture, 1815–1937.* London: Hutchinson, 1979.

Cheng, Pei-kai et al eds. *The Search for Modern China: A Documentary Collection.* Eds Pei-kai Cheng and Michael Lestz, with Jonathan D. Spence. New York: Norton, 1999.

Dawson, Raymond S. *The Chinese Chameleon: An Analysis of European Conceptions of Chinese Civilization.* London and New York: Oxford University Press, 1967.

Lach, Donald. *Asia in the Masking of Europe.* Chicago: The Chicago University Press, 1965–93.

Mackerras, Colin. *Western Images of China.* Hong Kong: Oxford University Press, 1999.

Mungello. David E. *Curious land : Jesuit Accommodation and the Origins of Sinology.* Honolulu: University of Hawaii Press, 1989.

Idem. *The Great Encounter of China and the West, 1500–1800.* Lanham, Md.: Rowman & Littlefield Publishers, 1999.

Idem. *Leibniz and Confucianism, the Search for accord.* Honolulu: University Press of Hawaii, 1977.

Spence, Jonathan D. *The Search for Modern China.* 2nd ed New York: W.W. Norton, 1999.

Individual scholars and officials

Feng, Youlan

Feng, Youlan. *The Hall of Three Pines: An Account of My Life.* Translated by Denis C. Mair. Honolulu: University of Hawai'i Press, 2000.

Pfister, Lauren. 'Feng Youlan's New Principle Learning and His Theories of Chinese Philosophy.' In Cheng, Chung-ying and Nicholas Bunnin eds. *Contemporary Chinese Philosophy.* pp. 165–187.

Idem. 'A Modern Chinese Philosophy Built upon Critically Received Traditions: Feng Youlan's New Principle-Centered Learning and the Question of Its Relationship to Contemporary New Ruist ("Confucian") Philosophies.' In John Makeham. *New Confucianism: A Critical Examination.* pp. 165–86.

Heshen

Nivison, David. 'Ho-shen and His Accusers: Ideology and Political Behaviour in the 18th Century.' In David Nivison and Arthur F. Wright, eds. *Confucianism in Action.* Stanford: Stanford University Press, 1959. pp. 209–43.

Hu Shi

Grieder, Jerome. *Hu Shih and the Chinese Renaissance: Liberalism in the Chinese Revolution, 1917–1937.* Cambridge, Mass.: Harvard University Press, 1970.

Hu Shi. 'Science and Philosophy of Life.' Excerpts translated by Wing-tsit Chan. In *Sources of Chinese Tradition*, Vol. II. pp. 375–7.

Kang Youwei

Hsiao, Kung -chuan. *A Modern China and a New World: Kang Yu-wei, Reformer and Utopian, 1858–1927.* Seattle: University of Washington Press, 1975.

Liang Qichao
Chang, Hao. *Liang Ch'i-ch'ao and Intellectual Transition in China, 1890–1907.* Cambridge, Mass.: Harvard University Press, 1971.
Huang, Philip G. *Liang Ch'i-ch'ao and Modern Chinese Liberalism.* Seattle and London: University of Washington Press, 1972.
Levenson, Joseph R. *Liang Ch'i-ch'ao and the Mind of Modern China.* Berkeley: University of California Press, 1970.

Liang Shuming
Alitto, Guy S. *The Last Confucian : Liang Shu-ming and the Chinese Dilemma of Modernity.* Berkeley: University of California Press, 1986.
An, Yanming. 'Liang Shuming: Eastern and Western Cultures and Confucianism.' In Cheng, Chung-ying and Bunnin, Nicholas eds. *Contemporary Chinese Philosophy.* pp. 147–64.
Hanafin, John F. 'The "Last Buddha": The Philosophy of Liang Shuming.' In John Makeham. *Essentials of Contemporary Neo-Confucian Philosophy.* pp. 187–218.
Yang, Xiao. 'Liang Qichao's Political and Social Philosophy.' In Cheng Chung-ying, *Contemporary Chinese Philsophy.* Oxford: Blackwell, 2002, pp. 17–36.

Mou Zongsan
Chan, Serina N. 'What is Confucian and New about the Thought of Mou Zongsan?' In Makeham, John ed. *New Confucianism: A Critical Examination.* New York: Palgrave Macmillan, 2003, pp. 131–64.
Tang, Refeng. 'Mou Zongsan on Intellectual Intuition.' In Chung-ying Cheng and Nicholas Bunnin eds., *Contemporary Chinese Philosophy.* pp. 327–46.

Tang Junyi
Sin Yee Chan. 'Tang Junyi: Moral Idealism and Chinese Culture.' ' In Chung-ying Cheng and Nicholas Bunnin eds., *Contemporary Chinese Philosophy.* pp. 305–26.

Xiong Shili
Ng Yu-kwan. 'Xiong Shili's Metaphysical Theory about the Non-Separability of Substance and Function.' In John Makeham ed. *New Confucianism: A Critical Examination,* New York: Palgrave Macmillan, 2003. pp. 219–51.
Tu, Wei-ming. 'Hsiung Shih-li's Quest for Authentic Existence.' In Furth, Charlotte ed. *The Limits of Change: Essays on Conservative Alternatives in Republican China.* Cambridge, Mass. and London: Harvard University Press, 1976. pp. 242–75.
Yu Jiyuan. 'Xiong Shili's Metaphysics of Virtue.' In Chung-ying Cheng and Nicholas Bunnin eds., *Contemporary Chinese Philosophy.* Oxford: Blackwell, 2002. pp. 127–46.

Xu Fuguan
Ni, Peimin. 'Practical Humanism of Xu Fuguan.' In Cheng, Chung-ying and Bunnin, Nicholas eds. *Contemporary Chinese Philosophy.* pp. 281–304.

Zhang Bingling
Furth, Charlotte. 'The Sage as Rebel: The Inner World of Chang Ping-lin.' In idem ed. *The Limits of Change: Essays on Conservative Alternatives in Republican China.* Cambridge, Mass. and London: Harvard University Press, 1976. pp. 113–50.
Laitinen, Kauko. *Chinese Nationalism in the Late Qing Dynasty: Zhang Binglin as an Anti-Manchu Propagandist.* London: Curzon Press, 1990.
Shimada, Kenji. *Pioneer of the Chinese Revolution: Zhang Binglin and Confucianism.* Stanford: Stanford University Press, 1990.
Wang Hui. 'Zhang Taiyan, the Individual and Modern Identity in China.' *The Stockholm Journal of East Asian Studies No. 7,* 1997, pp. 89–124. Trans. Torbjörn Lodén.
Zhang, Taiyan. 'Explaining the Republic of China.' Trans. Pär Cassel. *The Stockholm Journal of East Asian Studies,* No. 8, 1977.

Zhang Junmai
Zhang Junmai. 'The Philosophy of Life.' Excerpts translated by Wing-tsit Chan in *Sources of Chinese Tradition.* Vol. II, pp. 370–2.
Jeans, Roger B. *Democracy and Socialism in Republican China: The Politics of Zhang Junmai (Carsun Chang), 1906–1941.* Lanham, Md.: Rowman & Littlefield Publishers, 1997.

Zhang Xuecheng
Nivison, David S. *The Life and Thought of Chang Hsueh-cheng, 1738–1801.* Stanford: Stanford University Press, 1966

Zhang Zhidong
William Ayers. *Chang Chih-tung and Educational Reform in China.* Cambridge, Mass.: Harvard University Press, 1971.

CONCLUSIONS

C onfucianism has been used as a tool by political leaders to legitimize their rule but also as a weapon in the hands of critics and reformers. In the twentieth century people have held diametrically opposed views of Confucianism in terms of its potential to promote modernization.

These different functions and appraisals pose a challenge to the student of Confucian thought: is Confucianism essentially a tool for rulers to legitimize their rule and an obstacle to modernization? Or is it rather a powerful weapon in the fight against oppressive governments and a dynamic force in promoting modernization?

There are different questions involved here, the answers to which may also be different. At the most abstract level there is a question about the social dynamics of Confucianism as such, in any society, at any stage of development. Is Confucianism as such *essentially* a conservative or a dynamic force? Against the background of the brief historical overview in the preceding chapters it seems quite obvious that the only reasonable way to answer this question is to say that history shows that it can be both.

How then does Confucianism relate to modernization and modernity? To be able to discuss this question intelligibly and with any degree of precision we should distinguish at least three different major questions involved: (i) Does Confucianism have the potential to initiate a modernization process in a society? (ii) Can Confucianism promote modernization once the process has begun? (iii) Once modernization has basically been achieved, how does Confucian thought relate to modernity? If there is such a thing as post-modernity, how does Confucianism relate to it?

When addressing these questions one must also try to consider the meaning of the key concepts involved: 'Confucianism', 'modernization', 'modernity'. When we go back to the question whether Confucianism has the potential to initiate a modernization process, we must first ask ourselves what the modernization process is actually about. In a broad sense 'modernization' refers to 'the transformation from a traditional, rural, agrarian society to a secular, urban, industrial society.'[1] The core of modernization is generally considered to be industrialization, but it is usually taken to imply a lot more in terms of technological, economic, social and cultural changes. Often modern science, market economy and even democracy are associated with modernization. Does then Confucianism have the potential to initiate such a process of modernization?

As we have seen 'Confucianism' can mean many different things. For many scholars in pre-modern China Confucianism was undoubtedly inextricably linked with the social structure and political system of imperial China, and as such Confucianism was most of all concerned with safeguarding and perpetuating the prevailing order. The question becomes more interesting if we ask ourselves whether Confucianism as referring to a core content of the discussions among Confucians for more than two thousand years concerning man's place in the universe, human nature, ethics etc. has this potential. But one more distinction has to be made. Does our question mean whether Confucianism would have the potential to initiate modernization in a global context where it had not yet taken place? This hypothetical and counter-factual question may serve to remind us that the causes behind modernization as it first began in Europe are still quite enigmatic. Why did the initial phase of the process of modernization, which took place in the sixteenth to the eighteenth centuries, begin 'in the countries of northwestern Europe – especially England, the Netherlands, northern France, and northern Germany' which at the time were in most ways less advanced than China?[2] One may seek the answer

---

[1] Quotation from the article about 'Modernization' in *Encyclopedia Britannica* online.
[2] Ibid.

to this question in different fields – science, economy, culture etc. We may note that two of the fathers of modern social science – Karl Marx and Max Weber – sought the answers in different fields. While Marx saw the emergence of capitalist society – which is very close in meaning to modernization in a wide sense – as resulting from inevitable contradictions within the feudal mode of production, Weber paid more attention to the role of Protestant Calvinist thought. Scholars after them have come up with other explanations. But the fact is that we cannot claim to understand exactly the causal processes involved here. What we do know is that modernization started in Europe and then spread around the world, and it does seem reasonable to regard modernization as having first resulted from an unusual and rather complex constellation of factors.

We cannot be sure if and when modernization would have happened in China, or any other place, if it had not occurred in Europe. Many scholars, especially economic historians, have found 'sprouts of capitalism' in Ming and Qing China. These refer to tendencies in the economy and do not appear as the effects of Confucianism; rather it seems plausible that these tendencies in the economy had some effect on the Confucian ideas of scholars such as Li Zhi in the Ming Dynasty and Dai Zhen in the Qing Dynasty.

Thus, it is hard to believe that Confucianism would have had the potential to initiate for the first time in history modernization; and for that matter we may also doubt whether Calvinism really had this potential.

The next question is if once modernization had started in Europe, Confucianism had the potential to initiate this process in China. With regard to this question we should recall that even before the Opium War it appears that individual Confucian scholars – Gong Zizhen is the most famous example – wanted thorough reforms, and it is conceivable that these scholars would have been prepared to use Confucian thought to promote modernization. When in the latter half of the nineteenth century some influential scholar-officials wished to adopt Western learning as a 'means' to realize fundamental Confucian values, this opened the way for Confucianism-supported modernization. The Reform Movement of 1898 was an abortive attempt at speeding up modernization, legitimized in Confucian terms.

As for the question whether Confucianism can promote modernization once the process has begun, I believe that the answer must be that it *can* but that it will not necessarily play this role. The development in Singapore and South Korea during the past two decades or so seems to prove that Confucianism does have the potential to promote modernization. We should also ask ourselves what in particular within the Confucian tradition it is that may play this role. Especially in an initial phase of industrialization the Confucian sense of duty and focus on study and applying what one has learnt in practice may well be important factors in this context.

On the other hand, it seems likely that the focus on 'good governance' rather than on formal and objective rules in mainstream Confucianism is more at odds with the requirements of modernization. When Xu Fuguan argued that Confucianism may contribute a kind of subjective perspective to democracy, which is missing from the Western forms of democracy, he may have had a point. But for the growth and evolution of democracy the emphasis on legality as an impartial objective framework, within which to implement policies and act out political differences, seems to be more important than this subjective perspective.

Once modernization has basically been achieved people will to an increasing extent feel the freedom and responsibility to define themselves. Under these circumstances we may think of Confucianism as one of mankind's great spiritual traditions that individual people have access to and can use to enrich their lives. This is a theme that we shall shortly return to.

The crucial question is how people choose to interpret Confucianism

There is no doubt that Confucian thought has been important in shaping the consciousness of people in China and other countries in East Asia. Since modernization is the result of human endeav-our it is therefore also quite reasonable to ask ourselves how Confucianism relates to modernization, and we may discuss this as we just did in the preceding section. But in this book we have also seen how the basic Confucian notions and ideas lend them-selves to different interpretations, and in this perspective it is tempting to say: 'Confucianism can be an obstacle to moderniza-tion but it can also promote modernization.' To say this should not be understood as to avoid taking a stand; rather it may reflect some insight into the social dynamics of spiritual and intellectual traditions.

Maybe the question is not so much how the basic Confucian ideas as such relate to modernization and modernity as how people choose to interpret them and what roles they assign to them.

In this book I have tried to describe Confucianism not in terms of a set of fixed and permanent doctrines but rather as a continu-ous discussion of some fundamental questions concerning the human predicament. The discussion has given rise to a living Confucian language or discourse which can be used to express different meanings and to serve different purposes.

The wholesale rejection of Confucianism in twentieth-century China can be understood as an aspect of the break-up of the empire; likewise the vitality of Confucianism in the dragon economies and in post-Mao China also has its historical causes. In other words, the basic tenets of Confucian thought lend themselves to widely different interpretations and different social functions.

In his seminal work *Confucian China and its Modern Fate*, first pub-lished almost forty years ago, the late professor Joseph Levenson argued, if I have understood him correctly, that while Confucianism had been combated for a long time as an impediment to building a strong and wealthy China, once this combat is over and Confucianism has become disarmed, as it were, it emerges again as a cultural legacy to take pride in – almost like a historical relic exhibited in a museum. Maybe this perspective captures an import-ant part of the background of the rehabilitation of Confucianism that has taken place in post-Mao China.

Confucianism as a source of identity and moral rearmament

Emanating from Europe, it is not surprising that attitudes to modernization in other parts of the world are often rather mixed. Modernization is considered both a blessing and a threat. To the extent that modernization entails economic growth and affluence it is a blessing, but in so far as it replaces indigenous cultural traditions, especially traditions upheld by the social élites, it becomes controversial and is often perceived as a threat. In the eyes of many people, not only in East Asia but all over the world, Western-style modernization is seen as having produced not only affluence but also a moral crisis.

Attitudes to modernization are often mixed within one and the same person but different groups of people also take different attitudes: evidently cultural traditionalists often perceive modernization more as a threat while radicals welcome it. Traditionalists will see Confucianism as a possible antidote to the moral crisis which they think Western-style modernization produces.

On the psychological level modernization affects people's sense of identity, and especially the identity among the cultural élites. Replacing traditional creeds and religions with some imported alternatives gives rise to a sense of rootlesness and uncertain identity.

The most important factor today which attracts people to Confucianism in China is, I think, the quest for a non-Western national identity. It is somewhat ironical that Confucianism whose adherents throughout most of its history have described it as being universally valid is now becoming a major source of a specific Chinese identity.

Clash of civilizations or enriching world culture?

The forces of globalization bring cultures into close contact with one another. This may lead to confrontation or to mutual enrichment.

Pessimists believe that after the end of the cold war, the clash of civilizations is becoming a major source of conflict on the international scene. In his famous essay on the clash of civilizations, the American political scientist Samuel Huntington identified Confucian civilization as one of the major contending civilizations in the post-cold-war era.[3] One cannot rule out the possibility that the clash of civilizations will indeed be an important source of international conflicts for a period of time. The terrorist attack on New York on 11 September 2001, and the increasing tension between large parts of the Muslim and Western worlds may seem to confirm the reality of Huntington's pessimistic prophecy.

But closer contacts between cultures and civilizations also open up the possibility for mutual enrichment. In this perspective cultural globalization offers great promise. We can hope that the meeting of the great civilizations will result in a repository of world culture containing cultural traditions that peoples have shaped in the course of history, accessible to people all over the world as a source for enriching their personal lives.

Confucianism certainly deserves its place as one of the major cultural traditions in the world. Making Confucian discussions on the human predicament, from Confucius to the Modern New Confucians, accessible to all mankind would indeed greatly enrich world culture.

---

[3] Samuel B. Huntington, *The Clash of Civilizations and the Remaking of World Order*, New York: Simon & Schuster, 1996.

INDEX

INDEX